speed

kentucky ham

william s. burroughs jr.

speed
kentucky ham

the overlook press
woodstock • new york

First published in 1993 by
The Overlook Press
Lewis Hollow Road
Woodstock, New York 12498

Speed Copyright ©1970 William S. Burroughs Jr.
Kentucky Ham ©1973 William S. Burroughs Jr.
Foreword © 1993 Ann Charters
Afterword, "The Trees Showed the Shape of the Wind" © 1984 William S. Burroughs

Speed and Kentucky Ham were first published by
The Overlook Press in 1984
in separate hardcover and paperback editions

Library of Congress Cataloging-in-Publication Data
Burroughs, William S. Jr., 1947-1981
Speed/Kentucky ham.
I. Title.
PS3552.U75S64 1993
813'.54   83-42919

ISBN: 0-87951-505-8

Manufactured in the United States of America
Seventh printing.

Introduction

To find the origin,
Trace back the manifestations.
When you recognize the children
and find the mother,
You will be free of sorrow.

LAO-TZU

William S. Burroughs, Jr., was born in Conroe, Texas, on 21 July 1947 to Joan Vollmer Burroughs, the common-law wife of William S. Burroughs. Nicknamed "Billy" as a little boy, he lived with his parents and older sister Julie (Joan's daughter by a previous marriage) in Texas, Louisiana, and Mexico City for the first four years of his life. Drugs influenced his life from the beginning: his mother had been addicted to Benzedrine since before his birth, and his father was a morphine addict. With his parents' need for drugs, they moved frequently to new locations to evade the law.

v

The Burroughs family finally settled in Mexico City where drugs were more accessible than in the United States. On 6 September 1951, in Mexico City, four-year-old Billy was present in the room at a party where his father accidentally killed his mother in a drunken game of "William Tell." Burroughs shot his wife through the forehead with a Colt .45 while trying to hit a cocktail glass she had placed, at his suggestion, on top of her head.

After the death of his mother, Burroughs junior lived with his paternal grandparents, Laura Lee and Mortimer P. Burroughs, for a short time, in St. Louis. (Julie was sent to live with her maternal grandmother in Albany.) In 1952, they moved to Palm Beach, Florida, where his grandparents opened an antique shop and sent Billy to the Palm Beach Private School. A few months after the tragedy of his wife's death, Burroughs senior told his friend Jack Kerouac that he hoped to make a home in Panama with his young son, but after he was acquitted of accidental homicide, Burroughs senior left Mexico and moved to Tangier in 1953. There he lived as an addict and worked on the book that was published in Paris in 1959 as *Naked Lunch*.

Before Billy's fourteenth birthday, he saw his father on three brief but vividly remembered visits to Florida. He had an affectionate relation-ship with his grandparents, who took him into their home, as he later wrote, "without reticence and with great compassion." As he grew into adolescence, he became increasingly difficult for them to look after. In his first autobiographical novel, *Speed*, he describes himself as a "fat, sweaty little kid who rode an English bicycle." He liked to play the guitar, but he felt so inept with his hands that his schoolmates nicknamed him "Billy Beer Can," because he was "the only person in the world who couldn't crumple one" with his left hand. When he was thirteen, Billy shot a boy through the neck, nearly killing him, during what Billy called "his own little breakdown." His grandparents sent him to a private sanitorium in St. Louis for "psychological rehabilitation," but they brought him home when he threatened to run away.

In the summer of 1961, after Billy's fourteenth birthday, his father invited him to live in Tangier. Before the visit, like most sons growing up with absent fathers, Billy had idolized Burroughs senior, but his father recalled that his time with his son in Tangier was "strained and hollow. We never really came close in Tangier. I remember listening to him playing his guitar after I had gone to bed in the next room, and again, a feeling of deep sadness."

Billy Burroughs gave a more detailed account of what happened during his visit to Tangier in his second autobiographical narrative, *Kentucky Ham*, although apparently he didn't relate all the traumatic events he experienced while he lived with his father. Billy describes himself as being "square, pink, fourteen, and American" before he embarked on the trip, clutching a science-fiction anthology he bought in Florida to read on the airplane and to help him deal with his fear of flying. His grandparents had told him that his father "was an explorer, probably because of his South American sortie for [the drug] Yage," but soon after arriving at his father's house on the Marshan, Billy learned that the territory Burroughs senior was most intent on exploring was inside himself.

In Tangier Burroughs senior introduced Billy to hashish and marijuana. His idea of entertainment was playing endless experimental word montages by his literary collaborator Brion Gysin on the tape recorder for his son. Billy recalled that he "would stumble to the roof occasionally, stoned out of my squash," and there he would see his father "transfixed and absolutely motionless, right hand holding the perpetual cigarette, lips parting to the sun, and himself stirring only to drop it when it burned his fingers. When it was finally, absolutely night, again, the sudden rush to the typewriter."

When Billy left his father's house to return to his grandparents in Florida, he "wondered" how his father felt about him, but there was little communication between them. He had been witness to Burroughs senior's involvement in hard drugs, however, as well as fascinated by his life as a writer. (Billy's impression was that his father "transcribed" rather than wrote *Naked Lunch*.) Billy's experiences in Tangier were major influences on the direction he took after he got back home.

In 1962, Mortimer Burroughs died, and Billy was left alone with his grandmother, Laura Lee. He called her "mother," and she was sympathetic and kind to him, but she was unable to offer much guidance to her adolescent grandson. Six years later, when Burroughs junior wrote his first autobiographical book, *Speed*, he began his narrative at this point of family crisis, a period of oppressive sadness in his widowed grandmother's house, which he summoned up in a heightened poetic metaphor in the opening paragraph of his book: "When my grandfather died, we let the roof get a little grey and the two banyans in the back yard took each other in their arms and, weeping, filled with spider webs."

Billy began spending most of his time away from home, playing hooky with friends, hitchhiking to Miami, getting drunk on beer, experimenting with the drugs available to affluent Florida teenagers in the early 1960s—paregoric, Benzedrine, acid, marijuana—and feeling guilty in the early hours of the morning when he finally arrived home to fabricate "a soothing story" for his grandmother about where he'd been and what he'd been doing. With characteristic humor, he realized that when he'd gotten back to the comfortable sofa in Laura Lee's livingroom "sometimes I made her horribly sad passing out while I was talking about how much sleep I'd gotten the night before."

Before he was fifteen, Billy realized he had a drug problem—"I never know when to quit. I've always wanted to continue beyond X point. That is, I've always been kind of dumb." *Speed* is an account of his growing addiction to amphetamine after he and a friend ran away to New York City and hung out in various crash pads for five months, until the fall of 1962. In a mounting spiral of drug confusion and paranoia, his addiction to speed led to his arrest on two occasions, but he was released both times when bail was arranged by his father's close friend on the Lower East Side, the poet Allen Ginsberg.

After Billy's second arrest in New York City, feeling suicidal—"if I'd had a gun I'd gladly have blown my brains out"—he and three friends drove back home to Florida. At the end of *Speed* he stands alone in the yard outside his grandmother's house on the quiet street in Palm Beach, "depraved speed freak me, with my crater-pocked arms," smelling the jasmine in her garden and wondering at the banality of the scene: "how the hell could this prim little environment have produced me?"

Back in Palm Beach with his grandmother, Billy's condition deteriorated still further. Without her husband, Laura Lee drifted into senility and had to be placed in a nursing home in St. Louis a few years later. She was aware of Billy's addiction and did what she could to help him, but he soon realized, as he wrote in the opening page of *Kentucky Ham*, that after his months in New York his addiction had progressed to the point that "I wasn't using speed, it rather seemed that my entire metabolism had developed a speed deficiency." More ominously, speed had become a necessity "to hold off" the idea of suicide.

At seventeen, Billy was arrested in the parking lot of a Florida drugstore trying to pass a prescription he had forged for Desoxyn. In *Kentucky Ham* he describes how Laura Lee contacted his father in London, and Burroughs senior came to Florida to help his son through his trial. As a minor, Billy was sentenced to four years' probation, with a mandatory cure at the Federal Narcotics Farm in Lexington, Kentucky.

Most of *Kentucky Ham* is a description of Billy's experience at the hospital from 1964 to 1965 "drying out." In the last chapter, he tells what happened after he left Lexington and enrolled in an experimental school in Florida, the Green Valley school, run by the Reverend George von Hilsheimer, who "specialized in adolescence" and became Billy's close friend. Hilsheimer provided what the biographer Jenny Skerl called "some much-needed guidance and stability." Burroughs junior dedicated *Kentucky Ham* "to the Rev. G.V.H. who engineered my cure and who knows damn well that one vice is as good as another."

Kentucky Ham concludes with Billy's experiences after Hilsheimer sent him and other students to Alaska for a summer job working on a fishing boat. After Alaska, he returned to the Green Valley School, where he met Karen Perry, whom he married in 1968. At the age of twenty-one, Burroughs junior wrote *Speed* (first published in 1970); he followed it from 1969 to 1970 with *Kentucky Ham* (first published in 1973). With contracts for his books and confirmation of his talent as a writer, Billy's "street days" appeared to be over, but alcohol became his next addiction. In 1974, he and his wife separated, when she could no longer tolerate his alcoholism.

The last decade of Burroughs junior's brief life was spent in Boulder, Colorado—in the vicinity of the Naropa Institute, a school for Tibetan Buddhist studies—where Ginsberg founded and taught at the Jack Kerouac School of Disembodied Poetics. In 1976 Burroughs junior suffered a liver collapse and underwent a liver transplant in a Denver hospital. In his third autobiographical book, *Prakriti Junction*, he describes the months of hospitalization when he suffered the after-effects of the operation and endured a painful convalescence. This book, begun in 1977 and 1978, was apparently never completed to his satisfaction.

As Skerl understood, Burroughs junior continued to work on the manuscript of *Prakriti Junction* "until his death, writing on matchbook covers, napkins, envelopes—whatever was at hand—trying to record his suffering and to find meaning in it." Aware that his body was rejecting the transplanted organ, Billy moved back to Florida in January 1981, hoping to heal in the sun. He was visiting George von Hilsheimer when he suffered a second liver collapse, and he died of liver failure on 3 March 1981.

When Burroughs junior became a writer he was indebted to his father's first published book, the autobiographical novel *Junky* (1953), which told the story of Burroughs senior's addiction to morphine at the age of thirty in 1944. In Ginsberg's introduction to the first edition of *Speed*, he wrote that the narrative "shows traces of characteristic Burroughsian laconism and precision regarding genius fact. . . . What's completed is a story-coherent account of impossibly wobbly subject: inside the Methedrine universe. [Burroughs] Senior had done his first job with the junk universe."

As a second generation Beat writer, Burroughs junior also had available to him the model of Kerouac's autobiographical novels, the series of books constituting what Kerouac called his "legend." Autobiography has always been a favorite American genre, and Kerouac insisted that the novel of the future would be confessional literature, people telling the stories of their lives because, as he said, "stories last forever."

When writing about his life, Burroughs junior was only in this early twenties, younger than both Kerouac and Burroughs when they wrote their novels *On the Road* and *Junky*. The fact that as a young writer he was so close to the horrific experiences he had gone through as a teenager underscores his vulnerability for the reader and adds considerable pathos to his narrative. Burroughs junior wrote as if he were the young Holden Caulfield in J.D. Salinger's *Catcher in the Rye*, twenty years later. Billy's misfortune was that his timing was all wrong: he embarked upon his archetypically rebellious adolescence during the widespread drug experimentation and social upheaval of the 1960s instead of the relatively stable 1940s.

In his books, Billy's tone conveys the wacky bravado of adolescence rather than his father's characteristically laconic adult bite, as when he wrote in *Speed* that after dropping acid, "The rest of the day was full of the type of L.S.D. experiences that you can look up in Life magazine or some like periodical." As the poet Anne Waldman realized, Billy was all heart, and he scattered nuggets of advice to his young readers in his narrative, ranging from his practical statement "If your friends watch you go, go back" when hitchhiking, to his impassioned advice about "your [legal] rights" during a drug bust.

Kentucky Ham is a cautionary tale about the perils of drug addiction following the law enforcement procedures set up by the Harrison Act; the book ends in a plea for the legalization of drugs. Burroughs junior argues that his life story was evidence that the current system of punishment and rehabilitation just didn't work. He understands that "these guys [the police and the narcotics agents] are fanatics" and that he "belonged to them" after his arrests. At the same time, he is realistic about the inevitable course of his self-destruction as a drug addict. He feels that the cure offered him by the doctors at the federal hospital in Lexington was a sham, but he pays attention when an inmate there taught him that the only way to cure a junky was to "put in a new brain."

If *Kentucky Ham* is the story about how Burroughs junior got busted and rehabilitated, then *Speed* is his account of his addiction to amphetamine (A) and Methedrine, and his experiences with the two other drugs favored by his sixties generation, L.S.D. (acid) and marijuana (reefer). Being arrested makes him wise up fast. In the New York City jail he finds that "everybody I talked to knew more about American power orientation than the most intelligent of political professors. And they knew exactly how it affected them. Cops-and-Robbers is part and parcel of the American Way."

Burroughs junior took drugs to escape the psychological pain of his existence, but he found that the drug experience became a horror all its own. He understood the disaffiliation of the 1960s, that "the postwar Beat Movement may have been religious but excluding a few archaic nuts, most of the folks I know today want nothing more than to wipe their asses with the whole country." Drugs caused him and his friends to decompose—when he got to New York and met a girl he used to know in Florida, he found that "all her fizz was gone"— and *Speed* climaxes in what must be the most nightmarish acid trip in American literature among the dark back alleys, the filthy crash pads, and the ghostly all-night coffee houses of the squalid city.

What Burroughs junior was searching for was authenticity, the ultimate truth of his own identity, which he found when he defined himself in his books: "Far better to retreat truly into a thousand tragic selves than to be a teen-ager in reality." He was smart enough as a "screwed up kid" to hold on to his sense of humor, remembering while stoned that the best he could do would be to see "things the way they really were in perhaps five different ways."

Speed and *Kentucky Ham* are two of our best records of the so-called "youth rebellion" that overflowed into America's streets in the 1960s. During this period of tumultuous cultural change, Burroughs junior recounts a conversation with some of his "square" school buddies after his arrest in Florida that confirmed his belief that he "had the good sense to go insane during adolescence." In his life he might have hung "right over the edge," but as a writer he was redeemed by his love for capturing the sound of words on paper and his genius for nailing both the precise physical detail and the unforgettable poetic image in his descriptions to buttress what he called his "story line."

Read together, these two completed narratives constitute the saga of an exemplary twentieth-century American unsentimental education, in which the generosity of Billy Burroughs's spirit and the resilience of his voice have transformed his "surrealist desolation" into literature.

Ann Charters

speed

1

For ten years, I lived on a street lined with royal
palm trees at the north end of Palm Beach where
the houses get smaller and some of them have no
servants. For nine years, our house had been just
as manicured as the next, but when my grandfather died, we let the roof get a little grey and
the two banyans in the back yard took each other
in their arms and, weeping, filled with spider
webs.

My grandparents ran an antique furniture
business on Worth Avenue before he died and the
house was full of the creaking stuff. I think the
rooms used to be divided up into different peri-

ods but after he was gone, my grandmother sold a lot of it and scrambled up the rest. We had a lot of old Victorian articles with taloned paws carved on the legs; one coffee table actually had wings.

I never spent any more time at home than I could possibly help, and I can still remember some of my dismal trips to and from Miami, how my sleepy friends would leave me off at the downtown Greyhound Bus Station on their way home. It was usually around three A.M. by that time, and there was never a bus running until four-thirty, so I'd sit around the crummy restaurant drinking gritty coffee and maybe chewing my lip half-time to some waitress' invisible transistor radio.

Earlier, on such a night, I'd have run out of excuses to give my grandmother over the phone long distance. "There's a flamenco concert tonight," or "The weather is so bad here that all the busses are delayed overnight," or "So-and-so's parents want me to stay for dinner," or "I rescued a babe from a flaming building and must stay for a celebration in my honor." Anything to stall, anything to stay a while longer, chasing after some cellophane scene.

But often as not, I was empty-handed for sure and would sit there chewing my lip and brooding over my lies all for nothing; I'd pay a sleepy hag and buy a random book. Upstairs, the waiting room was full of stiff-backed black benches designed to make sleep impossible but which only made it *look* impossible. Old men and young slobs leaning, drooping, falling over and lurching were hard not to watch—me usually being the only one awake. Sometimes, though, there would be one old creep awake among all the sleepers with a grisly crewcut and champing toothless gums. I'd catch his shiny eye and he'd look away; he'd catch mine, I'd do the same. I'd turn to my science-fiction book, thirty-five cents with a robot on the cover.

If I were driving home, as sometimes happened, I'd be on the turnpike about now, snapping awake just in time as I left the road maybe with my shirt smoking from a lost cigarette.

So I'd read about the green monster until I was dropping cigarettes on the floor there in the station, and I was always looking at the ashtray, it seemed, when the bus would arrive. I'd get out to the garage where it waited CHURRR-R-R to take in passengers, which at that hour were usually six or seven tired people totally without form. No one ever said a goddamn word on that bus. I remember a colored woman's hairnet in the silence as it was lit by the smoke-whorled beam from her reading light. Crisscross and lace. As the bus moaned north over familiar roads, I'd start the fabrication of a soothing story for my grandmother. I remember one time at a red light, a workingman looked up from his battered car and caught my eye. I looked away quick, feeling guilty.

In West Palm Beach, I'd be out of money, but

take a cab home anyway. I always sat behind the driver and, as we crossed over the bridge, I'd study the backs of his hands and the fat of his neck. The streetlights flicked off while I was in the cab, if the bus had been on time. And the cab always pulled into the driveway and stopped fast, WHAM! The gravel scattered and I was home. Dawn. I'd smell jasmine and see my grandmother in the window pulling the awful pink bathrobe tighter around her, as the driver turned to me, money, money. "I'll get the money." So I'd get it and he'd hand me the change with his hammy hand not giving a damn but I suppose he had his own troubles. Maybe a fat bitch of a beer-drinking wife.

In the living room with me seated, at bay, on the sofa. "What did you do all this time? Was it fun, did you sleep? Did you get enough to eat?" Then my weary recitation and a dance to bed, sleeping like a rock. Sometimes I made her horribly sad passing out while I was talking about how much sleep I'd gotten the night before.

Then, for maybe a week, I would stay at home and play her favorite songs on the guitar for her at night. But the music would remind her of my grandfather because I used to play for them both, and she'd start to cry and wouldn't talk to me and I'd quit and go to my room not wanting to accompany a weeping fit. All it took was a few days and I was itching to get out for several nights at the very least.

So the idea of leaving had been coasting around my brain for some time, but it seemed strictly storybook, just a daydream like running off on a clipper or something.

In those late evenings, I used to wander around looking shrewdly for some big excitement, but always wound up at the Hut—which was a small drive-in restaurant facing the bay right near where one of the bridges came across from Palm Beach. It was one of these gathering places where every kid with a car—for miles around—would come looking for something. "Where's the party? Where's the beer? Where's the girls?" And I was there almost every night, on foot, watching the diseased pigeons mouthing up crumbs in the patio. Now and then I'd talk to some giggly girls for a while and marvel at how absent human beings could get and still be there. Sometimes, for fun, I'd pick out some broad as a victim and make her laugh until she wet her pants or blew her sody-pop out her nose.

I first ran into Chad there at the Hut one night when I was kind of drunk. I knew him vaguely from when we were in school in the fourth grade together, but to all intents and purposes I first met him there. His whole attitude was full of fear I could see that right off, and I always respect scared people who know what they're up against. We started hanging out right then, and it turned out that he was playing some sort of ultimate ping-pong too. All he could see ahead was himself wandering around the country visiting friends of his and getting drunk, and the idea scared him pretty bad. So we used to sit around philosophizing and we turned on together a lot. One day he tried the paregoric I was shooting at the time and then that was the first thing he wanted to do every day was go buy some P.G. One interesting thing he was always doing, was hitch-hiking back and forth to New York City. That idea of taking off for New York appealed to me right away and since he knew a couple of girls who would house us, we started making plans to get right on up there, ha, ha. We were a little lazy about it actually, because when you consider it, it's one hell of a walk and you don't just get up and go like in the movies. So we drove around buying paregoric and imagining the police were after us to give ourselves initiative. We used to drive down down side streets giving the shake to unmarked police cars which was all there was on the road.

We went into various drugstores signing our enemies' names on the books. Chad was very good at looking as though he was suffering from diarrhea, but whenever a pharmacist would say he was out of it, his whole facade was shattered instantly. "Right! Right!" he would say, laughing his head off. "You sure are!" I told him that maybe this was not good thinking, but he said what the hell, the guy already said we weren't getting any, and he did have a point there.

We spent about two weeks like this and it was

any door with a lock after we boiled the stuff down to this awful-looking brown molasses. We went in the bathrooms in hamburger joints, we drove out west of town to stop by cow pastures, we got off under street lamps and on side streets. When we didn't feel like hunting around for a safe place though, we went to this girl's garage apartment in West Palm Beach. She had a record player, a big stereo—which counted for something, and she was very nice about the whole thing. It wasn't her cup of tea, she said, but she did think it was all very interesting. Then one night she had a big party with all kinds of awful high school and college kids; got drunk, and impressed everybody describing how we cooked down the paregoric. We heard about that at the other end of town through some distant acquaintances and decided to step up our travel plans instead of burning her house down.

It was the night after that, as we sat around thinking urgently, that we decided the trip would or could be dismal what with all that walking and identifying ourselves to ham-fisted cops, who would keep us moving at the very least. So we borrowed some money and went on down to Miami with the sincerest intention of buying up some bennies and leaving the same day in a blaze of glory. But we got involved with some friends of mine which is what usually happens to any timetable, and we clean forgot New York for a while.

Here's what happened. It took us four hours to

hitchhike to Miami that day, and that day was hot as hell, so we were hoping for a swell foop and no trouble. But the man with the pharmaceuticals had gone to a friend's house, and when we got over there, he'd gone back. It was just so, on and on, *ad infinitum,* until finally we got disgusted and dropped by a gas station where a friend of mine worked.

As we came walking around the corner, there was Schell squatting between the gas pumps, and glaring at the traffic, skinny ogre him, just dared anybody to get his gas. I hadn't seen him for a while so we haw-hawed and slapped each other around for a few minutes. Then we all went inside to talk things over, he at his ratty old desk, me on a pile of old tires, and Chad leaning in the doorway. The sun pounded in through the windows on two sides of us and a smell of oil and grease snaked in from the garage. I asked him about A and he said, "No, there's none of that vulgar stuff to be had but come over to Richard's house later and see," I watched a bunch of Cubans wandering up the street toward the Orange Bowl, thought something about Guevara, and then remembered who Richard was. A priest was what, and in one of those vegetable visionary foundations. I think it was the Neo-American church. So I asked Chad if he'd ever had L.S.D. before. Because I thought if he hadn't, maybe the situation should be better and maybe I shouldn't be around. You never know.

A lot of people who say they ought to know, say that L.S.D. will never do permanent harm, but never's a big word in reference to mind and I think there's always the chance that some poor fool might crack a one-way dimension. I just don't like the feeling of being responsible for such things and besides, even if the damage isn't permanent, I hate explaining to the police why my friend is doing that.

But Chad assured me that he was acquainted with the stuff, and during the two hours it took to get dark, we walked out of the business district and finally, after many leagues, down the narrow roads into the green residential area where Richard lived.

On the way over, I got to thinking about my ape man heritage for some unknown reason and I felt pretty hairy by the time we arrived. Richard had a beautiful one-room place in a clearing. There were rafters in the roof too, and as we came in he was there impressing a dizzy broad from the University of Miami. They were talking about enlightenment, ha, ha, and the tranquility of the void, ultimate purity and related subjects. I decided that my steaming brute slogging through a million muddy years with just five fingers and a rumbling stomach wouldn't fit in here. Could he sit enraptured with a rose in his gory fist? So I just clammed up and talked philosophy for a while. I hate philosophy, so I steered the conversation around to telling Richard that we wanted to trip.

He said shit yes he had de ol' sakament handy, so Chad and I split a cube that didn't do anything much. So we bought another and split it intravenous. Richard and his girl thought the syringe unlovely to say the least and made us go in the bathroom to get off. Religious persecution, that's what it was but it was worth it. I sat still for a long time thinking about cathedrals, and Chad went and sat down real quiet and happy-looking.

As I came out of the bathroom rolling down my sleeve, I found Richard, Schell and the girl meditating I think is how they would have described it. The girl was sitting in the lotus posture with her head thrown back, and her tits absolutely seared the air. Or so it seemed to me through my loony eyes. She was very fine footage indeed, but I didn't think that she or anyone present would appreciate my idea of oneness with the allness so I just saddown.

Okay, so they were all high and they wanted to meditate, except for Chad and he was obviously incommunicado. That put me in the minors and I had to scrounge over into the corner to listen to the radio. The music sounded good, bop, bop, and a couple of times I felt like telling everybody that they ought to be ashamed of themselves for taking such a weird-ass attitude and sitting around like a bunch of castrated monks. What they thought they were, I don't know. Old Chinese sages, maybe. But it would have been a terrible mistake to say that and instead, I got on the phone to another session across town and tried to get them to come over. But they were all in the midst of God and didn't feel like driving. I didn't feel like walking six miles to the same situation, and the girl from the University of Miami wouldn't lend me her car, material and earth-bound though it was, so I gave it up.

All in all, though, we were a pretty compatible group and I didn't start railing on about ape men and ancestral blood so everything went along smoothly and nobody wound up whispering to themselves in the closet. Slight as it was, a little confusion did result when Chad stirred up some interest in what might be in a little attic among the rafters. One by one we climbed up on chairs to look and found dust, splinters of wood, and a rotten sofa cushion. Everybody else took it calmly, but Richard completely lost his holy up there. He started laughing like a lunatic and pelting us with debris. We were all sort of embarrassed and just ignored him and eventually he came down to do some explaining to his friend. I started to help him out with some impromptu Darwin, but right then everything and their voices went geometric and I blew most of the night waiting for a way back.

As form returned, Richard had turned out the lights because the night was wearing thin outside and the furniture and rafters were traced in silver. I got up stiffly and went outside into the yard to listen. Chad was lying on his back by a gardenia bush but I didn't go over to see how he was getting on because I hate to yak at people just as it's getting light. A bird flew by his face so close it breezed his hair and I thought, "God, I bet that was beautiful." Then I watched a tiny spider lower himself all the way from the roof of the porch and wondered how the little thing could manufacture so much web. It stopped right in front of my face as I sat there thinking how strange that such a tiny thing contained just as much life as me. I thought that the soul of the spider or of the bird that flew over Chad must be exquisite indeed to take such form.

Then the sun reached into the yard. I took a deep breath, accidentally inhaling the spider, and went back inside to help calm the panic. When people sit up all night, there's usually a kind of guilty confusion as the sun hits the curtains. The whole city was soon to move out there, and everybody emptied ashtrays and started looking for their shoes. A minute later, everybody was sitting back down and trying to look ready as if the sun had a question perhaps?

While we were sitting there, Chad came wondering in, and we had a quick discussion with Schell. We decided carefully that all three of us wanted to leave and started saying good-bye and thank you etc. Everybody thanks the host. I did

12

some quick bartering and came up with two more doses to take along because I never know when to quit. I've always wanted to continue beyond X point. That is, I've always been kind of dumb. Chad and Schell walked out the door and as I went to get my works the girl told me not to forget them and I said, "Boy, I'm glad you reminded me, yes sir."

So we got into Schell's lovely car all painted lovely and not garish, and moved out onto the street. I think we moved over one of Richard's kittens but I wasn't sure. We were alone on the road at this hour, awake before millions of others and as the wind eddied by and through the car, Chad started wondering what we were going to do. It's amazing how quickly some people can jump back into time, dead set on placing themselves, on copping a definite position between early and late, between outset and finale. I mean, I realize the necessity to go by stages when our life style demands that we think and see in chunks suitable for framing, but there are some days that can be taken in one bite. I didn't want to go by the hour that day, and said that we could go to the beach and watch the girls drip water and grin. Or we could go to Fairchild Gardens, get lost in the jungle and belly down in the moist earth, shaking water onto our backs.

Chad looked a little surprised when I said that and sat nipping the inside of his upper lip for a minute and watching the road. Then he said that he guessed he'd hitchhike on back to Palm Beach. I didn't know that he was so afraid of not being wanted around that if there was nothing stopping him, he'd go to get it over with. So we just thought that he had it in his mind to do something alone and Schell stopped the car to let him off on U.S. 1. I waited until we were some distance away and then waved to see if he was still watching the car. If your friends watch you go, go back. But he didn't see me wave, so I didn't think anything of it.

I settled back against the seat and Schell and I drove around looking for a street omen or something. At a red light we bought a paper from a little colored kid—God have mercy on him—and Schell started yawning. I asked him if he wanted to share my two doses with me but he just yawned again and laughed. He said that I was crazy and that he was going home to bed like any God-fearin' feller oughta do. So I ate them both myself, gobble, gobble, and as I got out of the car in Coconut Grove I told him he'd be sorry if I found the Soul of Man and a Cure for Cancer while he was asleep. But the prospect of missing out didn't seem to worry him too much and he drove off as I sat down under a tree to consider my position.

The shadows were still deep, but delivery trucks were already out and moaning, and it seemed that the day was going to proceed on schedule. For about half an hour, I walked up and down streets and across lawns, and a couple of old women squinted at me as they bent out of their doors to pick up milk bottles. What happened then was they went back into the grey guts of their houses and I wandered on down by the Grove park, starting to go into the Florida Pharmacy out of habit. But a great many people go there for breakfast and I didn't want to take the chance of running into a few specific bores. . . . "HEEEY! There's my man! What's happenin', maan?" So I went into the park to see if I could find some sort of wombish place.

As I crossed the shuffleboard courts, I hunched my shoulders a little, thinking about the fifty or so old players who would be there in a few hours clutching each other's arms and pointing at things. Like fond old women, horrors with bulging ankles and weak-bladdered husbands lurking in the shadow of the men's room.

A lot of old people seem to think that I'm a delightful young man and want to talk to me, and smile at me, and put their metazoic hands on me, ah, ah! But they they stare at me with their wise watery eyes thinking if youth but knew, while I sit there smiling polite and wishing, meteorite, meteorite, slough their brains away. "Never for me, the Municipal Courts," I thought, as I hustled to a far corner of the park where three banyans grow in a circle. Any other three trees would have formed a triangle, but banyans, the wisest, are always growing into each other. I lay on my back in the grass between them, safe and warm, and slowly became aware of a bug buzzing in the web of a rainbow garden spider. True Life Adventure and I climbed up to watch it woven in, wishing that my enemies weren't so unnatural.

When all three of us were finished, I slipped as I started down and scraped my elbow down the side of the tree. I watched the bark soak up a little blood and then went down by the bay at the end of the park where there were mosquitoes spiralling above the water. I sat on a rotten picnic table watching the oil on the surface and listened to the flagpoles clank in the wind. A little sailboat named *Mercy Two* was thudding weakly against the dock nearby, and I began to be afraid that if I didn't move soon, I'd have to stay there forever. So I got up and walked back to the street with the wind shuddering in my ears to come back.

I'd felt the same way before, but I've never been able to find the reason. Some kind of surrealist desolation and I kept wanting to look over my left shoulder.

I remember the first time I felt like that was late at night in a friend's place in Coral Gables. Everyone else was asleep and I was lying on an old brass bed trying. I was thinking about all the times I'd been the only one awake when a jet passed over. God, I hate them, and it sounded like a wind from the edge of the vacuum two hundred miles high and a thousand fast come to blast me right off the face of the earth and I thought how the room I was in hung right out into space. "Everything can be classed as stuff," I thought. "And so am I." And I felt how abruptly my body ended and out of touch with anyone else.

So here I was back on the street, definitely wanting to see someone now, and I remembered that Mad Liz was probably home and awake because she was pregnant. I still called her that from her demented days in the Neo-American Church. She used to be crazy as hell, always making noises when she ran out of words. Then one day she had a vision or something, turned straight, got married and never regretted it. I didn't remember quite how to get to her house from where I was but after a few watchful blocks I found a landmark in the person of an old church, and I knew the way from there.

As I clumped up onto her porch, I could see her dimly through the screen door. She was reading a newspaper on the floor when I rattled, and she looked up smiling before she knew who it was, and said for me to come in. I've never been in her house for more than ten minutes without her feeding me. She'd signed up on some plan providing free food if you buy an icebox and was really proud of herself. So she gave me some odd ravioli and while I was eating I tried to talk to her. She listened to what I was saying, all right, but all her attention was turned down inside her. She looked pale, too, and she never closed her mouth completely. Her whole aspect was kind of scary. I suppose my feelings would have been different if the little creep was going to be my kid, but as it was, I'd come to see Liz and two-thirds of her had gone to Child. So I said thanks for the food and went off down the road feeling a hearty dislike for vampires in general.

The rest of the day was full of the type of L.S.D. experiences that you can look up in *Life* magazine or some like periodical and just after sunset, I ran into a friend of mine who gave me a ride home. He was constantly giving me rides back to Palm Beach so he could talk to me. He always had enough benzedrine to reduce me to a gibbering idiot, but never enough to sell me any. We talked garbage all the way and then continued until dawn, over coffee in the Lido Steak House down by the beach. When the sun rose, we dropped off trying to verbalize satori and he drove me out to my house to say goodbye-goodbyegoodbye.

My grandmother was sitting pink-robed on the couch in the living room, of course, and I told her that I'd spent the night at so-and-so's house, blah, blah, blah, then went and stared around my room until late in the afternoon. I got me up then and

18

phoned Chad to tell him to meet me at a friend's apartment in West Palm Beach later that night. The friend's name was Paul Higgins. He was a great lover of booze and he had little or no personality, just sat around drinking every night surrounded by his bullfight posters and erotic fantasies. He received no invitations of any kind, not even those to say another word that you and I take for granted, and his meagre social life depended on people coming to see him. Whenever he'd see me on the street, he'd practically try to borrow my right arm so I'd be sure to drop by later if only to pick it up. So I was going there that night to meet a girl named Noni, and kill two birds with one stone, ha, ha. Noni was a lovely and abysmally stupid girl who had been attracted to me to savor the delicious danger of courting a misfit. She was seldom on my mind, but we were planning again on leaving the next day, Chad and I, and I wanted to be with her on the eve, if you know what I mean.

When I got there, all three of them were sitting around drinking beer. Henry Mancini or some music just as lousy cast a stupid glow over the whole room. I was glad to see Noni, though, and felt like this was going to be a good night. We went into the bedroom to be alone and had been playing for maybe five minutes, when she sat up and said that she wanted to eat some fried shrimp from Howard Johnson's. She didn't say that she'd like some or that she wanted some; she said that she'd like to *eat* some, for crissake. Neither that or the beer on her breath fit the scene I was trying to build but I said, "All right, let's go." But no, she wanted to stay there and have me bring them to her. I told her I wasn't about to go walking a mile to buy her some fried shrimp to eat, with heavy emphasis on the eat. In the silence that followed, I closed my eyes for a few seconds and felt something important slipping away from me. I didn't know what I was losing. It wasn't her, but it went with her. When I opened my eyes again, she went to get a drink of water and didn't come back. I picked the fuzz off the bedspread for a while, staring out the window, then I went and asked Paul, who was alone, where she went, as if I didn't know. "Shewenoff with Chad," he said. He was drunk out of his gourd and I stared at him for a minute before I went back in the bedroom, thinking how satisfying it would be to kick his teeth down his throat.

Everything would probably have been all right if I'd gone home then like anybody with any sense of timing would have done, but I sat around waiting for them, thinking about Chad and how he was obviously my inferior and how the situation was unfair and absurd. When they came back, I felt even worse and went and sat in her car with her and tried to talk to her, which was a mistake because my feelings were all blown up

20

out of proportion and I sounded like a madman. Sometimes, you know, something is so hard to get across that I give up trying to do it right and just recite lines as they come to me. And the weekday morning melodramas provided me with great filler material for this particular occasion. Like, "What did I *do*?" and every word I spoke twisted around on my tongue like a live thing and went farther and farther from my meaning until I hated her, threatened to beat Chad to a jelly, and went home in a shambles. I couldn't get that fried shrimp off my mind; and the beer. Somehow, the fact that such stuff could have played a part made the whole thing flat suffocating.

I hitchhiked part of the way home, straining the silence in the seats of the cars that picked me up, and I walked the last mile to my house stiff as a Nazi with some unidentified tension.

My grandmother was waiting on the sofa when I got home and it hadn't been but minutes before she wanted to know what was wrong with me. I started to tell her I was hanging right over the edge, but instead I started an argument. I sat there thinking beer and shrimp and letting the exchange build automatically to where I called her a calculated name. She shut up then, and went into her room all hurt.

My reflection stared at me viciously from a big window across the living room until I got up and went to my part of the house, twenty-five steps exactly. Shut the door softly and I sat on the bed looking at my record player ten minutes before I saw it. When I did, I stuck the earphones on my head and made the music loud. I didn't know what I was doing aside from rocking and I must have been crying like a baby because she heard me all the way on the other side of the house and came to comfort. You can't ever tell how much noise you're making with earphones on and when I saw her and realized what was up I felt that someone knew now and that was the worst of it. What I wanted to do was ask her to help me; what I did was say, "Get the hell OUT of here!" She refused. She said she wouldn't leave me in my condition. I thought about mental hospitals and said please in all the ways I knew but she still wouldn't go. So I stood up and grabbed her all weak and frail, and the strength flowed out of me as I shoved her out of the room and locked the door. She stood in the hall weakly rattling the knob and saying she was going to call the police. She said she was afraid I was going to hurt myself. I yelled, "I'm not going to kill myself, for God's sake, I just want to be alone!" and finally, she said she'd be in her room if I needed her and went away. An hour later, I shook my head and got up to tell her that I was confused, blah, blah, that I was going through a phase, etc. etc. etc. and not to worry. She listened all wrinkles and knowing more than she said and finally told me that I needed sleep. That sounded like good politics to me so I went and forgot the whole thing.

The next morning, before I could wake up, the phone rang and it was Chad on the line saying, "What are you doing? Hurry up, man, I'm down by Staten's Drug Store and T Bone's coming over to take us out to the city limits." I said, "Huh? Oh, yeah, New York. I'll be right down."

2

I went and told my grandmother that I was going camping for a few days to try to think things over. She nodded benevolently but thoughtfully and said if I thought that would help to go ahead. An extra pair of pants and a blue shirt and I was out in the sunlight heading off.

I felt whore and hound this morning, raring to go, and I was glad to see Chad and his duffel bag standing by a big fountain, the one nervous and the other bent. Chad looked as though he thought I might try to strangle him, but hell, today was the day; we were leaving it all behind and I didn't even think about the night before.

We sat on the fountain in the mist that flew from it snorting and pointing until T Bone drove up in his old Rambler. He was half asleep and scratched his hairy stomach all the way out to the highway, while we tried to get him to come along and bring his car, ha, ha. But he was hung up for a while with some girl and couldn't leave until he could convince her to come too, or something like that. We almost had him convinced for a while there but he swore he'd meet us in New York and kicked us out across from an Atlantic Service Station on U.S. 1 just where the speed limit turned to fifty-five.

T made a U-turn and drove off back to town, and there we were, on the edge of town and outward bound. On the other side of the thumb, we winked back at scowling parents, driving their kids to pieces. I had a sheath knife in my back pocket in case I had to carve any belly, you know, and Chad kept saying, "That's a concealed weapon!" So I put it on my belt and he really didn't like that at all. You know, that's a *revealed* weapon. We finally compromised and I wound up wearing it in sight but behind me. I don't know what I was wearing for a belt, but it must have been some stretchy material because the knife hung back there like a tail.

It was a hot morning, and after two hours with no luck, we decided that people should know where we were going, so we threaded through the heat waves to the gas station and asked the guy if he had some cardboard and a magic marker we could make a sign with. He gave us a marker and said, "That's right, boys, you gotta have a sign. Lotsa folks that's goin' a long ways'll think you're just goin' to the next town if you don't have a sign. I used to hitch all round the country 'n I always had a sign." And he said there were some cardboard boxes behind the garage as he gave us the marker. We walked around back on broken glass and made our sign. Back by the road, we put it up so the speed limit read New York City, and we got a ride right quick. As we ran to jump in, the station attendant lit a cigarette and waved to us with the hand that held the match, to put it out.

Our benefactor was a fat boring businessman who didn't say a word all the way to Daytona Beach where he let us out saying by way of apology and a little plaintively that he had to go see his mother. We walked along the road looking for a shady spot to hitchhike from and worrying about cops. They're pretty eager in Daytona; always trying to catch some poor slob giving teenagers a bad name. As soon as we staked out under a tree, an old clunker Plymouth with a couple in it stopped. "Hop in," she said. "You're taking your life in your hands, but you're welcome."

It was a big old car inside and we had plenty of room for us and our stuff in back. We relaxed with our feet up on the duffel bag and looked out the windows at all the cars that wouldn't have picked us up. Our driver said his name was Michael and that they were going to Washington D.C. which was fine with us. He was brimming with their story which was about how all they had was this old car and about seventy-five dollars. They planned to get married and take a little apartment in Washington, and hoped like hell that he could find a job. They'd wanted to be married and stay in Florida, but their parents had given them par for the course, so Michael had kicked Susan's father up and down his front yard just before they left. In spite of that, he wasn't too smart and kept tearing hell out of the gears trying to beat other cars out of stoplights. But the car kept moving, and Chad and I didn't say anything. We were never anything but inanely cooperative when we were hitching because a lot of people will throw you back on the road if you so much as belch. Chad tells me he's lost many a ride by falling asleep with a runny nose. I thought that was pretty funny; I could just see him dripping and oozing with his head back over the seat while the driver stared real hard at the road with his lips pressed together.

That night, it seemed as if we'd been driving through Georgia forever when we stopped at a roadside we-have-everything place. Susan was asleep and the three of us went across the gravel to the halo from the bare bulb above the door, and I got clay under my fingernails from off the latch. Inside, there were all sorts of country products and a big can in the corner marked Gargoyle Arctic Oil, the sound of which I love more than any other words I've ever heard.

I bought a mass-produced barbecued beef sandwich and a glass of milk for myself, then we just poked around awhile. The proprietor was a knobby, obliging old hick and he watched us all real close to make sure we didn't try to lift any fertilizer. I wasn't about to try to rob because I have a supersititious fear of old store owners in out-of-the-way places. Besides, if he was out here all alone, I thought he might have a knobby old shotgun or something. Suddenly, Michael got a wild look and ran straight at the old guy from across the store, and I was expecting fireworks when he stopped short and asked the man did he have any fireworks. The old man said yes, he had fireworks and right there, before our very eyes, Michael went and bought fifty dollars worth of the damned stuff. He turned to us with his eyes aglow and said, "When we get to Washington, I can sell this stuff for four or five times what I paid for it and get us a really fine place. Come on, let's go show Susan!" Chad and I looked at each other knowing this guy hadda be crazy. But we all piled back in the car, yes, and Michael shook Susan so hard I heard her teeth click. He explained his big plan and sat there grinning till she threw a handful of firecrackers in his face screaming in her sexy cracker voice, "you take them damn things right back inside! What if we got stopped with your fool driving? We'd be in trouble, and we wouldn't have any money, and, oh you stupid ass, shit, shit, shit!" And all this time she was throwing stuff around the car. Well, Chad and I were ducking roman candles and were kind of glad when he went, "Shurrup, bitch!" and clouted her on the side of the head even though we were inclined to agree with her. We thought that would maybe quiet her down some, but she jumped on him and tried to stick her fingers in his eyes. Before she knew it, he got her head under his arm and was smashing her in the face. Chad and I were just getting ready to intervene, ha, ha, when she got loose and jumped out of the car. He made a wild grab at her hair but missed and turned to us all frustrated and said, "Goddamn it, I'll never get her now, she's faster than I am." I started to say something encouraging like oh, I bet you can, Mike, when Chad interrupted in a small voice saying, "Uh, hey, uh, hey Michael, look out, man," and pointed. Out in front of the car Susan had an enormous brick and was winding up. Mike hollered like a foghorn, "Susan, you chuck that thing, and I'll beat the everlovin' SHIT outa you!" She threw the brick on the ground and ran off down the road sobbing and spitting like a bobcat. He yelled after her, "You get back in this car or I'm leaving you right here, so help me." She didn't answer so he started the car and drove about a quarter of a mile up the road and stopped. "I gotta go back and get her," he said, and jumped out the door.

We sat there thinking how strange until they came back, she screaming how "We're getting rid of them at the next town goddamn it!" meaning us, and him going, "Shurrup, bitch!" Wham! But after about fifty miles they cooled off and she apologized and said she was sleepy, so they got in back and we moved up front so I could drive. After they fell asleep, we felt like we owned the car and got a great and true kick out of driving along into North Carolina with Florida way back there and New York up ahead. We whipped along, thinking about the day, and talking big about how we ought to pick up speed and shove them out of the car.

Michael woke up a little after dawn to take the wheel, just as spunky as ever, and started crashing through the gears again with his head cocked to one side. He got silly enough to where Chad made a few meek remarks about how maybe, all things considered, it might be better to drive gently, but Michael knew this old car like the back of his hand, yes sir. So about noon, the transmission went all to flinders and the car would only run in first. It was some holiday or other and most of the shops and junkyards we called were closed, and there's something rotten in town when you can't even get into a goddamn junkyard. Finally we found one though, and we wound over to find out that maybe the guy had one that would fit, and maybe it would work if it did, and that it would take at least six hours to put in. The boss had the key to the shop and maybe he'd drop in today. Chad and I had a swift talk, shook hands with Michael, said good-bye to Susan, and left feeling guilty. There wasn't much we could have done but we felt bad about leaving them anyway. There they were, wanting to get married in Washington and stuck with a dead car full of illegal fireworks in southern Virginia.

We lugged our paraphernalia three miles up to the highway and set up the old sign. We were standing under a beautiful shade tree and a little kid with a fat stomach and a dirty friend came and stood behind a crate to watch us. After a long time, we were expecting Mike and Susan to drive by and wave when a soldier in a Volkswagen stopped and the kid was overcome with giggles and joy, but his dirty friend didn't blink an eye.

The soldier was in the Special Forces and told us about his knife-twisting exploits in Vietnam all the way to Washington D.C. where we decided to get out and try to find a friend of mine who had gone to Arizona. It takes maybe six hours or more to get to New York from Washington by thumb, and we didn't want to arrive at two or three in the morning, so we hustled, in a lame sort of way, down towards Du Pont Circle, which is Washington's Washington Square at one end of Georgetown. On the way we bought some rhinalgan nasal spray, the traveller's companion, to keep up the old tradition and stay on our feet. Then we blew two dollars on a cab to take us the rest of the way because we didn't feel like walking or asking for directions. As a matter of fact, Chad hated to ask for directions under any circumstances. He thought it was strictly from bad policy to talk to strangers.

Now Du Pont Circle is literally a stage. It consists of a big fountain with a promenade around it, surrounded by a lot of benches facing in. And every night, every nut in the great city of Washington comes to walk round. An occasional true madman drifts, haloed, through and out. We were pretty punchy by the time we arrived though, and everything may have seemed weirder than it was. In Greenwich Village, the people look as though they might be going somewhere, at least around the block again, but this really was a circle, and the effect was frightening.

We sat there blowing on our feet and wondering if we could explain our presence away in case somebody dropped a cage over the whole place. There were more girls there than anything else, and one of them was making a big squealy cute thing out of wading in the fountain so she could lift her dress, while another lost her wig and ran off in tears. We sat there staring at variations on this theme for hours, and about four-thirty, I started dreaming while I was talking. I was taking trees for stained glass windows and Chad waved his hand in front of my face, too bad, so we moved down the street for a cup of tea. The Circle people would walk round and round, then go to this restaurant a block away to get their second wind. We shared a booth with a couple of queers in drag who couldn't have been over sixteen. One of them asked where we were going and Chad said New York. She just stared blankly and said, "Mmmmm Hmmmm."

Well, we drank our tea one, two, three, and went back to the Circle where the crowd was starting to slough away in group chunks of three and four. We lay out on some benches and tried to sleep, but the nose stuff wouldn't allow it. So we gave it up, stood up, and stamped our feet in time as we turned around once and then twice. Chad said he was going to find a lert, and as we walked away a girl with long blonde hair ran across the Circle laughing like a pale finale comet.

Neither of us had any idea how we got there from the outskirts the night before, so we took a bus and wound up on the wrong side of town in front of what looked like an ocean, and the next one took us back where we started from. So we walked to another stop and tried again. This time we went in the right direction and got off by an old ramshackle sign shop on the edge of town.

The third car that came by stopped and it was two liberal young men, one white and one black. They made endless pointed remarks about each other and kept looking at us to make sure we saw what good friends they were. But we sat in the back picking our noses and going, "Yeah, ha, ha," whenever it would fit.

A few miles from New York they let us off at a gas station restaurant and we sat on a bumper in the parking lot thinking how unkind of them not to take us all the way even though they were going someplace else. Then we went inside to get something to drink and it was so clean we almost left. The place was full of families who kept their children hushed and businessmen with dollar-sign tie clips. As I reached for the sugar, dirt slid from my shirt sleeve onto the counter and Chad asked the waitress for a list instead of a menu. We finished fast and got back outside away from all the eyeball.

Well, we're getting near New York indeed now, and it took us four hours hanging around the parking lot to get a ride, and then the guy made us give him a dollar to take us as far as the Holland Tunnel. We stood there forever. Most of the cars that zipped by were coming from an airport over there and when a few busses passed us, we went over to see about getting on one. We had no change and four bus drivers refused to break a dollar before Chad ran into the Delta ticket office, good folks, and got change. The next driver looked annoyed but he let us on and down the tunnel we went.

3

The next image I can remember was the two of us, there we were in Greenwich Village, part of the great phenomenon, just arrived and celebrating on a couple of hot dogs. Things started rolling right away. We hadn't been there six minutes before a familiar face floated free of the crowd and told me that an old friend of mine was living with her just around the corner.

Gary was one of the people I used to fool around with in Palm Beach before he became unsavory and had to leave. As we hove into view, he was sitting on the steps of his hotel chewing the fat with a little psychologist who was running a survey. There was a girl there who was saying why no, she wasn't ashamed of being a lesbian, no, of course not, why should she be? "Well, how about you?" said the good doctor, turning to me. I like to answer questions about myself, so I went along with his quiz until all of a sudden he started pestering me to come to Bellevue so he could show me to a doctor. He said I wouldn't have to stay if I didn't want to and that I wouldn't be committing myself in any way. Well, I damn near laughed my ass off. He got kind of upset at that and walked off down the street looking over his shoulder.

All this time, I was saying hello to Gary and introducing him to Chad and both of us to the girl. After the nut left, I told Gary we were dead on our feet and asked him if he knew where we could get some methedrine. As a rule, it never occurred to us to sleep while we were in New York; we just figured that when we needed it, it would come get us and isn't nature wonderful? Chad stood in awe of the human body. Anyway, Gary said with a manly flourish that we'd come to the right place and sold us a dime's worth for a nickel. We did it up and suddenly he started looking very strange and I sat still, breathing carefully. When I stopped sweating, I said wow and how much did he want for a gram? Fifteen dollars, and off we went to find it.

On the street I remembered a girl named Vicki

that I'd grown up with who was supposed to be attending N.Y.U. We walked into the first building we came to, and there she was, so help me God, and taking a twenty-dollar bill out of her purse. I promised her that I'd come to her hotel for a visit soon, and we went back and copped from Gary. And it didn't even seem strangely simple at the time.

Half an hour later and thoroughly stoned, we stood laughing our heads off on the street trying to think about where we were going to spend the night. I spat once, with an effort, and bubbles flew away on the wind. I watched them go, moving fast, and the street was blurred behind them. The Washington Square Arch shot by. So we went and blew most of the money we had left on beer, twenty-five cents the glass at some famous old pub with sawdust on the floor.

A little later, Chad called those two girls uptown and found out that they wouldn't be back until midnight. We decided that it wouldn't be manners to arrive then—without notice anyway—so we started down to the East Side in hopes of ferreting out a poet friend that I thought might render temporary aid. But we got hung up. Down around Avenue C I spotted a colored guy sucking an orange and swishing in a crouch from side to side. Crazy as hell, and I said to myself, "I gotta ask this guy." So I did and he pointed to a window above us and said, "Ask him,

WooEEE!" I turned and looked at an empty window and he told me to wait a minute. Then a pale wild-eyed guy came and leaned out like he was looking for something. I asked him if he knew where this friend of mine lived, and he said, "Yeah, vaguely, wait a minute, I'll be right down, you can help me move!" So a minute later, he staggered down onto the street with an enormous pile of trash and gave some to each of us. That's me, Chad and the laughing man with the orange, and we started walking back to the West Side. By the time we got to his place, we were on pretty friendly terms and he invited us up to try some wonderful speed he'd been saving for a special occasion.

We fell into his ten-dollar-a-week, bloodstained closet all out of breath from seven flights of stairs and stepped around the plastic syringes that littered the floor. He got them legally because he was diabetic, but you could say that he misused a few of them. He had all kinds of odd drugs lying around and he couldn't have been more generous or desperate for company.

So we sat around shooting the shit and talking, dissolving this in that, and all of a sudden it came out that he'd been going with a fashion model named Victoria, that I'd loved in Florida. Out of all the people in New York, the chances were pretty big against my running into him, but the way things were going, the coincidence didn't rate much more than a smile. His name was Fred and I told him I wanted to see her right then that minute, and I jumped on him to tell me where I could find her. But he got all wall-eyed at that point and said, "Uh, well, we're not exactly in touch right now, but I'll try to find out for you." It was a long time after that when I finally got a-hold of her by calling her at her hotel and catching her when she happened to be in. But I'll get to that; anyway, we kept getting higher and higher, and Flip, the orange-eater, was getting laughing hysterical and going, "Wow! WowEEE! Wow! WowEEHEEHEE!" So we decided that it was time to get on the street and walk some of it off. Flip played the bass and was crazy to get to the Village and find one. We did, and we listened to him play for about an hour, then he hollered like he was drowning for us to go on because he was hung up and we could find him there later, no doubt about it.

We were walking down the street and I was saying that I wished we had a joint to take the edge off it, when I looked down on the ground and found one, so help me. I said, "Saints Preserve!" and we cut down an alley to smoke it.

It was excellent grass and all three of us got high but it really fetched Chad. We turned a corner and he kept on going straight and didn't answer when I called to him. I told Fred to hang on a minute and caught up to Chad to ask him where he was going. He looked at me through terrified eyes and said he didn't understand why I was doing this to him. I thought, "Oh Jesus!" and what I should have done was let him go find those two girls uptown. Then he wouldn't have known he was crazy and could have gotten some sleep. But I thought about the subway, which scares me to death anyway, and how he might fall on them electric tracks or something. So I tried to get him to come with us but he said he couldn't face Fred and Flip. I thought he was just embarrassed and told him that they'd seen crazy people before, or something just as tactful. I was in no great reasoning condition myself and all I knew was I couldn't let him out of my sight until he started to come down, and that he'd disintegrate completely if I acted like a caretaker. Well, he wouldn't come back, and he wouldn't come back, so I hollered to Fred that we'd meet him back at his place later, and started walking around trying to talk it out of him. He kept saying he knew what was happening all right, oh yes, but he didn't understand *why*, which seemed like a pretty common affliction to me.

Bushwhacked by a sidewalk joint, for the next four hours we followed a zigzag course from the East Side to the West and back maybe fifteen times. Every direction I'd start to go, he'd say, "Oh, no! You're not getting me to go *that* way!" The fourth time we passed through the Bowery, I found three dollars neatly folded on the sidewalk and considered myself apologized to.

Chad was afraid to go back to Fred's apartment because he thought we were going to kill him there. We went back and forth, both of us getting more and more tense with him leading the field until finally, he got to where he wouldn't go up or down the street, and he wouldn't talk at all coherently, and he wouldn't shut up. At that point, I screamed at him for being an idiot who couldn't even go crazy without being rude and accusing about it. Part of that got through, and he agreed to go back to the apartment house if I'd walk in front of him, but then he balked at the door for another hour. I am no rock of sanity myself, and will react heavily off of nuts when I'm not completely together, and he kept giving out with this frightened snarl that scared the daylights out of me. His face rippled like a stream with torrents of emotions and reversals and ideas and in the middle of all this I saw the moon floating through a fire escape above the tenements and I had to grab a lamppost to keep from giving up and wailing. I thought about the people all around us who were eating, sleeping, fucking or slashing their wrists, and right then, a cop drove by looking at us real business-like. Quick then, I begged to Chad that we were a couple of lunatics and if that cop came back and asked either one of us the simplest question, we'd try to cover it up and wind up in Bellevue. That, thank God, sank in and we went inside, me getting a better grip on myself, and Chad staring around at things I couldn't see. We made slow time up the stairs for fear of ambushes at every landing, and the seventh flight was more hollow than the rest, giving out with a booming noise that was good for another ten minutes of panic and confusion.

At right angles to the hall at the top of the stairs and one step down was another, only three feet wide and very short with a floor of corrugated aluminum. I didn't like the looks of this spot myself, and Chad made an unprecedented noise that was very expressive. But Fred's room was there, so we went and banged on the door. They had been lying down, resting if not sleeping, and it took them a lifetime to open the door while Chad wondered what they were preparing.

The room was about six feet wide and twelve long with a bed along one side and a table by the window at the end. Immediately we got in, Chad whipped over and sat on the table and I expected him to flip out the window like Lloyd Bridges any minute. Flip sat on the floor, and Fred and I on the bed, all of us moving slowly and talking cheerful. I was all fagged out from walking so much and fixed up a big one, but I was so nervous I jerked the vein around and raised a lump half the size of a golf ball. I yanked the needle out and it was followed by black blood and a loud, victorious, "AHA!" from Chad. Fred and Flip were being as sympathetic as possible, not to be patronizing but it didn't seem to be doing any good. One minute he'd stare, then stretch and grin, then shiver, then sweat. Over his shoulder and through the window I could see a taxicab parking lot and an occasional pedestrian. It was very late. Fred took off, and in a rare spasm of cleanliness, shot the leftover blood into a piece of cotton instead of on the floor. This brought Chad bolt upright saying we couldn't fool him, goddamn it, he saw that trick with the cotton and what's in it? I told him if he'd pay attention to what was happening instead of acting so crazy, he'd know what was in it. I wasn't about to say blood. I was getting a little sick of all his accusing me of plots and felt like knocking him over the head so he'd sleep a while. Then he said, "I'm not as crazy as you think. I know you're going to get me drugged and try to kill me, but why? I don't understand *why!*" All the while he eyed the piece of cotton that Fred had then thrown cleanly into the corner. About this time, Fred got to thinking just what the situation could come to, and he announced that it was time to move the show out of his room. As we got up to leave, Chad said, "Oh, no! You're not leaving me here!" and made for the door after us. But he was too frightened to go out in the hall. After a minute, he followed us down the stairs, peering around the banisters like a lunatic caricature. We walked self-consciously around the street for a while, with him faltering around behind us, and finally he said in a somewhat steady voice that he wanted to go uptown. I went to give him subway fare but he wouldn't let me get near him, so I set it on the curb and backed off. He snatched it up and ran around the corner.

Back while we were hitchhiking, Chad had given me the number of the place he'd gone to in case we ever got separated. Now I felt horribly sorry for him, because I know what it's like to be that way. He was going through the worst kind of hell, but it either wears off, or it doesn't. So I hung around Fred's place for a couple of days, shooting and thinking and talking to give him time to cool off a bit. I hate like hell for people to go mad on me because I get all worn out keeping them from running into traffic or something, and trying not to wig out myself in the process. I may not like it, but I can't blame anyone for being crazy because rather than an unquestionable constant, I think that sanity is simply miraculous. I'm surprised that people can agree about any damn thing. Anyway, when I did talk to him he was in a pitiful apologetic mood and at the same time kept repeating that it hadn't been a drug reaction like I'd been telling him, that it was HIM, it was really him. I said yes it was a facet, ha, ha, and the only way to deal with it was to love, honor and obey the madman when he was up, and then to acquire some reverence for what goes on in there.

The girls had put him up for two nights, but for some reason, it seemed they weren't ready for any more, so we rendezvoused and went down to the Village to try to find quarters. Bingo! We ran into T Bone, come early, and had a big reunion. He had no place to stay either, so we joined up feeling like musketeers. I don't know what happened to Judy.

I'd heard that an ex-flame of mine had a place on East Fourth between A and B. I never got anywhere with her in the past and I was really anxious to see her for all sorts of tender reasons. When she opened the door I could hardly believe it. She was only nineteen, and she looked used up already; not weird, just blown out. And she wasn't using drugs either, it was just her goddamn attitude. Her place was a Grade-A dump with thriving roaches and piles of garbage stacked up by the sink. She and the guy that was staying with her both had the clap and wouldn't even get up off their asses to see a doctor. They just sat around scratching and complaining and caressing a horrible old communicable disease of a cat that shit under everything. I felt like kicking her down the stairs but we had no place to go and I asked her if we could stay instead. She said of course we could stay and I shouldn't have asked. There were five other people squatting there at the time and with our group, the total population came to ten in two rooms. So we settled down and I passed right out for the first time since I'd gone camping in Florida. Sometime later, I don't know how long, I woke up because everybody was screaming about something. It seemed that clean old T Bone had gotten upset by the dirt and stink and had thrown the cat out the window "for the benefit of all species concerned." I looked out the window at the blot seven floors away and started to congratulate him but Chris seemed pretty hostile about the whole thing, so I went, "Gee whiz, T Bone!" and fell asleep again.

When I woke up, Chad was fidgeting around scratching his arm so we got off. I was a little afraid it might make him crazy again, but I didn't object because he'd rested up and he could have got some himself without much trouble. He stayed stuck together, however, and he and T Bone went off someplace so I decided to go see Fred.

When I got there he was just hanging up an old shirt over a knothole that went through into the next room. There was nobody on the other side but an old man dying of cancer, but some of these old wretched cases that shouldn't give a damn will nail you and gloat about it on their death bed. Fred said he wanted to walk over to the West Side which was fine with me because I wanted to get around as much as possible in my little sphere. So he stuck some works in his pocket and out we went, breathing fumes and dodging around gangs of little kids.

The streets. I'd never seen so many different kinds of people in my life. So many people in dirty concrete, with handkerchiefs on their heads, babies in their arms, trash under foot, and way the hell over there in another world was the Empire State Building. Walt Whitman would have wet his britches. And the stairs that lead into black hallways below the level of the sidewalk! Somebody could go down one of those stairs to look into a garbage can and never be seen again.

Fred and I were just passing a bicycle shop when he looked over his shoulder and broke into a run. I started to wonder what was happening but I heard somebody holler, "Fred! Don't make me shoot!" and he stopped even though there were enough old ladies around that the cop might not have risked a shot. Of course I would have stopped too. In fact, I was slow enough for the guy to whip back, say you too, and drag us both into the shop. He took us to the back, showed his silly badge to the owner and told him he had a couple of criminals here and could we wait until the cops proper came. The man almost had a fit but said it was all right. He searched Fred and found the works and some prescriptions that it turned out were homemade, and when he found me clean, he told me in a deep dramatic voice that I had been walking with a Fugitive From Justice. Wowee! Then the cops came in fast and took us in hand. This was my first encounter with big city cops and I could feel the weather change as they walked in. "God DAMN!" I thought. "These boys could actually kill you!" and they could too; they came in, four of them, with their carnivorous faces thrust forward and immediately formed a circle around us, sizing us up feet to face as the probation officer told them what was happening. Then a squad car took us to the precinct where I stood around long enough to be questioned and dismissed. Fred was absolutely nailed, and as I left, he actually apologized for getting me dragged in with him.

Obviously I couldn't get a ride back, so I got good and lost trying to find my way to Fred's place. Since he wouldn't be seeing the street for quite some time I kicked the door in when I got there and took all the central nervous system stimulants, an old press camera, and about two hundred 26G disposable needles. I went and broke the news to Chad, and we mourned. We did.

On our way back from Gary's with a pocketful of methedrine after the sale of the camera, we ran into Eliot, an old school chum of mine, believe it or not. He was living with a girl named Dita, poor fool, and of course we went over to his place right away. His apartment was a lot like

Chris's except there was some food for about ten minutes and there was no cat. Outside the window on the fire escape there was usually a gang of little Puerto Rican kids running up and down. They used to make all kinds of strange paper shapes to dangle in front of the window late at night and scare Chad half to death when he was in the mood. The place had two rooms and there was a little back room with a filthy window facing a brick wall four feet away. In the muddle of the day, the light was like dawn and I used to sit in there dreaming a lot.

After Dita had really overdone the welcoming scene, flopping her bare tits around and almost bursting into song, Eliot asked me if we had any methedrine. I gave him some and he got off in a way that made me feel like I shouldn't be watching. I regretted turning him on later, because he grit his teeth when he came down. Most people grit some, but I appreciate it if they make an effort to keep their mouths shut and stationary when it's wearing off. Eliot damn near made the dishes rattle. And he made a flopping noise with his tongue that was horrible to hear. You hear a lot of talk about the horrors of drug use, but I think Eliot coming down was the worst one I ever saw. He'd been steering clear of meth for a while but that taste got him all stoked up again. When Dita saw the old fire back in his eyes, she packed up and went home to her parents on Long Island, which was the only sensible thing she ever did maybe. She only came by once in a while after that, and T Bone went to stay with some people in Brooklyn, so Chad and I stayed there with Eliot and visited Chris a block away every day.

The last place Eliot had stayed, he and a bunch of friends had been taking L.S.D. one night when a mangy pride of Puerto Ricans broke in and raped both the girls while a couple of them held Eliot and two other guys off at knife point. One of the girls was raped by her father when she was a little girl, so it was a big psychological thing for her. The result was one of those reactions: "She don't get around much any more." This isn't just local color, I mention it so you'll wonder along with me at the fact that Eliot never bothered to get the lock fixed on the door of his new place. All you had to do was push. He had enough money to buy a lock but never got around to it, and then had the gall to look at Chad and me wall-eyed when his radio got robbed. That made me madder than hell because I never rob anyone unless they die or go to jail which leaves me plenty of room, after all. I remember one time I boosted a guy that was only in a coma, and when he came to, the atmosphere was pretty strained for a while.

Anyway, there was no lock on the door, and pretty soon Flip started coming around with dark hordes of jazz musicians when we were out. That was all right, they needed a place to sit and we had some pretty out-of-sight music before dawn sometimes. There was one young kid that had just come to New York and never knew what to say. All these older musicians treated him like gold and I couldn't understand why. But one morning I woke up just as it was getting possible to see and he was talking through his horn real quiet and conversational, and I think I never heard a more healing sound. I wish I knew his name so you could watch out for him.

We were really happy about these guys being around, but pretty soon the place started drawing predatory A-heads like Spanish Eddy. Methedrine had taken him from crazy to nasty to brave and maybe you can imagine the combination. A kid about fourteen got away from a pharmaceutical warehouse once, with a pound of meth crystal. He and Vinnie, another charmer; poured acid on the kid's legs and he never walked again. But you never can tell, medical science is making great strides these days. Eddy went from place to place doing this kind of thing, and some people met him at the door with a gun which was about the only thing to do.

So when he started coming by, a lot of other people stopped, and Eliot started mumbling about locks under his breath, but nothing came of it. One day sweet Edward took all the clothes in the place to see if he could get away with it. He brought them back later in a good mood and turned everybody on, but it was a little difficult warming up to him. After he got off, right in the middle of a perfectly reasonable sentence, he threw a knife at me and laughed his goddamn head off. He was a regular Joe.

What with Eddy's ilk and the general dirt I had a growing urge to move someplace nice. For days, I'd been calling Victoria, the model, at her Barbizon Hotel for Women, and when I finally caught her in I thought hot damn, maybe she knows a clean place where I can wash up and feed my self, and nebulous thoughts of jobs, ha, ha, shot through my head. Now let me describe my condition so you can understand why it didn't work out that way. I had known her in Florida when I was in sound mind and good body. Now I was down to about a hundred pounds and my feet hurt. I hadn't slept for about nine days and was spacing at regular intervals. Spacing is when you're so high or punchy that your mind konks right out on you while your senses keep operating and you look like you're still there. It's really evil and the only thing for it besides sleep is more speed. And the batch of A that I had at the time was so poor that it was playing bloody hob-knuckle on my heart which was gurgling real romantic.

So I stumble into this lavish but tasteful lobby, and sit down on a couch spacing for several minutes before I realized I've got to call her on the house phone. I don't remember whether I talked to her, or whether the switchboard operator told her I was downstairs, but I was still there mumbling into the phone on my ear when a mass of black hair came up behind me and I got pecked a quick one on the mouth. Well, she was beautiful, and I no sooner got my mind running on an appreciation track, than she whisked me out onto the street. Victoria was one of these tall, full-of-life beauty machines and she wanted to go see some friends and of course she wanted to walk. You know the scene from television, I'm sure, striding down city streets, reflected in glass walls, camera pans to Rockefeller Center. Herb Alpert does the score. But I didn't want to walk, my feet hurt, and I said let's take a cab. When we got there, I asked the cabbie to change a five, and he looked at me like I'd hit him with a fish, so Victoria paid the dollar and I felt like I'd missed a move, sort of.

We stayed long enough to talk to her friends who thought hitchhiking was freakish, strictly from Kerouac, and for me to do up some more A and get heart failure. I have no idea how we got to her sister's penthouse, but there I was and her sister started going into astrology, and how I was a Cancer, and how she wasn't surprised I wasn't an *aficionado* on the subject. As a matter of fact, she'd never known a Cancer who could accept astrology. Her name was Melinda, and her man, as it were, was there. He was a longhaired, virile faggot soul singer and he looked like an aristocratic Hun. He was almost as beautiful as Melinda. There was some kind of joke circulating about how stoned he was at a party some nights ago. . . . After he left, Victoria and her sister dug out some hash which I turned down. "Oh? . . . Don't you turn on?" enquired Melinda with arched eyebrow. "Yes," I said, "But not now." I could just see me if I started smoking hash; they could have stuck a spoon in my mouth maybe, but I wanted to stay on good terms with these people. I thought, "Jeez, I'm in terrible shape," so I went out to the kitchen to fix another shot. Melinda came along because she was afraid it was heroin and she wanted to make sure I did everything right. When she saw it was just A, she went back and relaxed. Anyway, that one did it, I came out of the kitchen and everything went black. As I stood there, holding on to a pillar, I could just barely hear Victoria suggesting that we walk over to hear the Hun sing in Istanbul, or some place that sounded like that. I straightened up a little and said, "Well, uh, it was nice meeting you, Melinda, etc. etc. Victoria? When are you at your hotel? And I think I better get on back downtown, things to do, mutter, mutter," and then I was back on the street clutching my heart and heading for the subway.

When I got back, T Bone had come around from Brooklyn to turn us on. The stuff he had was good and smoothed the jackhammer out of my heart. Then he, Chad and I went for a walk to get nowhere special and to look at the streets.

Now T Bone had a pretty intense reaction to Bowery bums. He had this complex about how low can a man go, and was always running up to some slob sleeping on a grating and shrieking. "Get up! Get up! You're better than that, man!" But if one of them had held out his hand he'd probably have stuck a quarter in it. So would I, so would you, what are you gonna do, buy him razor blades?

There was a big pile of lumber in Washington Square that year that we adopted as ours to sit on. We'd about run out of proceeds from Fred's apartment and we stood around harassing passersby for funds. T Bone thought that the trouble with me and Chad was that we weren't ambitious enough, and he went around dead serious asking for five dollars. I never got much of anything except cigarettes. I don't know why, but people used to stop and offer them to me.

Sometimes, sitting there in the park surrounded by grey buildings, I was taken with fits of fear and expected the sirens to start way down low like the Titans arising, and before they could reach a scream, I was sure that somebody's side was going to drop a hydrogen bomb on us. Me that is. But I always kept my mouth shut, even when I was really scared, because how would it sound to say that you expected to be atomized any goddamn second? On this particular day, though, it got so bad that I could feel the ground trembling and the trees seemed to be aching to burn. So I stood up, trying to look casual, and said, "Uh, Jesus! Why don't we go over in the streets and poke around?" It was the trees and the grass being in the middle of the city that started it off, I think, and all I wanted to do was get off this island ground zero. I've lived most of my life in one fireball zone or another and occasionally it just gets to me.

So we'd gotten over into the crowd, me with my hands in my pockets and still scared when I spotted Dana swaying on the corner like she'd just then been set up by the stage director. I was really surprised at the change in her because she used to be a gasping Catholic, and now, not two years later, here she was decked out in granny style and so stoned she could hardly talk. She told me to come up to such and such hotel where she was staying to see her, and to hang around out front and get somebody that lived there to say we were with *them*. She couldn't take us in with her she said, because the desk clerk thought she was a prostitute. I said we'd come by the next night and went off thinking about the changes in people like her and Chris. I started to tell Chad and T

Bone about the implications, but Chad said he never knew the bitch, so why bring up her case. And T Bone wanted to go see the coffeehouse that Chris worked in. It was a little dive that you could miss easy if it wasn't for people hollering at you to come on in to where some lean kid was banging on a guitar. The entertainment was usually rotten and they couldn't sing because they didn't have a license. In New York, you got to have a license to sing for people. But whether the show was good or not, I thought that some of the fat bastards in suits, out slumming, could afford more than they gave. Time and again, the poor child on the stage would explain that the entertainers weren't paid and had to depend on the basket. And time and again, these cocksuckers would jingle their car keys and smile real smug as if to say we couldn't fool them with such a poor hustle. The usual night's profit was about a dollar for everybody. I mean one dollar for everybody, and most of the time they were so tired they spent it on cab fare back to the East Side. But that night we were rich, having sold a driver's license that had been lying around Fred's place, so we paid the cab and bought a loaf of bread and some bologna to boot. Back at Chris's we had a little party and those who were so inclined had a great time firing loads of methedrine that somebody'd brought over. Eliot came over and gnashed his teeth.

T Bone beat it home when morning came, and Chad and I spent the day getting higher and higher and watching the cockroaches crawl over everybody that had fallen asleep. We were betting on whether the roaches would do something or other, I don't remember what, but if I thought it might be good to sleep, I changed my mind about it.

That night, we arrived at Dana's hotel and after about forty-five minutes we found someone who would take us in with him. We rode up in the elevator with a couple of annoyed-looking businessmen, and as we knocked on Dana's door I said to Chad, "Did they look like cops or what?"

4

After a long pause, Dana let us in. I thought if
she'd invited us over the least she could do was let
us in inside of two minutes. The single room was
part of a suite that joined with another room they
couldn't afford through the bathroom. Dana introduced us to Johnny and Marion and started
running off about cocaine and did we want some?
I said I thought I could choke it down and she
said all right but I've got to bag some up first. She
fumbled around for almost half an hour spilling
it on the floor and saying, "Damn! Shit!" before
she finally handed me a nickel. I added it to a
dime's worth of methedrine and took off. I'd just

put the works down and was wiping a drop of blood off my arm when one of those businessmen came breezing in with his arms stretched out like poppa bear, saying, (And I think he must have had buck fever, because he said his first statement like a question) "Don't move? Don't anybody move. Just stay right where you are." Everything hit me at once and Dana started going, "ShreeeeK! Oh, Raaaaaaagh! Oh, please don't arrest us!" over and over. Two more detectives came crashing in through the bathroom, giving contradictory orders and waving guns around so we turned and put our hands up on the wall. One of them came over to me and said "Arms," like he was reading off a list. He looked where I was still bleeding just a little and said, "Oh MY, here's another one." Dana was still screaming and I wanted to shove my fist down her throat. If she had any class at all, she should let the fuzz know it, but on no, she had to gibber and drool and ask them to let us go which wasn't too damn likely. I was having my own problems with my metabolism. It was going so strange that the wall in front of me turned colors. I was just a little worried that my heart would kill me right then, but it didn't work out that way. Behind me, the cops were making almost as much noise as Dana as they ransacked the place. After they roared around for about two hours saying, "Where is it? You can save yourselves a lot of trouble if . . ." one of them took initiative and started asking for identification. When I went to reach in my pocket, my arms had gone to sleep and all I could do was grope like a spastic. He made a face and said, "Never mind. Get your hands back on the wall." They kept tearing things apart for another hour or so which I couldn't understand since they already had works, etc. etc. but I didn't feel up to making any comments. Someday, some flatfoot is going to find IT, and the world will come to an end.

Finally the ringleader said, "All right, let's take them downstairs," and one of his boys started jingling his handcuffs but he said, "No, we've got to take them through the lobby normal." "Politics," I thought. He made appropriate promises about his marksmanship and down we went, past the grinning desk clerk and onto the street. We walked to a windy corner that hung right out into space and two cars came out of nowhere like sharks, one for the girls and one for us. As we started off for the precinct, I noticed there was a handle inside the door next to me. That was surprising, and I thought of making a run under fire, but I was afraid some innocent pedestrian might get blown to pieces. Nobody was talking. Chad was staring straight ahead and I didn't like the way his face was set in the passing lights. Johnny was trying to look bored. I really don't know how the people on the sidewalk felt.

Once we got in the wire cage at the precinct and I got a chance to talk to Chad, I knew he was about to wig, which could be serious here. His eyes were wild and he kept saying that we'd been set up by Dana who was acting cool now and making a worse fool of herself than before. A set-up crossed my mind, but Jesus, who cared if it was a set-up or not, we were still busted. But Chad seemed to think they had a very special place for him alone which was true of course but I didn't say so.

Eventually, we found out that Johnny was going to the Tombs because he was over twenty-one, and we tender young kids were going over to the Brooklyn House of Detention. I had a sudden inspiration and said I wanted to make my phone call, but they said I could call from the House of D. They took Johnny off and stuck us in a paddy wagon with about twelve other young lepers, all of us handcuffed together. And off we went, rattling around in the dark and singing no songs. It was daytime again, we'd been in the cage all night, but inside the wagon it was black. All I could see was a couple of cigarettes burning and somebody was sniffling. We could see girls at crosswalks through chinks in the side if we cared to look.

I seemed to have gotten a little unbalanced in the course of all these events, and as we crossed the bridge I took one awful spasm of fear. "Oh,

God!" I thought, "What if that stupid driver goes off the bridge!" And I could see us falling down, rising off the seats and landing together in a heap with our wrists broken as the water rushed in and the cigarettes blinked out.

But we got there safely, of course, and the gate screeched open and the wagon stopped in the courtyard. I was sitting by the door and a couple of Puerto Ricans said, "Get up, man! Get up!" but I thought they were just jiving and I didn't move. Next thing I knew, a guard yanked the door open and I caught a belt across the back of my neck. "Get up off your muthafuckin ass, you dumb punk!" I thought, "Are you addressing me, suh? This couldn't be Hialeah," as I got the hell up and out. A pale man came and undid some of the cuffs so that we were lined up by twos. Chad was in front of the line and he kept looking back at me like he expected me to do something which I didn't. The House of Detention stands awful high and as we passed in out of the sun I thought, "Oh, God, look at me now."

We all sat in a bullpen that was remarkably clean but I don't think the cleanliness made anybody feel any better. We waited to be fingerprinted, devaluabled and showered. I liked the guy who took the prints because he said, "Just relax. Just take it easy and let me turn the hand for you. I know you're nervous, but just relax." And I was grateful for the shower in spite of the setting because I was really filthy. Awfully skinny, I noticed as I jumped back into my organic clothes, took two blankets off a big pile, hooked an extra one and sat in another bullpen. I waited for Chad to come through, but I didn't see him again but once, as they carried him screaming over to the mental side. That fucked me all around because even if we didn't get along too well all the time, he was my partner after all, and I couldn't know what was happening to him now. Besides the grieving for his fear, I felt pretty lonely without him. I'd never been locked up before and here I was in a bullpen with all these criminal types, thinking I was different from them and should somehow be exempt or something. But nobody seemed to notice that I was out of character, and they marched us on an elevator ten at a time to take us upstairs. I hadn't slept for many days or eaten but a few hot dogs, so I was watching transparent waterfalls pouring out of everything and feeling the proverbial bugs under my skin as the guard went through the indoctrination speech like a tobacco auctioneer. "Now you better understand that, or you may cause yourselves a lot of trouble." I'd hoped for a cell right away, but we had to sit in the dayroom three hours—until four o'clock. I plumped my blankets down and sat on the floor. The dayroom seemed to stretch into an infinity full of benches and wild-ass kids playing cards and screaming over the noise. I thought, "Screaming people tend to keep screaming unless acted upon . . ." and then somebody spilled coffee on me and woke me up. I sat upright the rest of the time and finally the bell rang and I got to my cell. The only bell I ever felt so grateful for as that one was when I was in grade school.

The bottom stainless steel bunk in my cell was taken by a poor fat colored kid who had been there a month awaiting trial for threatening to blow up the Statue of Liberty. I wondered who the hell was responsible for that. What authority will answer to locking this kid up? Huh? He would walk out when he got to court, of course, but his family couldn't make bail so he had to sit there talking to himself until his date came up. At least I assume he was talking to himself before I got there, because he talked to me like some kind of machine. He talked about his mother, and he talked about his girl, and he talked about how he was going to be good if he ever got out of this alive, and he talked about with God's help this and with God's help that until I was ready to throttle him. But I didn't have the heart to tell him that I didn't give a damn about his wretched mother and please to pray to himself, so I just lay there chewing my teeth and saying, "Yes, I think she'll forgive you," and "Yes, I pray sometimes," and "Yes, I think He answers." Up and down the tier, the Puerto Ricans were banging out Latin rhythms on bedposts and bars and singing popular love songs.

I stayed awake the two hours until dinner listening to my boy rattle on and on and then I ate too much because the meth was wearing off. I puked a little and sat down waiting for ten o'clock when we could go back to our cells. The dayroom was a big triangular affair filled with long tables and backless benches. The wall between us and the outside was laid with milky glass in honeycomb-like design and you could see if it was getting dark, but you couldn't see outside. There were maybe seventy other young rejects there, and weak chins and rotten teeth, knife noses and turned-up eyes all came over to ask how was I man? and Shooooee! Did I look sick! What did you do? they wanted to know, and offered all kinds of warped legal advice before I even told them. Across the room, I heard some guy bawling that he was "gonna get a writ of hocus-pocus."

I ran through my story, blim blam, trying to keep my eyes steady on the guy I was talking to. He was a sinewy, snaggle-toothed white kid with hair like Tarzan. His hair was something. It wasn't like mod or like anything for that matter; it was just flat savage. He listened to me talk, watching me with an easy pinpoint attentiveness that you see a lot of in places like that. He was paying strict attention to me, but I couldn't even keep my eyes on him. I'd see him straight for thirty seconds at a time, then the whole room would leap and roll. I think my eyes were convulsing down and to the sides, but there was no sensation in my head, so the action seemed to be in what I saw. And the sight of the room lifting and snapping like that got me to thinking about the bomb and how it would be, listening to the sirens after the guards had fled home with the keys, and my story got proportionately disjointed. This was the first time I'd experienced it, but it's happened enough since then for me to know that I go a little crazy when I get locked up. A whole lot of crazy fears come during the first hours before I can face the fact that they got me, pardner. Sometimes I'm afraid that a fire will start, or I'm afraid of the bomb, or I think the radiator is about to explode, or I can feel my marrow just straining to produce leukemia. Anything to overwhelm the fact of incarceration, I suppose that is why it happens. Pretty obnoxious mechanism, though.

But the kid I was talking to listened to my garble, not thinking me strange, so it wasn't long before I realized there wasn't much I could do about anything really, and I cut the fear loose. Then I just talked cops and robbers until ten, not particularly scared any more and not really conscious either. At ten, I lay out on my grateful back up top, with my blanket over the springs. I felt sleep catching up to me as Gestalt shifted and the spaces between the bars floated free. The beat down the tier took up again, ringing off the bars, but nobody sang this time. It was complex now, maybe thirty captives in separate cells listened hard and patterned together as my cellmate's tears and prayers fell unconsciously into time. Every bit of light went out, shapes ran melting through the dark as the rhythm slowed and stopped, and the last I heard was the click of the hack's heels as he passed on the catwalk and the kid finished, "forgive me . . ."

Then the lights were on again and between the shocks of the bell, the hack yelled, "On the gate! On the GATE!" I snapped onto my feet and stood up by the bars to be counted. The rest of that day comes in pieces because I'd had a taste of sleep and everytime I stopped moving I passed right out. I remember asking to make my phone call and I got a form that they told me to fill out with the message and the number. I could think of a couple of names but I needed a phone book which the guard thought was a real knee slapper. So no call went out and I sat in the dayroom hoping that Dana or somebody had made bail and would help me. Once in a while I looked up to the windows wanting the light to be gone. No one came that day except a couple of ferret-like fellow thralls, one of whom said I looked pretty fucked up and they both offered to give me their coffee at dinner. I ran through a lot of suspicions about that before it occurred to me that maybe they just felt a little sorry for me looking as I did like a living backlash. And I got to thinking that perhaps I wasn't so out of character here. After all, I'd committed a crime for my own reasons and I wasn't sorry. My cellmate was sorry even though he hadn't done anything and so he deserved to be. But I knew my position was rotten and for the first time I knew that it was imposed on me by the other side. Up until then, I'd thought I'd been breaking my own rules and never even knew what side I was on. But now it was pretty clear who made the laws, and I cronied up to these guys, albeit a little clinically, finding out similarities and differences. We had it in varying terminology, but everybody I talked to knew more about American power orientation than the most intelligent of political professors. And they knew exactly how it affected them. Cops-and-Robbers is part and parcel of the American Way.

So we killed time talking, mostly about dope, and I didn't learn anything new except that it was possible to talk with only slight interest in the words exchanged and forget the passage of time. We could sit there and talk for four hours, we three, about how to stay on your feet drunk, or about what we ate for lunch. Forgetting time in talk, we sat around laughing and slapping one another's extended palm as token of affection, understanding, acceptance and etc. etc. etc.

The extreme rapport I felt with my two buddies in the dayroom of the House of Detention, I think is an accepted outlet for the lunacy people get in the lockup. In the dayroom, we were more than brothers, but a month or so later when I saw one of them across the street, we waved and that was it.

So two days passed while we talked time in the corner, feeling this transient and undying affection for each other. Mario laughed through his brown snaggle teeth like rusty barbed wire, and then the guard called for me to get my blankets. He took me downstairs using keys at least ten times and I sat in a cell thinking hallelujah bail while they went through channels.

Finally I was escorted to the gate and the goalie took a deep breath, turned as slow as a stroke victim and pointed down the street. "Now, as you go out the gate," he said, "turn left and go to the end of the block, then turn left again and go to the corner, then turn left again and go halfway down the block on the right side of the street." He talked slower and slower like a record running down and he yawned before he said, "That's where your bondsman's office is, and you got to sign some papers or you're likely to be picked right up again. Now . . . you got that?" I said, "Yeah, g'bye!" and bolted.

Some seconds later the bondsman bought me two hot dogs and gave me a glass of milk that I glommed so quick that she said here, and gave me the quart. I sat in an easy chair plucking fur from off her fat old cat and staring at the street while she rustled with papers and rubber stamps. Finally I signed there and she told me it was Allen who had gotten me out. He was a poet, a friend of the family, ho, ho, and he was the guy Chad and I were looking for when we fell in with Fred and the laughing man. She said that he wanted me to come right over to talk about the law I'd broken. She gave me bus fare and as I got on my feet to leave, she asked me what I was using that had gotten me busted. Methedrine methedrine; she asked me my age. Eighteen, I said and she got all soft and protective which I thought was sloppy and out of place. She said she didn't see how we poor kids did it and I said thanks etc. and went to catch a bus.

5

Allen lived on the fourth floor of an East Side
apartment house that was typical except for the
hall downstairs which was clean and a sort of cool
blue. Out his window and across the street, there
was a massive construction project gaining momentum. Probably it's a building now, but when I
was there, it was all huge girders lying in white
sand under a living crane waiting for its chance.
Allen had a big bushy beard and a kind voice.
The top of his head was bald as we talked about
lawyers and me and all kinds of things, under an
Indian deity with the head of an elephant. There
were finger cymbals lying around the bookshelf

and he had a lot of fine recordings. I could maybe have changed my attitude there if things had been different. But I must have been possessed or something and was too much in a fog to do anything but accept help. Allen called my father in London who said he'd handle the finances but I couldn't talk to him. "How's the weather in London?" I would have asked.

Allen and my father had been friends long before I was born. He knew me as a little child but I just couldn't relax with him. I was too involved to stop and after he told me to, "For God's sake, be careful, they're fanatics," I left, thinking well so was I, and went off looking forward to some speed after my four days' rest.

There was no one there when I breathed open the door at Eliot's, and I sat in the grey light in the back room for a while thinking that someday I'd go back to Allen's and relax for a spell.

That decided and forgotten, I walked over to Chris's through the early afternoon. They were all there just awakened, and they'd been wondering, in a rib-scratching sort of way, what had happened to us. I told all and wound up by asking how or where I could find bail for Chad. Of course no one could help, but at least I made the gesture. I went over and looked out the window through the fire escape to Manhattan. Million-dollar deals over there, government moves, U.N. scenes, big stuff happening. And it all filtered down to me in the form of weary plainclothesmen, impossible phone calls, and Chad still incarcerated. I felt a little nauseous and when I turned around, there was a stranger named Spanish Johnny sitting across the room. I disliked him at once for his too tight Levis and fine-trimmed beard. His eyelids pulled tight, giving him a slightly mean Oriental look. But we were friends in less than an hour. I was amazed later at how many friends he had, and how they all knew him personally, not just by sight. I remember how he cried one time when he heard of some friend in jail, punching his palm with his right fist that had "Love me" tattoed on the knuckles.

When I turned around from the window, he was sitting with his early-weaned black cat on his shoulder sucking its tail. He was just back from Rikers Island and he talked about getting a straight job as he stroked the animal. He was full of ideas about staying clean but they didn't last and in a week he was peddling A in Village bars trying to raise money for his own apartment. All his furniture he'd donated to Chris until he made his own place. But he was enthusiastic about any place he slept, and was always trying to improve it. He and I spent all day one Saturday cleaning up Chris's place. There wasn't much you could do after you'd scraped up the cat shit and nameless goo, but it was an improvement to crowd three old beds into one of the rooms. Plenty of place to sit, and at night the mattresses could be dragged onto the floor to sleep ten in relative comfort, except for the leaks in the roof. And we made a fake spider web to hang decoratively on the window.

There were only five people living there regular but come two or three in the morning there were usually four or five others sitting around looking anxious and they couldn't very well be turned out to the elements, brother. I remember one night when they had a full house, one of the transients was wounded by a twenty-pound chunk of plaster that wet-rotted free of the ceiling. It wasn't mortal or anything, but he needed some stitches and we took him to the hospital. He couldn't get over being beaned like that and kept saying, "I was lying on my back watching the ceiling and I saw it coming! I saw it coming and I just lay there and waited for it! Wow! Wow!"

But the building rarely decomposed upon us and the usual night was built around a crazy pothead poet in dire need of an audience. Almost without fail, this guy would swoop in after everybody staggered home from the coffeehouse, and turn everybody on so he could read his poetry. Desperation with long hair, that's what he was. He had hair like Alice in Wonderland in those old drawings, except stringy with dirt, and his ectomorph face was toothless at twenty-seven.

But he had a pretty good reading voice and after he got everybody high as a kite, he'd start; all the while watching every face for a sign of appreciation. Some of his stuff was very much worth listening to, but everyone was usually so exhausted that they'd drop off one by one until it was the two of us left alone. Then he'd turn to me, his voice trilling with heartbreak and say, "But YOU dig them man, don't you?" And I always said yes yes as I rocked back and forth on my methedrine heartbeat. So he'd hand me a bunch of reefers and read on and on until he'd drop his tattered notebook and fall asleep with his hair wild as in a wind as his lips formed the last words in a whisper, then caved in on the gums. I'd sit there a while smoking higher, listening to all the breathing, and sometimes one of the heaps on the floor would talk in its sleep. There was always water flowing somewhere, and the sound of a cat calling in the street would rise from a point of light gleaming from a belt buckle or the corner of an ashtray. I'd sit there maybe thinking back to Palm Beach when I was a fat kid on a bicycle, or even further back when I used to swim in the ocean seven hours a day. I'd wonder what the hell I was doing here on the Lower East Side, then token crush a couple of roaches and go back to Eliot's. That's how it was 'most every night unless Johnny and I would take off and go to the Village for fun or business.

Johnny believed in steady sales for sure profit, but I used to hang around for some trusting jerk to come along that I could maybe rob blind. On this particular night, I found one named Sharkie standing around Washington Square. A few years back, when I'd known him in Florida, he'd been a fanatical pot smoker. It was illegal, man, it was hip! Wow! It was balls to him, he loved to smoke and would say so at the drop of a hat. Now it seemed he'd graduated to hashish and he said he hadda have it, hadda have it. I had no idea where any was, so I went down to the bar that Johnny was working. Johnny sent me to a friend of his who lived right downstairs from Chris. I went back, took Sharkie in tow, and started east, him going, "We're gonna cop, right? You can do it, right?" As we walked on down, he started getting jumpy and asked me if many gangs operated down here. I said yeah, but they all know me so don't worry.

When we got there I left him quaking out front, found 6D and introduced myself through the door as a friend of Johnny's feeling like an idiot. But he let me in, Charles was his name and he was so calm and casual that I relaxed right off. Any friend of Johnny's was a friend of his, blah blah, and I bought a dime's worth of hash, cut it in half and charged Sharkie twenty for it. No, I'm not proud of myself, it's just what happened, that's all. When I handed it to him, his face mottled in sexual red as he shoved it into his pocket. He fingered it obscenely as he looked up and down the street like James Bond and said that he'd be back that weekend with more money. I was saying that was wonderful when he flashed down a subway entrance without a word and I never saw him again, but he's probably looking for me.

I went back to where Johnny was trying to make an honest dollar and told him we were relatively rich. We both agreed that the twenty should be saved but copped a gram and went to turn Charles on. We were looking forward to his hi-fi and we heard Billie Holiday faintly from the bottom of the stairs. We hauled ourselves up, gripping the smooth and shiny black banister with our left hands just like everybody else.

After I'd left earlier, Charles had taken a fit of paranoia, thinking I might have been a cop come in from the night, and he was glad to see me with Johnny, they being old cronies. He never got worried without tangible reason, but when riled he'd sometimes take measures before he knew exactly what was going down, like he'd flush everything illegal down the toilet. The last time I saw him, he was on the three A.M. street loading up a Volkswagen bus. He was on his way to California and no time to say why, gasp, gasp. Johnny laughed when he found out and said he thought Charles would enjoy San Francisco.

So he was relaxed and relieved to see us together and took a toothy big shot of crystal. Then John and I had some and we all relaxed into our own thoughts and listened to the music. I was thinking about Fate and odds and ends and how they seemed very much against my sojourn up until now. I had walked right up to Gary, then to Vicki and twenty bucks first try, then Fred. I brooded superstitiously about the joint on the sidewalk and the three dollars later. It was all very spooky and then someone thundered on the door. Charles wasn't expecting anyone, so he was all ganglia and eyeballs in an instant. He pussyfooted over to the door like a slapstick husband sneaking in late from a bar, and mumbled something at the latch. He had a great door, it had a sort of a cookie sheet thing hung on it for a burglar alarm that thundered like tenpins if anyone so much as brushed against it outside.

So he stood there and looked over his shoulder to say, "We don't know no Noni, right?" I said, "Yeah, I know her." He opened the door as I stood up thinking complications, and she came springing lightly into my arms like the Queen of the May saying, "Oh! Oh, I've looked for you so long!" She wore silk slacks and she smelled of lilac. I didn't know what the hell to do, I hardly remembered her, and here she'd crossed the miles from her Boston art school and seemed other-dimensional as she grabbed me in this apartment decorated in shades of brown, she flashing memories of dates at the drive-in and parties over at midnight. Better for all, I thought to get this young vacuum off the premises, so I said, "I don't, I . . . Well, I'll see you guys later." They nodded with their mouths kind of open and we left, down the stairs and onto the street. As we started west, I asked her how she ever found me. She said she wandered around the Village asking people if they knew me and somebody sent her to Chris's, probably as a joke, and somebody at Chris's sicked her on me downstairs. She just walked into New York City asking strangers for my address, and found me inside of two hours. This on top of what I was thinking about odds was too much, and I screamed at her that I thought that was a "likely damn story!" which upset her and I had to try explaining. She just got more and more confused until I told her not to pay me any mind, I just thought I was being funny. Nodding her head all wise, she said she understood, and I almost yelled at her again, but I checked myself and said, "Good." Then she said she knew some people uptown she could stay with and I was leery right away. I didn't want to make any more penthouses, but she said they were just students and would I pleez pleez bodyguard her through the subway?

So I stood next to her on the deserted platform, and when I heard the thing shrieking and foaming closer, I flat forgot it was a train and wished I was armed to the teeth. But a whiff of her lilac brought me with a thud back to the hassle at hand. We got on the first car; sit up there sometime, where you can see the tunnel ahead as the train banshees through the dark and the lights crack on and off.

I was pretty unnerved by the time we got to her friends' place and they wondered in stage whispers what was on my mind. I said, "Carnivorous albino badgers, the size of a boxcar," and they shut up. I only stayed a few minutes, obviously, just long enough to ask Noni if she could bail Chad. She said she was going back to school tomorrow and she'd try to find money. I told her I'd be around Chris's place and left. The subway was a little less awesome on the way back. By the time I left New York, I could look bored and read the posters like anybody, but I still snapped my head towards any particularly loud splintering sound.

I didn't feel much like explaining to the fellers when I got back so I went over to Eliot's and shot some meth in him so he'd get out of bed. I told him about Noni, and he was chortling and saying things like, "You can't outlive the past," and "Were you going steady?" as I fell asleep.

The next day I woke into was dismal and rainy, and there was Eliot, gritting his teeth over something Italian. He didn't notice that I was awake and I didn't feel like saying anything, so I watched him eat. It was a strange operation, him feeding himself, because he wasn't bothering to really chew. He'd just shove a forkful in his mouth when it happened to be open and let his jaw come down on it and grit. I wondered how he'd ever started eating in the first place, because he didn't seem interested at all. He was glaring at the floor and not paying much attention to what he was doing, so once he didn't get the fork out ahead of the down gnash, and his fingers slipped away leaving it clenched fast, the end waving up and down with his chewing. I waited a tactful couple of minutes after that before I thrashed a bit, pretending to wake up, so he could stop looking stupid if he wanted to. He sat up a little straighter, took over control of his jaw and said, "Are you hungry? Good morning. I mean, Good morning, are you hungry?" I said I wasn't and he said, "Well, that's life." I could see he wasn't thinking too well and I wondered how it would turn out when he left to keep an appointment about joining the Merchant Marine. I could just see him gritting his teeth and saying in a cracked businesslike voice that yes, yes he's sure like to ship out, by george.

I listened to the rain for a while after he left, then went over to Chris's to find everybody asleep. The weather was rotten misty floating rain and I should have gone back to Eliot's and curled up with a good rat, but methedrine always makes me want to go someplace, so I got into a tattered old peacoat that I'd found somewhere and went out walking.

I had a puffy feeling in my lungs that morning that I'd have ignored usually but the mood of the day was such that I figured what the hell and practiced hacking as I walked along. It was so misty that day that I couldn't see much farther than the tops of the buildings and about two blocks ahead. And there was something about being able to see only the section immediately at hand that brought the size of the city to mind. I'd always thought the city was big but I just said, gee what a big city and that was about it. But this morning it hit me like a sledgehammer, me little bit of flesh inching through the canyons. Huge! Huge! I thought, and stopped on a corner to tell myself that it was all built for and by people about my size. But I couldn't believe it, who could build New York?

So I was hack coughing along in the rain feeling small to the point of folding up into nothing, when a pincer grabbed my sleeve. There was only an enormous thumb and forefinger on the hand, it was a lifetime deformity, the others hadn't been lost. I looked at the bum at the end of the arm and he said, "You and me's all right, see? Gimme a quarter, y'know?" Well, I hauled back and hit him in the teeth. He let go and I stepped out of clutch. I'd seen bad protoplasm before, but this guy seemed like he'd sat down at some formation clinic and signed up to be horrible. He didn't say anything, he just stood there facing just to the side of me with his freak hand to his bloody lip. He watched me wall-eyed for nearly a minute, working his pincer in the mist, and I didn't leave. This man was as awful as anything on earth. He was a rock-bottom man and to chalk him off as a bum was ridiculous. Then he said, "Gimme kooowater!" I threw a quarter at him and took my leave as he bent to pinch it off the sidewalk.

Maybe it was just the day and my mood, but I was shivered to the core. When he stopped me, I was thinking about myself on the streets as a little flea or something. But he said, "You and me's all right, see?" and then there were the two of us skittering around in there together. Then a whole flood of faces that I'd seen but not accepted came flooding back into my head, like an old bum with pus oozing from his eyes in great gobby tears sitting in a rainy doorway. All the faces that were too wrong or foreign to be considered until now, came spooking back to tell me stories. And I didn't want to hear from the human catchall battalions, because they were coming through too clearly and all wrong. I could have killed that bum had he held onto me, but he was so hideously necessary. We're all all right, see? I felt that the stage director had made a rotten mistake and I wasn't ever have supposed to have met this man.

It was maybe twenty minutes before I stopped feeling like the most sickening joke in the universe, and I ducked out of the rain into the nearest building and climbed to the roof to get my bearings. Once up there I stared awhile at Manhattan flying through the clouds in chunks, thinking about how the rain ran down my neck, about Victoria, and wondering who goes into New York and never comes out again.

The street below was deserted, and I honestly couldn't face thinking it out then and I suddenly got disgusted with the whole entire business. "Fuck it," I muttered, "Maybe the government will look into it," and ducked under an eave to take off. I tapped some crystal into my hand, caught some rain, drew it up and shot myself to pieces. It was a good deal too much and I felt as hot and moist as a sponge in the jungle. The sweat vomited up from me like the rain came down and it was hard to breathe. The sky filled with whirling shapes and my hands and the rooftop they dug into threatened to disappear pettishly until I got my senses. The skyscrapers in the mist writhed like monster cobras, of course. It was a good half an hour before I could do anything but hang on for dear life, but the thought of the placeholder with the pincer was cut loose and I started feeling ambitious and overjoyed. I stood up chuckling at my escape from the fact and stepped down the stairs clicking a beat with my heels.

I yanked my ideas way out of reach of possible relapse and remembered Vicki. I would go to N.Y.U. and deliver myself for a visit as I had promised. I had no trouble finding the place, but I don't think I was the kind of stuff that usually came on the premises. There were various well-dressed collegiate girls sitting in the lobby talking primly to nice young men as I came flapping in out of the rain like a goofy bat and walked across the mirrorlike floor squelching water from my shoes. The clerk looked at me in a meaningful way, but I was ready and shook my head to spray him a bit, sucked his little beady eyes into my dilated ones, and asked him to check and see if Vicki was in *S'il vous plait?* He picked up the house phone almost gagging and I turned around to catch a polite steel-wall smile from a young lady and a dark look from her male friend. I sucked some water off the hair hanging in front of my face, pushed it back and said, "Well, HI there! Great day for ducks, right?" I was a little exuberant maybe, but the combination of my escape in the nick of time and the crystalful of joy had me feeling like I could stay mine enemy with a mere blast of toothy grin. I think I was crowding everybody just by standing there. Matter of fact, I was probably damn lucky some football player didn't crowd me down the mail chute.

The clerk said that Vicki was in and she was in

Room 1112, sir. I obviously turned his stomach, but he called me sir anyway, so I told him he was a brave stout fellow and squelched onto the elevator. As the door slid shut, I turned around and saw him leaning over the counter pressing his lips at the puddle I'd left. The elevator shirrrrred up to the eleventh floor, making me heavy and then light and there were stars dancing before my eyes when I stepped out.

Vicki was a friend from clear back to grade school. We both attended Palm Beach Private and I hope they don't sue me. I remember the Monday morning assemblies when the school fascist patrol would run up the flag and the head of the English Department turned purple tooting his trumpet. I was a fat sweaty little kid who rode an English bicycle and was embarrassed to be naked in the showers after the do-or-die compulsory sports. One day I grabbed a potato chip from a buffet table that wasn't serving yet for some school function, one lousy potato chip, and the principal mentioned it to the whole student body along with his opinion that I was chubby. And it had a lasting and scarring effect on my life, yes Lord. I blame everything, *everything*–the whole human condition and the loss of the Soul of Man—on the principal of the Palm Beach Private School.

I never knew Vicki until about her fifteenth year when one day, the school, Palm Beach, and her rich rotten parents finally got to her and, using an older boy's lack of interest in her as a springboard, she dove into a complete collapse. Oddly, it seemed, her paranoid alchoholic mother's dirty jokes couldn't cheer her up, and neither could her fat eunuch father, who had fled from his castrating young wife into a room off the parlor and old age. He wrote dreadful poetry about Eros at night and told Vicki that she really should get a grip on herself.

I was just then recovering from my own little breakdown. I had tried going off to boarding school and made a wreck of myself, so naturally we gravitated together. I liked to make people laugh and I did that for her and told her no, she wasn't crazy, and that anybody in their right mind would be disturbed these days. Sometimes her mother would call me in the middle of the night to come help and I'd hear Vicki wailing in the background.

So I helped her over the pit, as it were, and she rewarded me by being a true and valuable friend from that time on. Most people are faltering, terrified wretches with their power-struck minds in the toilet, who make excuses right, left and sideways, but Vicki was honest about it when she was weak and she was honest on her feet.

So I stayed for a long time talking to her and her roommate, listening to records and fooling with her guitar. She told me that she liked N.Y.U.

and was meeting a lot of great people. All the while her roommate acted very polite and a little crowded. Vicki told me that I looked like a slobby bum and recommended that I take a shower. I did, and though I'd already gotten wet I must have dropped a pound of dirt. I shaved and dried my hair that was pretty shaggy now, but I liked the lunatic way it funneled rain between my shoulder blades. Vicki dried my clothes in a machine somewhere and I felt a better man after my wash-up. We sat a while longer listening to music, me with my mouth open thinking about how much the dirt on me had numbed my sense of touch.

Vicki sees people pretty clearly and from the way she looked at me a couple of times I knew she was wondering what I was doing here in New York, not making a living and obviously running high octane. But she kept the peace and took me out to dinner instead of asking. I was glad she didn't want to talk about it because my understanding of the thing went only as far as the idea, vague enough, that it had something to do with my image. She asked her roommate if she wanted to come with us, but she said no, her boy friend was coming and smiled that polite chromium lie, so I grinned real keen and her smile cracked a bit, but I quit it there because she was Vicki's friend. As a matter of fact we met her boy friend downstairs as we got off the elevator. He was

92

bright and eager when Vicki introduced us, gripping my hand and hauling himself up to me with a piercing valedictorian expression. Oh, he was going to go far and no monkey business. As we walked down MacDougal, Vicki asked me didn't I think he was a mean motor scooter and a bad go-getter. I chuckled at that over the menu. It was a good restaurant, air-conditioned and such, and right outside the window, the hip kids were massing for the nightly wander. I had a fine steak that went straight to my head. I didn't even remember to put A1 on it. In more lavish times I always used a lot of awful stuff, but I ate this thing completely before I even thought about salt. When we were through, she bought me a pack of cigarettes and went twice around in the revolving door before stepping out on the street beside me. We separated on the corner and as the rain started up again, I stood on the curb with a mint disappearing on my tongue.

The lights had come on and the street was full of young people. Boots on the girls, very sexy, slogan buttons everywhere, army surplus shirts and wide belts were all around and most of the people looked pretty upset. They looked tense and annoyed and they weren't kidding. The post-war Beat Movement may have been religious but excluding a few archaic nuts, most of the folks I know today want nothing more than to wipe their asses with the whole country starting with the president. I mean its garrison belts and heavy boots. Open defiance of the law. It's a disgust reaction. The media carry reassuring descriptions of the love-ins and how they wore flowers in their hair, but miss or ignore the fact that there were thousands there and most of them loathe their parents. I read some article by a foremost psychologist, ha, ha, who thinks that these are the businessmen and political leaders of tomorrow. "A healthy phase," he says, and not to worry, soon they will shave and shear and take the reins of our runaway tin horse. No, I know a lot of these "hippies" and neither they nor their friends have any intention of punking down to America. They are sick of it and its leaders. Guard the military schools closely, and keep up the school spirit with vigor, because your prize kiddies are escaping right out from under your noses, folks. But they have to damn near kill themselves to do it.

I was standing there on the curb dreaming revolution when a cop came over and said to break it up, fella. There was only one of me, but I broke it up anyway and went down the street in a well-rounded way. I could see four or five more cops up and down the block keeping people from sitting on steps and generally giving everyone confidence.

I walked by the place where Chris worked and wondered where the hell I thought I was going anyway, so I went back and sat in. There were a couple of suit-and-tie customers snickering at the guy playing the guitar onstage, and saying, "When does the music start?" I thought, "Just you wait, Buster." Empty words, and the indigenous personnel were polite as usual and expecting nothing better from them. They sat there, the customers I mean, fingering their drinks and muttering something about the girls around here, whisper mumble, yeah, yeah, that's what I heard. Finally one of them came over to me saying *Like* and *Man* and asked me if Chris could be had without much trouble. My brain reeled with sarcastic replies but this was a place of business so I just said nooo, nobody in here makes money whoring, my friend. He said, "Come on, man, I'm hip, just introduce me to her." I said with a smile that I'd cut off my right arm first and he went back to this table and had words with his pal. Obviously confused, they got up and left, the poor bastards. It was supposed to be so easy in these coffeehouses. I sucked up what they left of their drinks and went out to see how the street was coming.

I was walking over toward Washington Square when I heard somebody weeping in an alley. I went to see and there was a girl about fourteen crouched in a doorway saying, "I don't understand, I don't." I asked her what was the matter and she looked at me through acid eyes and said, "I don't understand," and rocked back and forth, staring at the pavement and crying. Not thirty feet away, the crowd murmured by in the lights and atmosphere. And here was this poor child, maybe a runaway from your hometown. No jumping-off place for her, somebody left her in the alley. I stood there not knowing what to do and hating everybody but her and me. SOME-body had to be at fault here and I couldn't help feeling ashamed as I fidgeted around looking for help. Just then a cop came sniffing around the corner and said to me, "Let's go, fella, best thing's to leave 'em alone," like it happened every night. I said, "No, listen! That's just what's wrong!" He'd started back out of the alley, but he whipped around then and said, "If you don't get out of here right now, I'll take you in for contributing to the delinquency of that minor!"

I said, "Right, officer, right," and went back to the coffeehouse. About half an hour later I watched an ambulance come quietly up the street and pull into the alley where the cop was waiting. "It's going to be a hard night for somebody," I thought and hollered, "We got a good show! Come on in!" A couple of guys burst out of an apartment house across the street as if it was about to blow up. I watched them run down the block attracting cops at the other end who started gliding over to head them off, as a red plastic telephone landed next to me. I looked up and a little kid on the fourth floor giggled. I decided I wasn't in.

Don't ever let anyone tell you that Florida is habitable in the summertime. The heat and moisture can drive you out of your mind and fungi will claim for its home anything that is organic and stationary, so keep moving if you go there to retire. Of course you can go to the beach, but I hate it there and only go about five times in the course of a year, feeling like I have to take my medicine.

But there was always cold beer on hot days, Orbit Beer to be exact, with cartoon pictures of space ships and Saturn on the can.

Geordie and Gary were living in West Palm Beach with an enormous guy named Jan. It was 1961 and my nickname was Billy Beer Can because I was the only person in the world who couldn't crumple one with my right hand.

I spent most of my days and some of my nights there getting drunk and silly and lusting after Barrie-Jane who lusted after Geordie. She was blonde and she looked just right to me at the time except she had a wart next to her naval that she called a birthmark. She used to get madder than hell at Geordie and Gary for smoking pot, and I used to get madder than hell because they always went upstairs and wouldn't give me any. They were three years older than me and I'd never turned on yet, so they probably just didn't want to waste it on me. I used to sit downstairs trying to squeeze a beer can and appealing for a joint to all the gods of every religion I could think of. But I suppose there's a time for everything.

About the end of that summer Gary became unsavory in the town's eyes by virtue of clobbering some girl that hit him with a guitar, and he left town. Geordie had already been to New York and whatnot and he left soon after.

That was a pity because their company fed some obscure hunger in my fourteen-year-old irrational self. I never saw Geordie again until the day before my trial in New York when we passed each other on the street about eight o'clock one evening.

We both turned to look at each other grinning under a street lamp by some garbage cans. Geordie has always presented an air of madness in the past but now he seemed to have acquired the reality—with his long hair pulled back in a ponytail, from a gaunt really gaunt face that reflected light from high Indian cheekbones above a huge white toothy grin.

He lived on East Fourth only a few blocks west of Chris and we went over, me looking forward to seeing Linda, his wife. She used to have a Volkswagen with a skull and crossbones decal in the window and she wasn't too smart. But she was really a sweet kid and I wanted to see her.

She was holding their baby as we came in, and I won't say she was as changed as Chris, but she was somewhat the worse for wear; all her fizz was gone and I lost interest in talking to her. There were various and sundry freaks standing around, it was one of those places, and they wandered in and out of the three rooms, periodically going through the many-step procedure of opening the door to the hall. It had three beams barred across it, numerous locks along its length and a police lock—which is a heavy iron bar propped against the door with braces. A lot of work had gone into making the fort secure and believe it or not the windows were covered with electrified chicken wire. This was all because the police had cracked in the door the other night whooping like savages and waving unwarranted pieces of paper. The search turned up nothing as the place happened to be clean at the time—which was rare and lucky—but Georgie wasn't going to be taking any more chances, no sir.

His place was one small room bigger than Chris's or Eliot's and one of the rooms was furnished very fine, with sofas and a coffee table. We settled down there in the light of two brass lamps to smoke a little tea and talk about Palm Beach, interrupted at intervals by a tall pimply-faced kid who was running around with a piece of broomstick trying to kill off them little orange men. Geordie told him to sit down and leave them alone, what did they ever do to him? But he just chased them into the next room and banged around in there.

There was no A there at the time, but they were expecting an ounce or so soon, said Linda in a dull voice, looking at the baby that she clutched to her. That poor kid, Geordie's ideas on children were from somewhere out in left field and he had big plans about teaching her to shoot a gun as soon as she was big enough to hold one. He'd already tried to shoot her up with meth on numerous occasions "to get her ready" he said but Linda would always head him off, thank God for that. Now I'm no A. S. Neill by a long shot but I am pretty touchy about how people treat their kids. But I figured that this child was already doomed, so I just swore at him for a brutal lunatic and let it go at that.

I left a short time after that, ha, ha, and looked back to see Geordie waving his scarified collector's item arms, and shouting something about his own business.

On my way over to Eliot's I called Allen to let him know I remembered that my trial was the next day. That might be a wishful memory but at least I hope I did; he was looking out for me as it were, and I should have made it at least that much easier for him. I often forget what I owe people until it is too late. For example, it occurred to me for the first time that night that I might have dropped Chad a line while he was awaiting trial. If it had been the other way around, with me in there, I'd have been praying for word every day.

So the next morning, after a big hassle of getting lost and going to the City Hall or something, I sat in the back of the courtroom with Dana and her friends waiting for our names to be called. They called us up as they brought Chad out of a little door in the front of the room behind the bench. We walked up before the judge past Dana's bewildered parents and I stood next to Chad, feeling good to see him again. He gave me a disgusted look whispering why the hell couldn't I even have managed a postcard?

That knocked me down a little but I came out about even emotionally because our overzealous lawmen had had no warrant so we got off on illegal search and seizure. We all went into a back room, us, the arresting officers, the judge and our lawyer. The Powers that Were held a pow-wow around the judge at one end of a long shiny table, us waiting like a ragged bunch of weeds at the other. It turned out that we were free to go if we would sign some papers promising not to sue for false arrest. We signed gladly and went out into the hall to congratulate each other and go through the wow we're free number. The cops came over to kiss and make up saying, "No hard feelings, right? Cops and robbers, ha, ha, everybody got a job." I don't know what came over me, but I shook hands with one of them who laughed in a sinister way and said, "I bet I get you all back within a week." "Rots a ruck" I wished him, and we all went out on the street together. Chad and I split up from Dana and her crew right away, wanting never to look upon them again, if possible. As they drove off, Dana waved out of the cab smiling and said, "We'll see yoo!" And Chad hollered, "Horrible BITCH! Not if I'm alert!"

6

Back at Chris's and both of us high on some speed we'd dug up someplace, I asked Chad what had happened to him in the House of Detention. The Puerto Ricans there spoke mostly Spanish, but it seemed that every time one of them spoke an English word, Chad thought that it was some kind of signal to the others to let them know it was about time to strangle the American. It got so bad that he wound up cowering in the corner of his cell and his cellmate called the hack to take him over to the mental side. He spent he didn't know how many horrible hours there before he finally got his senses, and then he just sat there waiting to hear from somebody. That brought us to me and why I didn't write to him. I didn't try to explain and just told him I'd forgotten. He said he'd learned a thing or two from my silence but he wasn't going to hold it against me because it went further than that. He went off then, to visit T Bone in Brooklyn and left me feeling low mean vile vicious and rotten.

But I figured what the hell and got myself on foot to find Johnny on the West Side. Johnny was getting speed at a discount at this time because he was also selling it for a guy named Hans, who lived in the Village. For every three grams he sold, he got one free, and he could buy one for ten. I caught him coming out of a bar just after he had sold his three grams and was on his way to pick up the commission. I'd been up to Hans's before but I didn't want to join Johnny tonight, me being fresh out of court and wanting my freedom forever. Besides, Hans bored me to tears. So Johnny went on, saying he'd be back as soon as humanly possible which would probably be some time because it could take forever to score off this guy. He was a crazy young Nazi-type dreamer, born too late, and he spent hours pacing back and forth yelping about organization and how he would revolutionize the sale of methedrine on the West Side as never before. And how! Everyone who sold for him would carry a Derringer with a permit and, oh yes! there would always be a crack lawyer constantly at the ready. He wore a very wide-brim, slightly floppy hat that was somehow very Third Reich and once he was firmly established, he said, he would lead terrorist raids to clear the East Side of all the amphetamine vermin like ... and he'd take a deep breath. Like Spanish Eddy! At this point he expected you to collapse with admiration when all you wanted to do was cop and get out of there—having interrupted him two or three times already asking to do business.

So it would be a while before Johnny made it back and I wandered around with the crowd for almost three hours by which time I felt tired enough that all I wanted to do was go back to the East Side and sack out. I didn't feel like doing any more walking either so I went up to Hans's to try to borrow a dollar for cab fare.

Once I got inside though, and was sitting there with all those drugs lying around me, I was sorry I'd come. I had sort of promised to myself that I'd stay away from places where drugs congregate, if not the drugs themselves, and when some people came visiting I could have made it out the window by the time they knocked the second time. But manners prevailed and I just tried to hurry the deal that should have taken thirty seconds, but Hans kept saying, "Oh, yes, I'll get your dollar," and then getting involved in something else. When another knock came, I wanted more than anything else in the world to let etiquette be damned and knock everything over on my way to the fire escape. Then Hans unlocked the door, leaving the little chain still hooked, and the police kicked the door on open.

Strangely polite and respectful, they let us stay seated and went through the apartment talking calmly to each other and without any razzmatazz. I had no idea how much contraband would be lying around the place but I didn't think it would be too much—just A and some works—but they found something illegal every two minutes, it seemed, and I just sat there feeling worse every time somebody started looking over a new package in the light. There was a half-pound of methedrine crystal and I was unhappy enough about that, but when they found a couple of guns, besides some heroin, I started giving up. Just before we left, they uncovered a tear-gas gun and some live hand grenades and that was the living end. Right as we were about to leave also, a couple of guys knocked on the door wanting to see Hans and were yanked in to join the party. They came in really in shock and they looked so stupid that I nearly laughed in spite of the scene. I figured that they probably wouldn't be held.

Hans and the girls seemed to think that the whole thing was some sort of bloody joke and laughed all the way out onto the street and into a paddy wagon. This was to be a well-documented police action so now I understood why they'd been so polite. There were news photographers running past us like black cats on the path going flash! White teeth, and as we came out the door, we met with a rousing goddamn cheer. This was right in the middle of the Village and a big crowd of hippies had been drawn by the waiting wagon and photographers. They were all on our side but that didn't make Johnny or me feel particularly good. A diversionary riot was more what I had in mind. We got in the wagon disgusted with our grinning buddies and glaring at the crowd of cheering cretins. Cheering! What the hell was there to cheer about?

At the station, we were allowed our phone calls, and I started to call Allen but I couldn't get up the gall. Once was enough I figured, and stayed in the cage. I was real brave about it too. After they turned loose the two guys that had come late, Hans broke out some meth that he'd hidden in a questionable place on his person and we sniffed it up when the Man wasn't looking. I'll never understand why we were treated so nice after the newsmen were gone; they let us talk and they must have known we were sniffing something because we were all in the same cubicle and we were snorting up a storm for maybe ten minutes. That made us all feel a hell of a lot better and we relaxed and rapped until about three A.M. when they took us out of the cage and into another room. In there we were stood up in front of a closet with a one-way mirror in the door and somebody behind it said that we were us. A strange cop said to our chaperone that, "Once they're through with that case, we'll have a whole new one worked out for them." As we filed out, whoever it was behind the door went Brrraap with his tongue and I felt like crashing in there to stomp on him as I'm sure everyone else did, but I just muttered and grumbled as they put us back behind the wire and we never heard another thing about it. I think it must have been just to unnerve us.

Along about dawn and by some mistake, I was shipped to the Tombs with Johnny and had breakfast there—or, actually, a baloney sandwich. The other, older captives there were real nice to me and all wanted to give me, poor youngster, the benefit of their experience. Breakfast was brought around in the form of a big binful of sandwiches and they told me that the trick was, when you went to get yours, to rob three or four slabs of meat out of other sandwiches and hide them in your own, which I did. Nice folks.

So I was sitting in a long narrow eating room lined with cells in three stories and with mopping trustees, just sipping my foul coffee, when who should march in with a bunch of men all dressed in grey, but Geordie. He told me in a distracted voice that the police had simply waited outside his impregnable door until he'd opened it to let somebody out. By chance though, Linda had gone out sometime earlier so he didn't think it would be too long before he made bail. While we were talking, somebody got the message that I was but a tender youth and I was raked out of there to be walked up and down long halls lined with bullpens full of captured criminals. As I passed a particularly crowded one I heard someone call my name. I turned around wondering who in hell it could be and then I saw Fred pushing his way to the front of the cell. The hack let me stop there just long enough for Fred to slap my palm, then grab it and say, "What's happening, man? You too! How ARE you?" I never saw anybody so glad to see me.

Then the guard stomped on my heel real persuasively so we continued on the line. A fine upstanding citizen if he had any education at all, would be awed and frightened I think, by the endless labyrinth of gleaming steel and glass tunnels, passing pens of captured people that he never thinks about without wondering where his kids are tonight. There must be, at the very least, ten miles of cell rows and I doubt that I could have found my way out even if I'd had the keys. But the hack took me through the ways using no golden thread but his own keys here and the keys of a pasty turnkey there until after fifteen minutes he stopped, opening the door of a big bullpen. "In here."

The pen, in there, was full of other mis-sent

youngsters like me . . . all lined up on the benches built into the wall, and I sat down in a corner to mind my own business. Slowly, I came out of my thoughts because somebody was standing up by the bars calling Geordie's name. It was the tall pimply-faced kid who had been clouting orange men. He leaned against the bars yelling something like, "Guard? Wha? . . . Guard? Where's Geordie? I want to talk. . . . I want to talk to Geordie!" One of the keepers tried to explain to him that Geordie was on the other side of the jail and that maybe he could see him later, but the kid's voice simply rose an octave. "Guard?? Guardguard? Listen, give me your keys, huh? Just for a minute . . . GEORDIE! I'll just go and talk to Geordie. Geordie? I'll come right back, I'll just go and talk to him . . . Linda? GEORDIE!" This request of his raised some low amusement around the cell. The guy next to me rammed me with his elbow laughing and said, "He wants the KEYS, man, hear that? He wants to go for a walk, but he'll be right back." Then out loud, "Hey, GUARD! Giv'm the keys, huh? He'll be right back! Hura, hura, hura!" Well, it was kind of funny and I sat still for a while taking the grin off my face; then I went over to try to calm him down a little, but I'd have had more luck with a flaming spastic. He said, or sort of said, that the police had entered upon the premises after guilefully lurking in the hall waiting for their chance . . .

Geordie? . . . and he forgot that he was holding two ounces of speed in his pocket . . . "GEORDIE! Where ARE you?" . . . and garble, mumble . . . "Geordie, mutter mutter, gurk." So I gave up and went back to my corner. The laughing man with the supersonic elbow was getting a little disgusted now, and he said, "What's the matter with that guy? Whining and pissing like that? Sheeeit."

And right on those words, two faceless uniforms came with the keys to put me and twelve others into a paddy wagon out on the street. We were no more than one hundred feet from the outside wall.

Over in Brooklyn, I went through the showering and printing, "Just relax, just relax," and some of the guards laughed when they saw me and one of them said, "You back here already? GodDAMN boy!" I was sent to a different floor than before, so it was all strangers again, but after watching the radiators wall-eyed a while, I found some guys to sit with. They were a couple of A.W.O.L. sailors who'd stolen a taxicab and driven it into a liquor store window in the small hours intending to loot, but had gotten caught because they'd stayed at the scene of the crime and got drunk.

While I was in this time, I stayed long enough to go back to the Tombs for a thing—Bail Review. Bail review, on the receiving end, consisted mainly of waiting. Waiting in a Brooklyn cell for the wagon, riding to the Tombs, and waiting to be let out of the car, and then waiting a long time to go up to the room behind the court. After an interminable time in there, I stood before the judge for ten seconds so he could say, "Same bail," and that was the big moment that it was all about. I went back through the door disgusted because I'd entertained some mongoloid fantasy about being cut loose, and rejoined the crowd waiting for their moment.

Most of them were there waiting for bail review, but some were ready for their trial proper. These were mainly young colored guys in tall spirits who was gonna beat this rap or that one and who wouldn't have been caught in the first place if it hadn't been for some freak accident. They grinned and flexed and talked a bragging blue streak. The whole crowd sobered up a bit though, when one young fellow who went in the courtroom door smiling came back gasping and wild-eyed. "Thirty YEARS! That motherfucker gave me thirty years! Thirty YEARS years years," and he slumped in the corner like an old feather pillow. Everybody's grin faded in the dim light and no muscle bulged. I hate the judge and whoever vests his power in him. If those bastards didn't get laid last night, that might get you another five.

One of the boys awaiting trial could see his apartment where his mother lived out the dusty, heavy-screened window and was pointing it out to me when the Man came to put my group back in a pen downstairs.

Goddamn! I thought, more waiting and somebody ought to feed me. It was about five in the afternoon and I'd missed all meals due to administrative incompetence or disinterest. The pen was really crowded but I found a small place on one of the benches and squeezed into it. The man on my right was a little miserable Spanish fellow about five feet tall. He sat with his hands on his knees, left on left and right on right, and his head hung to one side but was facing up in like some kind of almost religious appeal. No audience. I'd been sitting there for maybe fifteen minutes when he slowly sagged onto my shoulder, and began shaking as if he were riding a motorcycle down railroad tracks and then he went stiff all over. He started grunting, then his eyes rolled back into his head, and a young guy grabbed his feet saying, "Jesus! Here he goes again; grab his head!" I took hold of his head and a couple of other prisoners held his arms. I dug the little man's face as the young guy cursed and raved about the doctor. The goddamn doctor, he said. They'd called him when the little man had taken the first fit and the bastard didn't get there until the end of the second one and then all he did was he said, "He's sick, is he?" and shoved a couple of pills down the throat of the poor weak huddled heap. Statue of Liberty, hell. Apparently, they did no good, because here he was gone off again. Suddenly he went limp—like a piece of raw sweating liver. He flicked his eyes around and tried to say something, but he couldn't talk so he just sort of mewed and licked his lips. Then another wave hit him before he could get his tongue out from between his teeth. His eyes rolled back all yellow and bloodshot and the tip of his tongue curled up and turned purple. The young guy dropped his feet and grabbed his lower jaw, trying to loosen it while I pulled back on his forehead, but then the blood came and in another second he had bitten clean through and was gritting the chunk loose. The amount of flow was amazing; the only sound in the cell was his strange breathing and the gnashing of his teeth. Everybody in the pen was watching, wincing and tasting blood and I said, "Turn him over so he don't drown!" So we held him straight on his stomach, me holding his head up so the blood would flow out. A belt or something for him to bite on just didn't occur to us. I don't think any of us had ever seen a seizure before. At this point the horrible fascination was broken and the people started rattling the bars and yelling, "Doctor! DOCTOR! Motherfucker, get down here! Sick MAN!" Long minutes later, the doctor came, untouchable in his spotless white coat just as the little Spaniard was starting to feel the pain in his mouth. "Epileptic!" He caught on. "Come and get him out!" he hollered to two hacks who came in and carried the poor wretch away.

After the doctor left, the cell was sickly quiet for a while and a few guys nipped their tongues lightly to see what it would be like. "UGH! Bad business," I thought and my eyes fell on the red-blue piece of tongue. I got up and tried to kick it under the bench, but it kind of rolled up under my shoe and I wound up scraping it under with the side of it. I felt a little sick and vengeful on my way back to Brooklyn where I found I had made bail.

7

It was Allen, St. Christopher Allen, who had saved me again and he met me at the door with a young friend. We went to get some coffee and I fumbled with the cup as I told him how it had happened this time. He asked me why I didn't have enough sense to stay out of places like Hans's and I didn't have a ready answer. I said after a minute that I had plenty of sense but that it didn't seem to help any. We went to his place to go through the lawyer bit again and while we were talking, a couple of dizzy college girls came to see him bearing a pan of homemade brownies.

Never look a gift horse in the pan so we took them out to Chinatown for dinner.

Over a meal of strange crunchy things, Allen broached the subject of my first four years of which I knew little. He was very interested that I recalled a certain careening drive on Mexican mountain roads at high speeds and the ha, ha, how-fast-can-this-old-heap-go attitude of my mother and a friend of hers. Allen had tried to slow them down, and my sister and I spent the trip on the floor of the back seat. Finally we hit something I think, and there was a little blood, but not much.

After we ate, the girls led us around Chinatown wanting touristy things, Allen wondering if they were really serious and we walked along behind talking about people that Allen wanted me to meet. As we waited for them outside an incense shop, he said that he had a morgue photograph of my mother with the bullet hole in her head if I wanted to see it. I said, "Yeh, I'd like to," I lied, and when he said it was overtown somewhere and he'd have to dig it out, I said there was no hurry, heh, heh.

After we got back to his apartment and the girls had gone back to some prominent Eastern college for women, I told him I'd be careful, more careful than ever, and walked over to Eliot's. I toyed with the idea of really getting clean and watching out, but it was only a passing thought.

Zoom! Chad was there all alone with a gram of methedrine, and after I got off he told me that Eliot had gone away somewhere, there to remain for an unspecified length of time, and the place had been left in my partner's charge. The rent had just been paid so we were set for almost a month.

So after various twistings and turnings, it was Chad and I again; now in a decaying apartment on the Lower East Side, and we were almost homeowners. In the days that followed, we shot all the speed we could get our hands on. And the hands got thinner and thinner every night in the candlelight. The Big Company had taken its electricity back, but by God, we still had the gas.

Upstairs from Eliot's there lived a militant-looking pot salesman that Chad had befriended to his grimy bosom. We were deeper in debt to him all the time. We'd take an ounce or two to sell by the nickel bag and make ten dollars profit after paying back the salesman. But just as we were about to set out to do business we'd always decide that selling nickels was the easiest way to get nailed and wound up smoking it. Our Man had pounds though, and never made any fuss at all, just dismissing us as demented crystal freaks. During this time, Flip started coming by again, occasionally bringing a gift of opium or some such; not often and it was usually adulterated, but the thought was nice. I made no excuses at all any more for my terror of being busted all over again, and a number of times when the steps were a little too heavy in the hall, I leaped through the bathroom window out onto the ledge. We did have a feeble lock now, but it could easily be kicked open and its effect was mostly psychological.

Chad would take a fear fit now and then too, and I remember one cold night when we were all sitting around smoking reefer and wishing the goddamn super would send up some heat. Chad had been sitting in a corner chair with his cannabis eyes agleam, and when, to everybody's joy, the radiator came on with a hiss he jumped up yelling, "I knew it! They're using gas now ... GAS!" and he ran over to open the windows. He stood in the cold draft with cars honking in the distance behind him, and wouldn't let anyone try to close them again. "Maybe you're ready to die, but not me! ... HEH NOW! Get back!" and he brandished a heavy ashtray that gleamed dangerously in the candlelight. It wasn't worth the trouble any way you looked at it, so we just wore coats that night.

I was going over to visit Chris just about every day now, and there was one folksinger staying there who seemed to be getting farther off his head every hour on the hour. This was about the time that Bob Dylan had fallen off his motorcycle, and awestruck waiting prevailed among certain ranks. Well, Brian was this kid's name, and one night he had a vision, poor child, wherein he knew, he really KNEW, that Dylan had died and the spirit of Bob had entered his heart. He was to be the chosen successor and it was a great and profound responsibility. And then he'd launch into some song he'd written about barefoot freaks meeting Chinese walls that never falls but your children were still growing. That's my own impression of his style and I probably don't do it justice, but even so there was something lost during the transmigration I thought. I told him he should have a heart-to-heart attack with himself, and then wait a few months out of mourning before he started billing as the reincarnation.

Brian looked up to me; he said I moved like a cat, and when someone says that about you, you can be pretty sure they're on your side. Everybody has a personal spell that they alone can cast, call it personality if you will, but it can become quite magical. Some people are sensitive to that magic and are easily taken. I am like that, I am constantly having to free myself from people after the initial beauty of their magic has led me to befriend them. Deep Southern gas station attendants with their friendly punches good-bye and their greasy gorilla hands. But then once I am close enough to them to talk freely it's "Smell that finger, boy, I got in her pants in ten minutes."

Anyway Brian was like that to a dangerous extreme. True, his Dylan vision had taken place behind psilocybin but *still!* He'd been taking a lot of the stuff lately, because he'd dragged some starving chemical guru in out of the rain and the guy was loaded down with it. "MMM! Exotic!" I thought, and ate an indeterminate amount with them one night. They sniffed theirs and got high before me, but after a while I smoked a bit of reefer and caught up with them in a surprising hurry.

"Well, I'm here," I thought as I looked around at the ebb and flow of outlines and the objects that were just starting to become verbs. There was a gathering peace and timelessness in the air and I sort of wanted to stay and enjoin it, but Brian was watching me and I was afraid he'd start saying things like, "What's it all about?" So when somebody says you move like a cat, you got to move, right? So I got up onto my methedrine footsteps to go out and walk. Up the block I went and across the street past the phone booth on the corner with the wind pressing my filthy faithful peacoat against me. It didn't mold to me though, being stiff with slobber and whatnot, the previous owners' slobbers of course, and it was more like hairy matted amour.

Chez Eliot, amid monstrous and growing piles of trash, I found Chad and a young artist girl sitting in the glow of the candle. He'd met her in the Village where she came regularly to go to art school. She lived with her parents on Long Island, and after her classes where they taught everything except vision, she would tease and whine over the phone to her mother about when she should come home while Chad stood outside the booth scratching. But she was pretty, after all, and when you have only one candle to see your garbage by, that counts for something. I suggested that we walk up to the Village and they were ready, so I snuffed the candle and we went out. We groped through the dark to the door, and into the dismal brown hall, then down the stairs littered with paper and rotting food. Turning left at the bottom, I smelled the cooler air from the street ahead at the end of the grey, flaking corridor, and saw the edge of a streetlamp's slippery puddle of light. My awareness was a rising tide all the way west, but the mushroom really spun as we approached the Village from an unfathomable direction. There was an enormous lot ahead of us and it was all dusty dirt, except for a big X where white sidewalks connected the corners. I took a bomb scare as I crossed the center, but it was such an obvious place for it that I almost laughed and didn't miss a step. But then, as we came up a quieter street towards the crowds, I began to feel really painful pressures out of nowhere like the heels of hands pushing, and they travelled from my jaw across my cheeks, around my eyes and onto my forehead. I was saying to myself that it was all in my head, ha, ha, when Chad asked me what the hell was wrong. He said my face was a little scary and I said that was all right because I was a little scared and to pay me no mind. I put down the little muscle rebellion by setting my features like a Nazi, but self-control wasn't enough. The Village is full of people who look quite alien and monstrous and I'm not speaking of hippies only, there are occasional soldiers of that lost battalion led by the man with the pincer, and the Village was dispassionately hostile to me.

Not wanting to stay on the street, I steered us all into a strangely lit coffeehouse to hear some flamenco, but I couldn't sit still for any length of time so I left them there and went walking up and down alleys and, stony-faced, traced a figure eight as I walked round the two blocks. I wasn't really running full of speed that night, but it seemed that I'd been running in overdrive for so long that I was leery of really stopping to take note of myself.

I flicked in and out of neon lights as I passed and repassed people picking sauerkraut from their chins in stall-like restaurants, and I started wondering if there wasn't a jumping-off place where I could relax for a while to listen down into my own self. And right behind that, from my personal sphinx, came the sixty-four-dollar answer question, Who am I? I didn't know. Kids don't know. "All right now, for three bucks on the sidewalk, and a landing place for body and soul, who am I in 1967?" I said to myself and laughed, but I sounded like a breaking window. I spent the next four hours chuckling uneasily as I re-repeated the walk from West Side to East wondering where to go and as who. Finally giving up waiting for an identity in shining armour, I spat arbitrarily on the street and faked it as a crystalline freak. Because of the hour and be-cause of the cold and windy drizzle, the streets were just about empty of other flesh. The build-ings were massive and sulky against the sky, glooming with schooning purplish clouds above me and above the scraps of paper they scrabbled along past my feet. On one approach to the East Side I was suddenly frightened to find that the earth was crumbling away under my feet. I felt like I was stepping away just ahead of an abyss that was steadily opening up right behind me, and I walked faster and faster, finally breaking into a run. I knew that if I stepped anywhere but where my feet landed, I'd be sucked right into the actual meatgrinder of another reel. "Try a stop," my better half whispered, "or you'll be flee-ing around forever." So I ran to Eliot's place and found Chad the caretaker alone with the candle. I stopped at the door to breathe a moment, then snuck to the chair by the bed still panting, through waist-high waste in the crazy shadowed candelight. Chad was staring out the window and didn't ask any questions and I didn't volunteer any remarks. We sat there in silence for some time, and the first thing that came to words was food for some probably natural reason. At any rate, hunger was a sign of life I thought, and I went after an old bag of rice that I remembered was in a cupboard above the bathtub. I tripped around in the black kitchen for a while, knocking things over with my groping bones, before I got hold of the rice. Then I put the rice down and lost it while I was looking for a saucepan. With the aid of a match, I finally got the rice and pan in their appointed places and lit the stove. I watched the blue flame until I figured it was cooked, then took it back, and we bent over the candle squinting into this fucked-up rice, without forks or even any salt. When we finished the stuff, or finished *with* it, the candle was near the end and I tried to say something to Chad about how important it was that our last candle was dying on us and soon the jagged shadows would . . . but my words missed and I frowned at my crazy sound. I looked to him for a helpful word, but he just grinned like a coyote, using what we in the field call non-verbal communication to say, "You actually think you can make sense? Ha ha! We'll both go together." Then he was sorry right away because he could see that I was unusually vulnerable, and he talked mundane facts about his girl Deirdre. I rallied again after a minute and went upstairs to see if the pot salesman might have a soothing atmosphere going. His place, it turned out, was big, with two very large rooms besides the kitchen and the rent was proportionately higher, so he split it with two other people. When they let me in, I was in the front room belonging to the two other people. Big brown mottled air plants were hung about to grow, there were straw mats on the walls and floor, and Bomba the Jungle Boy was lounging on the bed fanning his sweaty self. He had long hair on his tropical fruit head, and wore only a green jockstrap between his fleshy thighs. Or maybe it was the peel from the banana that his girl just stood there sort of squashing around her mouth. What the hell was with these people? I didn't know, I'd never met them before and they made me want to puke and laugh simultaneously so, saying, "Excuse please," I went and knocked on the potman's door. Those people were weird. I knew them from the street when they were dressed—as I did the salesman—but I never dreamed that they went into their place and acted like that.

"Come IN!" he said, and he should have added brace yourself, because the four walls were completely covered with silk. One wall was black, another unnatural bright blue, another insanity yellow, and the other very red. He was sitting in a straight-backed chair in the middle of the room with his arms crossed and bluish smoke from his cigarette curled up around the single glaring bulb in the ceiling. Chad had always been the one to come up here before, and I was a little taken aback by the atmosphere. His general attitude held me static for a moment as he sat there immaculately clean in black slacks and a white shirt. He was a little fat though, and his visionary genius glower didn't go with his thick-lipped face. I said, "That you, Ludwig?" but he only wrinkled up his forehead more. As a race, I've always found potheads pleasant to talk to, often in spite of their initial impact, so I said, "You wanna come downstairs and rap? You got nothing better to do, right?" He did, but I was sorry because he sat there in the dark, thrusting his hand in and out of a pile of trash while he told me about how he had sweated and even bled for everything he had, yes yesss. Chad wasn't awake to make sarcastic cracks and I didn't feel up to it so I just sat there disappointed and trying to change the subject away from his melodramatic stumbling years in Europe. There may have been a laugh or two in him but there was obviously no rest, so while he described a dirty European river I crept in the dark silently through the kitchen to take my leave. His seat faced away and I don't think he noticed the little bit of light when I slipped through the door.

I walked all the way to the Village before I remembered that Aaron might be reading his poems tonight at Chris's. They should have gotten back from work just about two hours ago and the idea quickly formed into an image of me sitting by the fake spider web listening to him read—all tear-struck while the others slept, and I started back thinking wonderful wonderful. A fraction of an hour later, and all out of breath, I was knocking on the door. Then a strange thing happened. A grey little mouselike girl that I'd never seen before came to the door. It was all dark inside even though it should have been light, and she blinked for a few seconds before she could say anything. The dismal creature was a stranger and I started to say something, but she looked up at me with her unbeautiful eyes and said, "Shhhh! They're all asleep, and I'm going too." Exhaling, I said yeah and went to sit on the stairs between the top floor and the roof. I was no more than four feet away before the lock clicked to behind me. I've always hated the idea of locks in general, and especially the sound they make as the people I just left lock me out. I always wait for my visitors to get well away before snapping the lock back, and I feel weak and mean if I forget.

So I sat on those seldom used stairs with my legs stretched out flat and stared at the steps between them. A leak in the roof was sending a steady drip drip onto the spot I was watching, and it had taken green. A little trickle ran from the pool down onto the next step, then the one after. I got caught up in the sound it made because the sound of running drippling water is one of the most timeless imaginable to me. It was no different there on the stairs than it would be in caverns much too deep to ever be found except by spiritual proxy like I was doing. I could hear it just so, just the way it was, and I ran my fingers through my hair, one . . . drip, two . . . drip, three . . . thinking how I'd like to give up my human consciousness and be found here the next day as a green carpet of moss, but not recognized. People seldom climbed over those steps and when it rained, I could drink cold water. The thought was like the sound of a flamenco singer in a torchlit cave, and narcotic, but I left it unfinished and lurched to my feet. "Stupid to sit HERE!" I said aloud, but made note that water would always be running and this was a thing I could come back to. So I went heavily down the stairs and onto the street feeling as though I'd rejected someone I loved and a little embarrassed, too. I thought, "Right. I should have stayed," as I beat my cowardly retreat feeling the flesh a-hanging on my bones and shaking whenever my foot would hit the pavement too soon.

Should have stayed, but here I was back in the Village again and the crowds had gone; the bars and night places shuttered, locked and barred, and me without my whip. I was making ready to wander off again when I saw two people hurry down the sidewalk and into a doorway. I went to see if I could get in too, and found a coffeehouse that was open till dawn. I thought for a minute, and no, there was no place else to go but into the Four Winds. That was the name of the place.

It was far too late for uptown people, or working people, or anybody who wanted to sleep. In fact, all those with a place to go to had gone, so I felt as if I had something in common with the twenty-odd others inside. I saw Brian sitting with a pretty colored girl he'd wanted to get next to for some time. That was good I thought, but I wasn't about to go and talk to them. I wanted no words with anyone if I could help it, because I'd been thinking personally so long that I wouldn't have made any sense. So I waved stupidly as I went for the back of the room. On stage, a couple of young guys played a mediocre raga as I fit myself into a stiff bench to listen. Brian and the girl were before and to the right of me and the stage lights lit their faces in a sort of halo the way a campfire will. They were very much together and when once or twice they caught each other's eyes they smiled shyly. That really got me, they actually smiled shyly at each other and if the lights had been brighter I bet I could have seen them blush.

There's a certain tear-jerking way that some

people can go slowly wide-eyed before any entertainment. I watch them at movies and in shows
sometimes, and if the action is good, their shoulders will slope and they turn right into open-
mouthed children. Some of them are so old you
wouldn't think anything could get through to
them, but the sight of one of them seen from a
few feet behind, catching the glow from stage or
screen lights, hits me as a miracle every time.
Beautiful, beautiful. These two were like that,
and I felt like watching out for them or something. That was a laugh though; I'd lay my hu-
morous ulnas radiantly across their shoulders
and say, "Don't you children worry about a thing,
just help me down the block, will ya?"

But there was another colored girl sitting with
another white boy on the other side of the room.
She was better-looking than Brian's love. As a
matter of fact, she was lovely by any standards,
and her straightened hair wasn't wrong for her
face as will so often happen to poor black girls
trying not to be. Her boy was white like Brian,
but there was something about them that seemed
to call for a spotlight. Brian was very fair-skinned
and his girl, I'll call her Mary, was very dark, but
together they were just a couple, while the other
two were an inter-racial couple. I could feel a
great backlash of sexual and racial suspicion between them. They were just proving grounds for
each other. He was a handsome blond guy who

sat there banging time on the table with cool countenance, and every couple of minutes, he'd kiss the girl or touch her hair, then look to see if anyone noticed. Ah, she was so very high class, and he was so lusty potent that it would have been obvious twenty feet under water in a kelp bed. They were inter-racial all right, just hanging around together for show, each waiting to rob an imaginary treasure from the other in some gruesome orgy of self demonstration.

Meantime. . . . An old bum wandered around the place begging a kind word or look, and during breaks in the entertainment, with a wrenchingly nostalgic and weepingly nasal lament, he warbled how he'd left his heart in San Francisco. His voice must have been downright peachy when he was young, but now everybody laughed and jeered at the old slob and he was so dull that he took it for applause and beamed.

The two kids left the stage, finally killing the raga they'd been threatening for the last half hour. I mean it was all right if all you wanted to do was listen, but they did mangle it up a good deal in the name of improvisation. The stage was bare then for ten minutes and the folks took up conversation or whatever and arched their backs, groaning and stretching. I sat there in my inobtrusive spot feeling like a sniper and watching everybody and listening to the general murmur.

Then the break was over and a young man

about twenty took the stage. I'd never before seen anyone so relaxed before people and so sincerely bent upon pleasing his audience. Once he began to sing, he sang steadily for at least an hour with no stops at all, and he never once sang a song. His music was improvised to fit short declarations and imaginary rhyming words, prayers and questions to the audience that he fit together in a continuous montage that came so freely and spontaneously that it wove together into one satoric sound that brought me back to and into the running water. It was beautiful and it slowly built to a climax that threw him into a mild convulsion that he kept the music following, and with his voice that rose to a high whimper and was choked off. His eyes nearly burst from his head with the strain and his head thrashed back and forth until I thought his neck would break. His lips moved but made no sound until the movement had passed. Then he shut his eyes and began a long low musical moan without guitar and let it grow louder and louder and just before it became a commercial type yowl, he snatched it back and sent it off again with music this time. At the end of an hour, in a drenching sweat, he was just coming in for a seabird sort of landing—no bearded or rough-voiced ethnic he, but a soprano giver of joy and one of genius—when a fire-and-thunder businessman in suit and tie burst in the door hollering, "GODDAMN IT! Don't you know we don't have a license to sing? Didn't one of these bastards tell you?" Blushing furiously in the lights, the singer said that he hadn't known and that one of the boys that was on before him had said to go ahead. The boss turned on the kid in question, bellowing, "What the hell kind of friend are you supposed to be, telling him that it was all right? You KNOW this place could be shut down in five minutes if the police dropped in! God DAMN you! Are you HUMAN?" Then he said to the whole place that we all should have known better and said that if anyone sang again, he'd close the place himself, right then. "Christ!" and he stomped into a back room wiping spit from his mouth with the back of his hand. All this time the singer stood on the stage looking from person to person, and when the proprietor disappeared, he said a hurried good-bye and ran out the door with his guitar on his shoulder, just like that.

The whole thing was horribly sad because the boss was right of course, and you couldn't sing without a license even if you were a true and real Angel. Old Heat would make you find bail. But then the bum started to sing in a quavering wail, mourning and whining, and that prompted a self-appointed bouncer to toss him out on his ear. "Too mean! Too much," I thought and started to leave but the prospect of wandering about like a windy feather stopped me.

There was no other place to go and I stayed,

but slowly now, I began to feel less connection with the people around me. Then, in a blare of trumpets, I discoverd that I was alone, and here for probably very different reasons than everyone else; no common bonds. Common bonds! What cornball! So I sat there still very much high but seeing things the way they really were. In a single night, however, I can remember seeing things the way they really were in perhaps five different ways. But this way of looking had a certain air of ultimate truth. The way things were, my awareness came in declarative snatches, my feet hurt. . . . A scrawny wrist . . . that girl . . . and then I got to thinking that the singer who had run should make a record. I couldn't get the idea out of my mind for a good little while even though I tried. Finally I shook it, feeling a little scared at the way such a dumb thought had just sailed into my head and taken over. Free thinking now, there was nothing but me and the crazy colors of the people and fixtures around me so I punked down to an attitude of resigned disgust and sat there listening to a one-eyed lurching long gaunt cripple play hit-or-miss staccato blues until nearly dawn. Brooding is not generally my style, but for a long time I stared at the stage with my chin on my hands thinking about how really dumb I was, and how ridiculous all my attempts at understanding were. I remembered that I was just a kid run away from home, drugging my brains out and getting in trouble out of sheer stupidity. What did I think I was doing here? I asked, disgusted at my disgusted self, and knew it was nothing—only grubby rooms, staggering highs, and what roaring incompetence. But maybe it *wasn't* nothing, I thought. I was trying to be something—anything, and not being very successful even at that. No great wonder that "Who am I?" was difficult, I thought, because when I boil it down I get a screwed-up kid and try putting that in your works and shoot it. And the humiliation of that, the help jammed at you from all quarters, the laughable attempts at understanding, the timeless, endless studies made on me and others are too, too much to face. Far better to retreat truly into a thousand tragic selves than to be a teen-ager in reality, and scream under scrutiny.

And now the light was a pale blue outside and the waitress was saying that they were closing now, they were closing up. I got up to leave with my rotten attitude, knowing what the boring passionless core of my unholy scramble for a personal style was all about. It was this—to become a man, a boy must prove himself, and I was out to be gutted and wired and starved just a bit. To see what was up. Then, later, to think about what had happened, and who would be doing the thinking then? A stronger flesh would surely come away. At least that was what I thought; I don't recommend it at all. I don't recommend it because you can go so far around the bend to where you might file your teeth and run amok in a supermarket biting only those housewives that are reaching for Cocopuffs or Alphabits.

8

As I stepped out on the sidewalk, I saw Brian and the guru ahead of me in the morning twilight. I called to them but I sounded like a dying old man. Clearing my throat, I tried again and asked him if he wanted to walk back with me. And I tried to smile, but the old face wouldn't hear of it, and I guess Brian knows the expression that resulted, but from the way he declined I suspected that I looked like a leechy old faggot. And I was too stiff to move with any finesse at all, let alone like a cat. But all told, I wasn't bothered too much and hobbled back to the East Side, all preoccupied, and with knitted brow.

I breezed in, fainting to see if Chad was awake yet. He wasn't, but he yielded up the bed when I came in. Really exhausted, I fell across it.

When I awoke that afternoon, we injected some more speed into our veins, my friend. We had finally given up all ideas of cleaning up, which was a far cry from our attitude on our arrival in the big city. We had wanted jobs then, and girls and money. We wanted to see the museums and the art, and we wanted to climb to the top of the Empire State Building on the stairs. But it never happened. Free choice it was, though, and in the next few weeks we ran ourselves into the ground, "What the hell, we are comrades in arms, blood brothers, and it's all in vein anyway."

Tie it up we did, and suddenly it was the morning I was supposed to be in court. I don't know what the hell I was thinking, but I was so doggy by then that I thought I'd just give the court a ring to say I was sick. Yes, I didn't feel quite right, and couldn't make it today. Maybe another time? Had I had a rose, I'd have held it in my teeth all morning with sanpaku eyeballs.

But Allen saved my neck again and came screaming onto the premises about my lack of brains, and how he was trying to help me, but goddamn! I said with a nasal twang that nobody fucking well asked him to look out for me as I pulled on a less filthy pair of pants, embarrassed

140

for my scrawny shanks. He gave me a dollar and I took a cab over to Hans's to probe him out of whatever fanatical fervor he was in.

He would have forgotten to go to trial too because he was pacing up and down his apartment Nazi-like and barking that the cops had wrecked everything, everything, but he swore to deal with them in the German way as soon as he became established. I swear, Hitler would have shot that guy on sight. When I told him it was time to go to court, he glared at me so that, for a moment, I thought he was actually going to try to strip me of my rank, but he said, "Good! Yes, finefine, but wait just a moment so I can go in style." After he took off, with his pupils dilating as I watched, he offered me some and dissolved a lump of pure crystal the size of a ping-pong ball. Bad politics to take so much before a trial I thought, but I was glad of the chance and I did up half. Half was a bit too much too, and I walked right out into traffic to find a cab and damn near got myself killed. But I cared not a whit and when we got in the car, I sat sweaty and happy staring at empty space all the way to the courthouse.

Our session of "What's My Line?" was on the third floor, accessible only by elevator. We stood waiting by the glowing button lost in the hazy dusty dusk that filled the enormous awe-some-ness of this cold cavern of justice, lit by a few ceiling lights that illuminated paths of dust float-

141

ing in the damp air. There was nothing in all that space, nothing—no chairs, no pictures on the wall, not even of the President. There were just two rows of forty-foot columns that stood silently from the floor to the ceiling while little people hurried between them like lost souls. "My papers! My credentials!" And away down at the other end in fine perspective, they gathered around a tiny pathetic warm-colored concession stand that huddled in the corner against the cold marble.

Incidentally, all the walls and columns were real marble—I shined up a spot with some nose grease, my very own—and of the highest quality.

Then the elevator came to take us up and we located the rest of our group waiting by the courtroom door among a crowd of frightened fathers, mothers and defendants. They all said that they could tell from halfway down the hall that I was stoned out of my kug and that I hadda be crazy, man, to come to court like that. Then one of them told me that there was someone in the back row wanting to see me. I pushed open the swinging doors feeling like a cowboy and walked into the courtroom wrapped in clouds to find Nancy sitting there with her long blonde hair!

Nancy! Good Lord, Nancy had read about my bust in the papers and she'd cut school to come to my trial. A long, long time ago in Coconut Grove, she used to give me peaches on hot summer nights. She smelled of lime perfume then, and I went to see her only when I couldn't score. She always wanted me to come, but was never grasping about it. I did come, now and then, but not often, and I stood her up time and again.

I remember one night I went to her on L.S.D. and cried my freak head off because "I wasn't worth a damn," and she was real sweet and soft, saying she loved me and got me through it. It had been years since then and I'd never seen her except in letters. I never wrote back, but it made no difference to her; she left her school to see me at the trial anyway. So I talked to her hungrily for an hour before my case came up. I didn't know what I was saying and I still don't, but whatever it was, there was a lot of it.

Then we beat the case the same way as before, and after saying YAY! I left with Nancy saying, "I'll see you guys later," and we went to her man's apartment. She lived with him when she was in the city and she'd asked him to go out someplace so she could talk to me. I shuffled into their lower but classy place all emaciated and muttering was she sure it was all right? And was she sure he didn't mind? No, he didn't like it, she said, but he would do it for her which I thought was kind of mean. She said that every time she'd seen me, I'd looked starved and she fed me a meal too big for my peanut stomach. We talked for a long time about what she'd been doing since I'd seen her and about what she planned to do in the future.

She said that John wanted to marry her and straightaway I objected to the idea in so many stuttered words. I had no intention of even thinking about marrying her myself but I also didn't want her marrying this John. As usual, in relation to her, I was selfish and beyond my rights, but she didn't object. Cautiously, we talked on, marking what we said and being careful not to get into any kind of fantasy until suddenly it was half an hour before the Man was due back. Then I beat a hasty retreat to my brand-new hotel room in the Village. Allen had gotten money from my father to stick me in a room there, hoping that having a place of my own would keep me out of other people's shooting galleries.

The room was a small one-bed one-dresser affair on the tenth floor and out the window I could see, across the street, Washington Square which was just starting to turn Autumnal. Here in this little room, I finally curled up with speed as I stared out the window waiting to see someone I knew. I saw Nancy only once more, no, I didn't see her, I talked to her on the phone and she said she could come see me for one hour before her train left. I told her that an hour wasn't enough and that it would only be frustrating for both of us, but actually I didn't feel like going through any tender feelings. So she left and I forgot her again.

I just wanted to sit around now and not think

about things like tongues and pincers or about the fact that pretty soon I'd either have to come down or die. It was very sad thinking about coming down.

I was getting quantities of crystal from Hans now on the pretense of selling it, but I used it all myself and went out now and then at ninety per to scrounge up money. Some I got from Vicki, and some I got from selling people ridiculously small nickels. As a matter of fact, I borrowed Vicki's record player with the purest intention of listening to music, but I ran out of speed that night and Hans was away, so I traded it to a queen for a measly dime's worth. It was a great dime though and I called Vicki the next morning to tell her that her player had been stolen. So, with my frayed morals, I was in the debt of one person or the other most of the time. I had speed, however, and hadn't slept or eaten for two weeks which was a bright spot. There were two sores on my sides where my ribs were stretching through, and strange strange, I'd started seeing faces everywhere. No matter where I looked, someone was there. Tiny people slept in my ashtray and a giant slouched, sulking, against the Chrysler Building. The trees in Washington Square were filled with faces from the past that blew in the breeze, even though I am still very young. In the mirror, my own face crawled with a dozen others making positive identification impossible, but

145

none of this was anything to worry about I thought because it was just a drug reaction. Chad was following in decomposition not far behind, tripping over my pieces, and he would come over now and then to fly the night with me.

My veins were all fouled up, me being clumsy and irreverent and it was long and bloody sometimes before I could get a hit. At every abscess or miss, Chad would say, "You're all fucked up, man, you're a skeletal frame, ha, ha." And I'd call him blind babe in mad world. He was a hollow framework to my eyes, like an erector set wrapped in cellophane, and every time he'd hit, I'd watch the electricity that kept him running crack and sparkle from forearm to elbow to shoulder and then to his brain, where sparks would flicker from his black eyesockets in a reek of electrical fire. I myself, labored under the illusion that I had died weeks ago at 1,000 mph ta ra! ta ra! and was running headlong on accumulating momentum into the approaching Fall. My grandmother was saying whenever I called her to come home dear; come home and go to London, my father was waiting.

9

One thing I did understand though, was that the rest of my natural life was about three months unless I got out of New York, so I said fine, great, when an old grade school friend of mine popped up out of nowhere and offered me a ride straight through to Palm Beach. He'd come over with Chad one night and I gave him his first shot of methedrine. He jumped for joyo frabjous day and when he could, he explained that his mother wanted this station wagon down there by a certain day. The day was named, so now I had a definite departure date and when the thing became definite, Chad and T Bone joined up for the ride.

The night before we left, a girl named Michelle came over with a friend of hers, and their exuberant pothead bopper talk and in jokes seemed to come from another world and in a strange dialect. We talked a little and she seemed satisfied with what we said but I was only aware of a fraction of what passed and that fraction was meaningless to me. The most of my attention was directed upon the faces all around us and on the Autumn creeping in reptilian through the window. "It's getting a little cold outside," I said, remembering a song by James Brown, " . . . and I wonder do you know what I'm talking about?" In answer, a scrawny bum from pincerland who was standing behind Michelle nodded vigorously and the skin flaked from his face in a rain of cockroach-like insects that swirled between us. She got up to go in the mist, and at the door, handed me five dollars asking me to get her some psilocybin if I could.

I counted to thirty and then locked the door, thinking that all she wanted from me was stuff. Then I sat for two hours by the window alternately watching my right hand on the sill like a snowy claw, and a Washington Square that looked all tinsel and balsa wood. I got up to get some more methedrine which I kept in the bathroom in the hall, and was surprised when my hand came along, but thought in a stupid happy kind of way that I could use it to tear the Square to pieces after I got off. It was hard getting off—and with a normal brain, I'd have been frustrated to the point of maybe actually giving up for a while. As it was, though, I was fascinated by the tactile difference between bone, muscle and the cordish vein I was trying to spear. Much later, as I put the works down, the phone rang. I picked it up, smearing blood on it, and it was Michelle. An old feeling came from somewhere that it would be nice if she wanted to say something personal or even romantic, but she just reminded me to cop for her. I said, "Yeah, I'll see you tomorrow night."

I was wide awake now to my fantastic daze and I cleaned off the phone, forgetting about laying waste to Washington Square. I sat on the bed with my chin on my knees all night. It was timely, me leaving the next day, because about four A.M. I started hearing whispers from the people in the bedspread and in the window glass, and though I was a little embarrassed at first, I answered them, thinking, why deny anything?

The next day, as early as the sun, Chad called my room from downstairs. The faces drew back, and I said for him to come on up. He sat on top of the bureau and said that Johnny and T Bone would be by in about an hour and that the jig was almost up. We decided to cop some A to take home in like a doggy bag, if Johnny could stand the delay. A couple of hours later, standing on the

sidewalk in the sun, we got up fifty dollars between us and Johnny's poodle. Then I blearily
went to try and get us four grams. We didn't get
out of the city until near sunset as it turned out,
because right after I gave Hans the money, he got
a phone call and had to go uptown with his gun to
tend to some obscure legal matter.

So we spent the day waiting reasonable lengths
of time between hopeful trips back to his apartment. I was the one who kept going up and
knocking to see if he was back, of course, and
each time I was more terrified than before. I can't
describe the way I felt about the possibility of
getting nailed on my very way out of town. Each
time, though, in spite of my anguished condition,
he still wasn't back and we waited some more.

Early that afternoon we were sitting in the park
across from the hotel giving it a good wait, me
wondering if the bomb had a face, when I saw
Allen slinking past the corner candy store behind
his beard. I went over to say good-bye and we
walked around the corner to a bookstore to talk a
minute or two between the shelves. Grateful to
him was what I was and I fell all over the English
language trying to get it out. I felt sorry we hadn't
gotten to know each other hardly at all and he
said he was too as we shook hands at the door.
Good-bye good-bye, and back to the park I went
to find my boys on the bench waiting up a storm.
Chad's artist girl had even shown up to say adieu

and they were going through an incredibly complex parting ritual.

I sat down with them as two colored guys came strolling up. One was toothy grinny and all full of, "Wow man!" and "Whuat you say?" He started spewing unintelligible jive talk punctuated with, "Right?" and, "YOU, my man. What you think 'bout that?" That kind of thing bores me to tears so I got up and walked over to another bench. T Bone and Johnny came with me but Chad stayed put with his girl grinning hiply and pretending he knew what the hell the guy was talking about. The colored guy's friend had been sitting a little ways off, looking bored, as if he'd just wait until his crazy companion was through, but now he got up and joined him in talking to Chad, who started laughing just a shade more mellow. I said to my buddies that I thought maybe we'd left Chad in a sort of compromising position, and that maybe we should go back to maybe talk and mix. I started over, and just as I came up, there seemed to be some kind of a crisis happening. The serious spade was saying, "Yeah? Yeah?" and then said to me as he galumphed forward, "You want trouble, I'm ready! C'mon now!" Here! C'mon!" and before I knew it he delivered a real painful clout to the side of my head. I stepped back, raising Michelle's umbrella thinking frightened maybe for an eye as his sidekick jumped in to hold him off, yelling almost pleadingly for me to get away and hurry! because his boy was crazy and would kill me. He danced around like a basketball player keeping between me and Monstro who frothed and foamed trying to get by saying, "YEEEAOOO! You just GET that umbrella up! You just TRY that!" and he choked and swallowed. Well, I saw no help forthcoming from my three husky buddies, two of whom really were, so I beat it down the street like a champ. Chad and the boys caught up to me on the next corner and as we walked across, I looked back to see that the enemy was nowhere in sight. Chad put his arm around his artist and said real tough that he was "gonna get a gun and go back and GET those guys!" I told him for God's sake not to be a complete asshole if he could help it and he said he didn't think that guy had any right to slug me like that, goddamn it. "Right, right," I said. "And where were you when he did it?" Then I shut up because its not fair expecting people to render aid in the face of possibly getting hurt.

So we went, then, to a cafe-like affair across the street from Hans's and sat outside to watch. After an hour, I saw him go in the door and told them to get the long-since loaded car running and to bring it around to meet me at the corner while I went up to get our cop.

This time, instead of just knocking on the door, I had to go in; the police knew it well and I was in a paranoid sweat being there all over again. In my fear, I thought how I'd been walking back and forth to this place all day obviously wanting to cop, and I didn't see how I could possibly not have alerted every detective within miles. I told Hans that we were in a hurry to leave twelve hours late and in spite of that and my obvious horror of the heat, he still took an eternal fifteen minutes to fork over. Then clickety zippetyzip I fled down the stairs and onto the street looking for the car and expecting the Man to zero in and frisk me to a jelly any second. But there they came around the corner and I jumped in slamming the door saying we'd got it and let's go for the love of God, never to come back no more.

The situation now was that there were four of us jammed in the front seat of this Ford Falcon station wagon which was really unreasonable and probably dangerous and unlawful besides, so we stopped a few blocks away to get things arranged. After half an hour or so, we got the luggage fixed in back so that one person could be laid out horizontal in the few inches between it and the roof of the car. It was cruel and unusual up there, as the victim would be thrown against the roof by the slightest bump, only to land on snaps and locks without benefit of padding. The first hassle of the trip, of course, was over who would take the first pummeling up there. Finally Chad gave in and slithered in feet first, the hero of the hour as the rest of us said thanks, you're great and other guilty bullshit.

But we were on our way now, and as we drew

near the Holland Tunnel, subtle changes came into the way the streets looked in the light of being only part of a thousand miles. I was stroking Johnny's pampered poodle and thinking about the trees on the other side, when Chad remembered some clothes he'd forgotten in some guy's apartment, and he set up hue and cry for us to run back to get them. I said forget them, and he said they were all he had. I said I'd give him more, and he said they wouldn't be like his own. You can't argue taste, so I lied and said I had the guy's phone number and would call him to send the stuff C.O.D. Okay . . . so we all shut up and drove out of New York. No conclusion; nobody took a deep breath or turned to look back, because we were twelve hours late and had time to make up. No time to think; how *about* that!

10

A good many miles out of the city and onto a freeway we stopped at a service plaza to get off. I was still holding all the speed so I went into the bathroom first to discover that three of our four grams were talcum or something just as useful. I went back and broke the news and no one had a rash so I kept the bad stuff, and T Bone immediately divided the good gram into four allegedly equal parts, saying that was all for each of us. Then all the way to Washington D.C. I was severely put down for getting everybody burned and by the time we got there I felt pretty much on the short end. We stopped at a gas station for some minutes while Chad called his father in Palm Beach to see if he'd be allowed home. I went in the bathroom to fire my bit and came out in a better mood. Chad was back in the car looking disconcerted because his father had told him that his room would be ready which didn't fit his persecuted image too well. I poked a little fun at him about that till he smiled and then tried to get everybody in good spirits, cracking jokes from my aerie up in the luggage. But everybody wanted to take their A at different times and didn't change their minds when I pointed out that then we'd all be up and down at different times. On top of that, nobody felt like talking or feeling good regardless, so I just lay up there on the baggage feeling privately mellow until the next morning. Then the jolt was wearing off, and the shadow of a monstrous long-delayed comedown hovered over me like some grisly bird. The weather looked so bad for me that when we stopped momentarily at a rest area all green with trees I dug out the talcum. I wasn't really sure that was what it was, and thought it might have been some hard-to-dissolve kind of speed so I tried everything. I stirred it. I shook it. I held it over a flame and stared at it and generally knocked myself out to the great amusement of my good buddies who laughed their compassionless asses off. That made me pretty mad. How could they laugh at what was happening here? I asked what was so godawful funny and they said they thought it was a scream to see somebody so intent on getting high. That wasn't it though, what I was doing was trying to hold off not being high. There was a great difference; I wouldn't have cared whether I was high or purple just so long as I wasn't getting straight. But I said nothing and looked at the goo I was working on which had turned waxy. It was absurd so I threw it out the window and we drove off, they snickering, and me cursing. There was no more and I knew it so the rest of the day I chewed my lip thinking of other things in a methedrine way. When we finally stopped at a restaurant I got Johnny to buy me a cup of coffee. He offered me a hamburger too and I turned it down even though I was hungry, thinking it would bring me down and knowing that I was nearly there anyway. Everybody else had a sandwich or something and the damned poodle had chopped steak. By the time everyone was finished, I felt that it wouldn't be long before I was too and my eyes had begun to jerk around just a little.

After three weeks high on methedrine the comedown isn't necessarily that bad, but the participant's frame of mind can steer it anywhere from mere exhaustion to suicidal desperation, with hundreds of nefarious variations in between. So I knew it was going to hit me terrible, and as I sat under a tree to the side of the road waiting for the others to come out, I wished I could stop time right then and stay between places forever, never to arrive; never to arrive anywhere, only to stay right here by the road for good I thought, saying fuck it to the whole wearisome business and if I'd had a gun I'd gladly have blown my brains out all onto the tree.

But we went on our way and it was along about seven o'clock as I watched some fence posts vipp vipp by, that the tears came welling up so insistent that I couldn't do anything but give out long outraged gasps. I turned to burrow my head into the corner between the door and the seat and with my right arm over my eyes, I clutched at the collar behind my neck. I didn't feel anything but bad and all I wanted was to get some A in me. Physically, I felt fine; the whole horror was in my mind and I had to face up but couldn't and I didn't think it was fair. Why should I have such an awful mess to face up to? Why not *them,* why not *you?*

The general reaction was, "Is it that bad? God, can't you control it?" I said, "You pat bastards don't know what's happening and never could!" They made me sick then, they were so so cautious of pitfalls, so protective of their souls, never risking them even for a minute. Chad was no better even though he could be swept along because he chalked it up to circumstances and would never willingly risk anything from his heart. I felt that the whole of existence was one great game of chicken and that people who never risked anything like my boys here, who sat in safety, clucking like old men, were unliving and had punked out of the mainstream of things.

So finally T Bone said that God, he couldn't stand to see me like that and gave me half of his share. We stopped at a gas station and Johnny gave me all of his. A few minutes later I came out of the bathroom sniffling like a snooty little kid and feeling better. It was my turn then on the luggage again, and we drove off in silence. I felt really cut out now because I was behind them all and they wouldn't speak to me unless I spoke first, and even then they wouldn't look at me. I wanted to talk now, but they wouldn't be about to talk to me as I'd used their speed because I was so weak I *had* to take it or cry as far as they were concerned. So I was the odd man out and without the scorn for their never-reckless thinking that had justified me when I was terrified and desperate. So I just sat up there and now and again they would talk in low voices about mileage or something but I couldn't hear them well with the wind whistling in my ears. I was being methodically disliked for weeping over methedrine and I was frustrated because they didn't really mean it and it was only a ritual. They were just acting the way they thought one should towards somebody who cries over drugs. After getting high and fooling with highs and expounding on the new ideas and outlooks gained, they still maintained a false morality about it, and felt that man should always be the master but they knew it wasn't so. I wanted to lay this down to them but knew I'd have gotten nowhere and said nothing all the way to Atlanta, Georgia.

We stopped there to stretch our legs and I went to the bathroom to wash my face as they went to the coke machine. I blew whatever composure I had mustered at the sight of my face, seen free of hallucination for the first time in a long time. My hair shagged out, ragged and hanging about my bony neck as I stared into some weird and contracted pupils, and my lips were cracked as if I'd had no water for days. I needed a shave real bad and the net effect was that I looked vicious and homicidal. I felt desperation pounding up again but held it in as I shuffled back to the car where we were ready to go again. But as I started to get in, I thought what the hell for, I wasn't with friends at all and I was strictly alone really, so why keep on? I backed off, trying not to cry, and told them to go on and that I wanted to hitchhike. Nobody knew how to take this except Chad with his characteristic irrelevancy, who jumped out of the car and said, "NO, goddamn it! I'LL hitchhike! Fuck it!" which didn't make much sense, but he seemed to enjoy the heroics, Johnny became reasonable at this point which was sorely needed and said, "Come on, you guys, for God's sake, we've come this far together and we're on the homestretch now, so let's not foul up now. Let's go." "Homestretch," I thought and figured what the hell, it wouldn't last much longer at any rate.

After that we all tried not to thicken the air and turned our attention to being worried about cops, because now we were coming to an area where we were a fine catch for the police and no longer just four of thousands of New York drug abusers. There was a green Cadillac that we'd seen off and on for the last five hundred miles and that was prime suspect number one. We concentrated on that Caddie mighty hard to forget the rest and when it pulled into the same station we were gassing in, we all got in the paranoid spirit deep enough to last us all the way to the West Palm Beach city limits. Fuzz paranoia can be almost a blessed relief sometimes, like an old enemy.

As we drew nearer to West Palm, T Bone started coming on really scared and demanded that we throw the works out. "They're legal here," I said, and he answered, "Are you kidding? Do you think they'd be legal if the West Palm Beach police got them out of the same car that you and me and Chad are in? And Johnny's reputation isn't so great either, so throw them out; you can get more!" I could get more at that so I chucked them, and ten minutes later T Bone pulled out a big pile of meth he'd saved until now. He said it was some that he'd copped on his own before we'd left but I had my doubts and if we hadn't been nearly home I'd have strangled him. The works having gone out the window, ha, ha, we sniffed it off a razor blade that T Bone passed around under our noses. I thought it was fascist that he should hold the blade for us but no one else said anything so I sniffed quietly and contentedly, but the third time around we hit a bump and I got a little cut nicked in the end of my nose. That broke the back if you know what I mean. Here I was returning home in tatters to my grandmother with dirt smeared on my face, looking scrawny and feeling hungry, and that was bad enough but bearable when painted with a little romance. But blood dripped weakly from the tip of my nose wrecking even that little image now and I held my sleeve against it till it stopped but I still felt ludicrous. Johnny said for me to watch where I bled for chrissakes, that was his mother's luggage back there.

So we were back in West Palm Beach, driving down the main drag in the early evening on our way to let T Bone off. This was the return and it was a little more dismal than I'd imagined it would be, but what the hell, eh? We dropped T Bone off and drove away across the bridge into Palm Beach, me with my cut nose. There was no ceremony, no pause to let down; Johnny just pulled up in front of my house and I got out saying, "Thanks a lot," like he'd driven me home from the bowling alley. They drove off, and I stood on the lawn looking at this little house with the lights inside and waiting for some conclusion to hit me. But there wasn't an end here either, and I stood thinking how strange that I lived there in that house, me, depraved speed freak me, with my crater-pocked arms. I tried to sink it in that I really lived in this nice neighborhood, me, me, whispering to phantoms, I lived in this manicured block with my ragged hair and long fingernails. A family full of young girls lived up the street and I thought about dragging one of them off to have my filthy way with her. It was amazing, how the hell could this prim little environment have produced me? But I was not so very strange and was only a freak by the standards I rejected so I quit my signifying. Then I took a deep breath, smelling the jasmine, and I went inside.

kentucky ham

1

The fool's way, the amateur's way, the easiest way
short of unconditional surrender. Speed-addled and
walleyed, some part of me must have known that
someone would smell a rat sooner or later, but I gave
it literally no thought, except for flashes of black
panic, as when encountering sudden loud noises.

When I returned, or rather imploded from New
York City (Viceville—I know a place where one can
buy retarded children for whatever use—$2,000,
give or take), I wasn't *using* speed, it rather seemed
that my entire metabolism had developed a speed
deficiency. Scoff at the scientific impossibility if you
will, Doc, but the result was the same. I once walked

seven miles at three in the morning to beg up three 15-mg yellow Desoxyn from off Johnny, a shooting buddy, and then lost one on the way back because I was a little crazy and the wind moaned directly from the face of the moon and the trees showed the shape of the wind. The wealthy were all abed as I faded past the homes so clean and otherworldly, clutching just enough speed to hold off the suicides. Back home, I drained every milligram from my two meager tablets and injected them while listening to Thelonious Monk's "Lulu's Back in Town." The music took on an unspeakably horrible death jangle, which I took the instant liberty of turning off. The silence was almost as bad, because my hearing is, at times, schizophrenically acute. What most people take for silence is really a grotesque bedlam of creaks and groans and distant howling thunder.

I got through the night, but plainly something had to be done, so, after casing five doctors' offices the next day, I decided on one and showed up after the doctor had left. The nurse was typing up the day's data in a side room and, as I asked her about an appointment for the next day, I, oh, so shrewdly, dropped a quarter, which rolled to the case where the prescription blanks were kept. The case was out of her sight and I grabbed a pad, made an appointment for the next day under an absurd name, which she took seriously, and I was on my way.

The prescriptions went like this: Desoxyn, 15 mg, #30 . . . one tab with breakfast. And them fuckers was potent. Scene was to fill the plastic bottle with water and shake it until all the yellow came off the pills, and fire the result mainline. Sure cure for constipation. Desoxyn is not a narcotic and the pharmacists didn't bother calling in to verify the script. I went from drugstore to drugstore and was literally swimming in what was now my element. The fact that a gust of wind would break my pace while walking didn't matter a bit. I felt terrific.

But, enter the owlish, Kafka-styled little character who checks the books every month. I assume he is bald. He *must* notice the sudden run on Desoxyn all from one doctor. So, while I even had enough to turn on a few buddies and spend hours just grooving around town listening to the car radio with my stash under the dashboard, the Big Wheels and small Cogs of Justice had already started to grind, matted as they were with the blood and hair of bad guys everywhere. Maybe on some cosmic day, some black hat, some feather on the camel's back, will just jam the machine completely, though I shall endeavor to be absent when the time comes. So, they'd been eying me suspiciously for some time before I made my fatal mistake—going back to the same store twice even though it had been weeks since I'd been there. I guess this is the proper place to mention it. From the pinnacle of my twenty-four years of wisdom, let me tell you young guys that if you think you're being watched, you are. Maybe, toward the end of the book, I'll tell you a few of the further-out surveillance methods, but would first like to establish a modicum of rapport with my reader. Nothing destroys a message as easily as dismissal for crackpot. You see, these guys are fanatics. This is *all* they do for a living, eight hours a day, six days a week; watch people and pluck 'em when they're ripe. And they're good at it. You can't tell who you can trust aside from lifelong friends. I had a buddy in Miami who fell in love with a girl, lived with her for six months, proposed, was accepted, and two days before the marriage she busted him and a number of his friends. She was flown to the West Coast the next day and John, that was the guy's name, let me tell you, he's one bitter mother. Of course, there are a few cops who are so stupid that they can't chew gum and walk at the same time, but leave yourself not be lulled into a false Keystone Cops sense of security. Them cats got computers and other shit working for them that makes 007 look like sandlot cowboys and Indians. I'll never understand how some of those guys can be so smart and so twisted at the same time. Maybe they got locked in closets when they were kids, I don't know.

So, I got greedy and Sanpaku as speed freaks are wont to do and went back to the same store. Henry's drugstore it was, in West Palm Beach, and if you're ever in the area, drop in and do something annoying for me, like try on all the sunglasses and buy a pack of gum. I wasn't at all sure that I could pass this one off. I had taken a fit of paranoia a few days previous, which can easily affect the mind. I would lie in bed at night, after cutting out paper dolls, making little pyramids out of household objects, or whatever momentous endeavors speed freaks engage in, and literally feel myself attached by psychic umbilical cords to every plainclothesman from there to Twin Falls, Iowa. This is where the stupidity came in. Because of that few hours panic, the next day I deposited shreds of that prescription pad in no less than seventeen storm drains all over town. Chad, an old shooting partner, was among my many cohorts who were well aware (How could they have thought otherwise?) that I had gone completely out of my tree. The next day, without speed, was like breaking glass and late afternoon found me at the same doctor's office going through the same song and dance. I really felt I should have brought a skimmer. But this time, in my hurry, I got a pad that was already printed up for codeine. I don't know what kind of patients he had, but a lot of them must have hurt. I was furious when I got home and the next afternoon was spent surrounded with all the various tools of alchemy, trying to convert them to blanks. And my best efforts were what got me. I mean they looked like something out of Jackson Pollack's nightmares. But when you want speed, as practically any kid can tell you now, you're ready to walk ten miles and pose for skin pix. Some of my friends have posed at one time or another. I never got around to it for some reason, but have disconcerted many a porn-shop owner by laughing uproariously for no apparent reason.

Lame as it was, the first script worked, behind a myopic old mummy who probably just didn't give a damn, which gave me the heart to bop on around to Henry's and get busted good.

So, I marched in, as innocent as you please, and handed this wrinkled and creased slip of Mayan codex over to an alert young pharmacist, a real go-getter. One of the most ominous sounds that one can hear in a drugstore while wearing a black hat is the click, click, click of the telephone behind the counter. Desoxyn is usually prescribed for weight loss and depression, so I was standing at the glass counter trying to look fat and sad when I heard Mike Marvel over there hit the phone. It's a mechanism of some kind (that explanation really gets us some place, doesn't it?) but at such times my hearing does its aforementioned thing, and when I heard the word "forgery," I said to the other guy who was standing nearby that I was going to the front of the store for a pack of cigarettes. I went, as slow and cool as my circumstances would allow. This was one of those big places, snack bar and all closed by now, and I walked as slowly as I could, trying to muster a semblance of interest in the latest brands of nonsense. I was in a world of hypnotic perspective and color; obviously not accidental and when I got to the other end, there was Dudley Doright, big as life, peering around the next aisle like a paranoid caricature. He straightened up as if for all the world he wiped his nose on the sides of Brillo boxes every day and said my prescription was ready, sir. The game was getting absurd as I reached into my back pocket to report lamely that I'd left my wallet in the car. "I think you'd better stay here," he said. The jig was up. "Whaddaya mean?" I squeaked. "It's not free is it? I gotta get my money!" The hypnotically colored aisles seemed to stretch into infinity as I quick-stepped out the door.

What I should have done was run for the car as fast as possible, but sometimes you can blow your cool by keeping it. Which I did. Sane reactions to negative stimuli have never been my forte. I got halfway across the parking lot, strolling along after my misplaced wallet, before I noticed Hank in the car motioning in agony and pointing behind me.

Like I say, I was a fool, an amateur. I should have gone out those doors like a bat out of Hell, but at that moment a heavy hand fell on my shoulder and I was spun roughly around to meet the eyes of that asshole pharmacist, standing proudly (behind) an enormous Negro plainclothesman. He (the Heat) had his enormous left paw upon me and held out his golden badge to me in his darkling right. Wisely withheld wisecracks about Cracker Jack boxes reeled through my head as I stood transfixed, staring at the badge, probably looking rather comical as three squad cars glided into the parking lot, like sharks, their fenders gently rising and falling as they passed the curb. One of them cornered Hank (I couldn't understand why he hadn't gotten the Bejeeziz out of there by then) and the other two nailed our separate little drama to the asphalt—the cop, the dolt, and me . . . frozen as in flashing blue ice from the cars and only the badge writhing in his huge hand as if endowed with momentary life.

So, we stood around in the parking lot being sized up, nightsticks tapping palms as if the two of us were going to take on six cops, Joe Frazier's brother, and a pharmacist, even though I would have liked a crack at the latter. I was paying him, wasn't I? And he was so pinkly proud like he'd just lost his virginity. They searched the car, a rented one, discovered Desoxyn under the front seat, but missed the syringe under the dashboard. They also noticed that we'd disconnected the speedometer, and during the course of my numerous interrogations, it was constantly thrown up to me what a rotten thing that was to do. Then they stuck us in the back of a squad car to wait for some hotshot detective, all lights still aflashing and Friday-night people driving by openmouthed.

I was looking at the back of the cop's neck through the heavy screen that separated us from the front seat and thinking how an ice pick would make it beautifully at the base of the skull when the Grand Narcotics Lizard General, whatever his name was, arrived. He looked at us with that absolutely mannerless curiosity I have encountered so often. Then he nodded to his goons who were fidgeting around, scratching their balls, and looking at their watches. "Run 'em on in," and with real B-rate "Dragnet" style, the city cop's half snarl of total dismissal, "BOOK 'EM." But this was a small town, you understand and he came across like Barney Fife.

On the way downtown, Hank told me he was going to try to cop an innocent-little-boy plea, like "he weally din' know what he was pwaying wif." I thought he was a little loony considering he was Irish, fiery-haired and six-foot-two. But *"De gustibus non est disputandem."*

Down at the station, the cops were gentle, almost apologetic but in a very evil way, like we *belonged* to them now. After all the fingerprinting and whatnot, we were put in separate solitary cells with metal walls, ceiling, and benches. But, we were still stoned from our latest invasion of the chapel and we could hear each other. The acoustics were *fantastic!* We stayed up all night banging rhythm on the benches and singing the blues. We did "St. James Infirmary," we did "Black Girl," we did field hollers and I don't know what all else until it was probably getting light outside and the rhythm fell out with one last rap on the bench that seemed to echo into and through everywhere and everything. I never saw Hank again.

2

Palm Beach, dreamland though it is, still retains many small-town characteristics. It's a small enough place that living there for ten years will, at least, have one acquainted with most of the faces on the sidewalk. It is one of the cleanest, safest and most beautiful towns I've ever been in and I think that if I had the money, I might actually live there. I would probably be completely out of place by now, even though I was raised there, because, by virtue of being raised there, I started out at the top, so to speak, and I have spent the major part of ten years increasing my downward mobility; even to the point of having a gold tooth put in and getting a beautiful four-colored tattoo of a snake curled lovingly around a rose, on my right forearm. And, it's rather amusing how I got the gold tooth. It was at a southern "play" college and one of a group of girls I knew had just turned twenty-one. She had copped some expensive champagne and they wanted me to come to her dormitory to do the "skweek, pop! fizz!" routine. So, since men weren't allowed in the distaff quarters, I rustled up some tools and an old baseball hat and came on like a workman. "Man in the hall! Man in the hall!" until I ducked into our agreed meeting place. The girls were there and so was the champagne, an unbeatable combo. "Life might be worth living after all," I thought as I suavely perused the label on the champagne appreciatively, which had a name sounding to me, for some reason, like an unusual venereal disease. What then ensued was scarring and traumatic. I'm sure you all know the good-natured bit about sucking up the inevitable foam from the mouth of the bottle. So I was all primed up to do the manly drinking from the mouth bit scene with the appropriate gusto, just to get things started on the right foot. A couple of the girls had already mentioned in a confidential way that it only took them one glass and all their inhibitions went right out the wyndoah? It's just awful? "Mmmmmmm, candy coated," I thought as I started to open the champagne, and what followed was instantly relegated to the "You Just Can't Win Department." The bottle skweeked, the bottle fizzed, and in anticipa-

177

tion of the foam, I blithely knocked out my left eye-tooth on the rim. There I was, Zorba the schmuck, sitting there, bleeding profusely and staring back at four delightful open-mouthed little creatures who were wondering what this lunatic had for breaking his lips. I stayed not upon the order of my going, and in the confusion that followed, me trying not to bleed on anything expensive, all I can recall is a vague "What the Hell did he do that for?" as if in an echo chamber.

But, I'd always wanted a gold tooth and now I was able to get one, albeit over the cultured objections of my grandmother who said, "Well, at least try to keep your mouth closed whenever possible."

Which naturally brings us back to Palm Beach. When I was fifteen, I accidentally shot a guy through the neck. One-fourth inch in any direction other than that exact spot would have ended one life and God knows where *I'd* be now. The whole scene was very much a drag. I won't bore you with the yowls and gore, but what I did was flee seventeen miles to the home of a girl. A girl that I worshiped. If she couldn't help me, then there was no ground called sanctuary. I go to the side of her house, hidden in the dark, just a few minutes before she returned from a date. She kissed him good-night and my heart almost broke, even though she'd only looked up to me as an intellectual buddy. But, this time, there was something happening that was even more urgent than love. I called her to the side of the house and told her what was happening. Okay, she said, she'd stash me in the fallout shelter, feed me, and try to find me a way out of town. My God, we were only children plotting in the dark, but even then, something deep inside me was entranced with the tragic day and I thought that this was surely the turning point of my life. I didn't know then if I had killed the blank character in the tumult of the day. But, she would hide me in the shelter (dig those words—the bomb was nothing, man. Nothing.), perhaps she would even come to comfort me later; I might even kiss her. That one kiss, love found and lost in an instant in the shadow of death, before I exiled myself to some far place—California, where I would surely be taken in and loved by the flower children. (I didn't realize it then because I was scared shitless, but the *romance* of the day was feeding a hunger that I'd never known existed and hasn't quit since.) One breakthrough of romance in the true sense of the word and . . . as a matter of fact, it *was* a turning point in my life.

Of course, her mother overheard, was very calming and sympathetic, gave me a cigarette, and drove me home. That night, I waked because of something hard in the bed. I know this sounds like an old Vincent Price movie, but it was real, it was delirious. I swear to Christ it was the gory bullet.

Then, the police came with typing machines and stumpy fingers. They took my gun and the bullet and it was over. My gunshot friend and I, blood

179

brothers until then, were always embarrassed and never spoke to each other again.

This is not just local color, I am running you this gauntlet so that I can say that by the time the story got about town, presumably scribbled on the backs of twenty-dollar bills, the story was that I had taken him with me to a vacant lot, turned and said, "Now, I'm going to kill you like I did my mother!" And had left the victim for dead.

Now, you see, we can get down to scene present. I am eighteen, gold-toothed "like some savage," and my arrest made big news. "William Burroughs and his associates are animals and deserve to be treated as such!" shrieked Judge Broberg, "the one-armed bandit," waving the stump that he got for incompetence under fire. I used to watch him swimming at the Coral Beach Club when I was a kid. Stroke, flip, sink. Stroke, flip, sink.

But, they got me alright, right there at Henry's drugstore. Fair and square, but it wasn't much of an accomplishment. I had "speed freak" written all over me in seven languages, so it was just a matter of time. And, then, the harassment started. All you young cats coming up right now, I want you to listen to this, because sure as shit, you're going to run into it soon. Sooner or later. Old Burroughs' proverb following statement: "I'm bust-proof," goes like, "Get out and don't come back." Anybody who claims they're cool and bust-proof, unless they've got a million, is a security risk of the worst kind.

I got bailed out that morning after the blues in my iron cell and went home to my grandmother, who was naturally all aquiver. We didn't say much to each other, parents always know, in advance, and have a remarkable capacity for doing exactly one of two wrong things: either saying nothing and just spreading general unpleasant nonverbal communications around the house (vibrations if you will), or coming on like gang busters with floods of misinformation about the effects of various drugs the kid has already tried. So, grandma was the silent type and I spent the afternoon using up what little stash I had left in my room. Then, there was the old knock on the door. See, they can bust you separately on all the various charges they have against you (you'd be surprised how absurdly technical they can get) and if they feel like being bastards, they'll just simply let you get bailed out and drop by, grinning, to play their game again. They followed me into my room so I could get a coat while my grandmother aged another forty years. While I was rooting in the closet, trying to ditch the syringe that was in the coat, one of the little darlings started going through my drawers. "You got a search warrant?" I said. "We don't need one," says he. "Like Hell you don't and keep your hands off my property!" They will *always* say they don't need one. Don't go for it, especially if there are witnesses. I mean if your bust is in some place other than the ilk of New York City or Chicago, make the most of your rights. Demand your lawyer, make your phone call, the whole television scene. And don't get embarrassed and think you're hamming it up. It's your skin. These cats usually will back down if you're right. But, if you're in, say Harlem, man, forget it. I know a guy who signed a full confession for something he didn't do because the cop told him he was going right out an eight-story window if he didn't. And he would have, too. He was black obviously, but even us honks gotta know our p's and q's. (What the Hell does p's and q's mean?) Don't sign anything and don't make any statement, they are experts at tripping you up later on minor contradictions. If need be, trade a bust in the mouth for one in the lock up.

This time they put on some kind of pressure and no bondsman would touch me, so I stayed in the Palm Beach County Jail. Scene: one wall, all cells. Two bunks to a cell. Mattresses, six ounces and strictly from perfunctory. No exercise. No reading material. No comfort for anyone over six feet. There's the ceiling joined to the floor by a maze of girders with rusty rivets that fill the other three-quarters of the room. On the far side, six heavily screened windows that look across the street to Belk's. Omigod, the swinging doors and the chicks and the cars, moving, going where they want to, even the newsboys, the pigeons, the whole scene was a nightmare, vertigo nothing. My cellmate claimed to be Mafioso, when poolroom was his style, if that. "They gonna get me out any minute. I'm important, you know. I, uh, can't tell you anything else, but you'll see."

But aside from a few phantomlike figures, mostly big black men in T-shirts moving against the windows at dusk, that's about all I can tell you about the place. I was gone. I was really half gone. As the weeks and months of Methedrine wore off, I talked to myself and to the kindly other prisoners who would whisper, with a kind of heartbreaking *respect* (it is very painful when someone really understands —respect is always the result). "It's time to eat, man, you wanna eat?" I ate once. I swear I have no idea what it was, could have come from a hospital bedpan, and vomited green foam flecked with red. After that, three times a day I would try to get up, and three times a day the floor would rush up to plant a grateful kiss on my right cheek; always the right for some reason. I should have alternated like Ben Hur. Strong hands, criminal hands, would lift me back to bed, me muttering about how weak I was. But I guess that dues is dues and one huge black son of a bitch, who was the kind of fella I was always afraid would rape poor me, even saved me a cup of soup against regulations. Regulations. "Prison regulations." There's something to let your mind just soak in for a few minutes. *Jail laws.*

When I was at my worst, when life, liberty, and the soul of man meant nothing compared to the buzzing of a fly (and them bastards bite sometimes —delicate balance of nature—Hell), THEN, they called for me. Be ever so careful. The cops know when you are weak, they are shrewd bastards. It is their living and they have fascist books that they take home to study; at least, the detectives. And it was the middle of the third day. I was taken to an air-conditioned room and placed in a cool leather chair. Detective Dan Noble had elbowed his way up from Miami to deal with me. (Imagine a name like Dan Noble!) "Trying to pass as a fag, I guess," my father would say, though what he really said was, "That son of a bitch!"

It was the standard routine, which you probably already know about, but I'll tell you how it feels in real life. While Big Dan stood in a corner with his arms crossed, sizing me up (I'm a goddamn pip-squeak, I'll never understand why they persist in doing that), another cop, whom I can only refer to as Porky, gave me a cigarette and told me to relax. While I smoked my first cig in three days, almost like a reefer, but mentholated, here it came. And they'll give it to you, too. If it ever happened again, I would say something obscene, get clouted, and go back to my cell. What is so hideous about the way these hyenas work is that you can never tell how you will react until the time comes.

This was it. I was offered extreme leniency (what-ever that meant, but I was too sick to think) if not freedom. All I had to do was set up a guy who had come to my door three weeks ago wanting to unload a quarter ton of Cuban grass. They wanted this cat bad. It would mean promotions, raises, maybe even a gold watch. When he came around before, I hadn't known him and thought he might have been some kind of obscure cop; besides, his car, a new Porsche, was in the wrong class so I refused. But this was no New York bust where the freedom fee simply rises with the charge; I was to be made an example of, so exhaling a breath of spring, I agreed.

I can say nothing in my defense except that I never did it. I will never throw down on anyone for bending at such times because you just can't tell when they're going to hit you. But, I didn't bend—I stalled. They let me out on the strength of my promise; I was to arrange the sale in a Holiday Inn. We would all be busted so no suspicion would fall on me. But I must say, young friends, don't believe that they'll let you go; they might, but it's entirely up to them. They even rented me a car so I could frequent the places where he hung out. I went so far as to drive by his house one night, but he wasn't there, so I explained to his friend that I was ready to do business, along with the subconscious warning that I had been busted and needed the money for lawyers and shit. Had he been there and willing, I might have tried to set up the deal. I don't know. I can only be honest. It was elemental. Survival.* Dog on dog. But if I had, where would I have been? Somewhere out in limbo. I just don't know—I may have broken

* Later note: no, it was *not* survival. It was comfort. This was not a capital crime, after all.

down and told him to get the Hell out of town, that he was really hot, but, at any rate, the deal would have taken some weeks to set up, giving me time for plenty of understanding that such a move would put me in checkmate.

Thinking back, I realize I was horrified to find myself nearing what I most despised and used the car that had been rented for my heinous purposes to drive to Miami by the most devious of routes and score an enormous quantity of morphine sulfate. (Until February 2 of 1971, these papers were more dangerous than strontium 90; I had to hide them whenever I finished typing, because I was still on probation and my guardian was entitled to walk in at any inopportune moment to inspect the premises.)

It was a funny trip to Miami. I leveled with my pharmacist in a restaurant beforehand and he quizzed me about this and that, but I picked up my dope by two and was home by five that afternoon. As soon as I got home, locked the door, put on some jazz, and figured everything was cool, I did in a grain or vice versa, just before the phone rang. It was Danny (par for the course) wanting me to come down to the station and make a progress report. "What is this, field maneuvers?" I thought.

Now, let me tell you something about Dan Noble. He was a huge predatory man who lived only for "The Bust" and walked with his head thrust before him and his shoulders back, as if all doors would open and most did. The problem in this particular case was that he had been a pharmacist before he had become a nark, which is bad medicine in anyone's "How to deal with" manual. When I came to the ratty office on the second floor of the Palm Beach Police Department (radiator peeling orange paint, somehow very official), Dan was there with Porky who looked rather sad. I repressed a desire to ask him, Porky, if he hadn't "bin gittin any" just as Dan bellowed, "Morphine! You little bastard," followed by whatever obscenities you wish to fill in, they all fit. And when I beat around the bush and told him, finally, that I couldn't go through with it, he shrieked, "Damn you! If this wasn't Palm Beach, I'd beat you to a bloody pulp here and now with my own bare fists!" I sent a silent prayer of thanks to Henry Flagler* and recall noting a distinct sexual intonation when he mentioned bare fists. It was something in his lips that I've seen on old men's faces at skin flicks when the chick is getting hell. I, poker-faced, visualized him writhing on the end of some medieval pike as his truly inhuman face of humanity came within inches of mine and he howled, like a dog run off from it's kill on a prehistoric plain, "I'll tell you one thing, buddy! I'm going to see you in prison! And when you come out of *there*, you're gonna be one hard-core mother-fucker or a faggot!" Now, I ask you, does this sound like the kind of man who is dedicating his life to alleviating the self-de-

* founder of Palm Beach

struction of others? There is simply no life *in* him, and worse, no capacity to receive any, I mean, shit! The things that have been done to *me* are *nothing*. Euthanasia for that cat. Anyway, then he delivered a Palm Beach, open-handed and restrained clout to my right ear and made me walk home, carless. Big deal.

On the way home I wondered if he'd slap together a search warrant to look for the morphine, but I decided he wouldn't because even though he knew I was a twisted Communist nigger-loving faggot/orgy weirdo, he recognized the fact that I had some brains and it wouldn't be in the house, as in fact it wasn't.

Something over an hour later, I got back to my mahogany-floored bedroom and took another shot. It wasn't an overdose by any means (but I'm sure you're *not* acquainted with those one in a hundred that just do every damn awful thing to you . . .). A strange metabolic urgency stirred and quickened as my statue of St. Joseph watched; broken fingers out-stretched and Himself unable to protest. Just as the rush hit me, my grandmother knocked on the door wanting to straighten my bed. I said the bed didn't need any such thing and that I was going to it now, but it was no use. I hid the still reddened syringe (it is very frustrating not to be able to clean equipment immediately) and let her in. Thirty seconds later, the cold wind before an approaching rain swept through my bowels and on to every extremity. I said, again, that the bed was fine but it was still no go. Women in general are strange enough, but old women are too much. She had to lift this, diddle with that, rearrange it, look at it, and put it back and God only knows how she couldn't tell how badly I wanted her away. The next time I opened my mouth to beg privacy, my jaw began to tremble. I got me up, cautiously, teeth clenched and vibrating, each vital against the next, not knowing what was happening and said, "Mother? It's alright. Really it is." I started to help her with the bed but, oh, frustration, when the body simply refuses! I fell on the damn thing in what I can only describe as a convulsion.

I was sweating and wrenching. I had never felt so cold in my sweet short life (94 percent) and my grandmother was saintly with her cold washcloth, which was the last thing I needed, something cold. I was suddenly very much afraid that I was going to die. I said, "Will you please, for the love of God, get me a doctor?" And frightened, she said, "Oh, Billy, you KNOW I can't call a doctor!" And I knew that it was obvious to her what was up, but I just simply couldn't care a whit.

About an hour later, I lost consciousness, which is a terrible thing to lose if you want to keep it, and when I woke up in the sweat yellow and clammy sheets, I took another shot, but nothing (side effects?) resulted this time.

It was something over a month before my trial,

and my supply lines to speed had been cut off, so I devoted myself to the opiates with a wholehearted horror of what was to come. I should have jumped bail, but I found paragoric, morphine, and Dilaudid extremely satisfactory substitutes.

About a week after the night of the convulsion, my father flew in from London to try to keep me from being totally hash-browned, southern style. It had been so long since he had been in America that he went into a restaurant wanting root beer and asked for sarsaparilla. But I mean to say that he was a pleasure to have around. There are times in a man's life when nothing can be so gratifying as to say something and to have it understood. And seeing, followed by understanding, was my father's specialty. Always has been. I mentioned to him once that Porky, who was usually with Dan Noble, was a fairly nice guy. He took me immediately to task, teaching me the proper means of dealing with the authorities. "Man," he said, "did you fall for that? That's the oldest vaudeville routine in *history!* Tough cop, nice cop. Laurel and Hardy!"

Weeel, I had fell, but won't ever again should the occasion arise. Make me no deals and I won't let you down, officer. Throughout the court proceedings, I followed my father's example of immaculate dress, punctuality to the minute, and speaking only when spoken to. If your timing is right, waiting rooms are unnecessary, but if you miss, never, under any circumstances, allow yourself to look comfortable in one. "Be attentive but not impatient. That's important. If a small mind with power begins to feel inferior, all Hell is going to pay. Above *all* (and this will be the hardest and most important to swallow), there is *no such thing* as a *nice cop!* Truth, like anything else is relative, and *believe* that, son, and you'll save yourself a lot of grief!"

My father, incidentally, takes a marked interest and often delight in the grotesque and bizarre. For almost a week during the trial hassles and appointments, he had been driving the "powers" crazy by practically materializing on time and answering all questions straight out of the manual of standard operating procedures. But, one morning he blew it completely for five seconds, it may have been less. We were being taken to meet my probation officer, and the flunky said that Mr. Panos would be with us in a moment. The name Panos was slightly mispronounced and I thought, "Oh, shit!"—because I saw the light of glee in Bill's eye. I could almost hear him thinking, "What! A probation officer named????" For just a fraction of a second, he was a long, yellow-toothed junkie, radiating Amazon headwaters and New York jazz scenes, as he asked, with a joyously piercing intensity, "Did you say *Penis?*" "No, I said Panos." "Ummm, yes, of course," said Bill, regaining his composure with science fiction speed. It was all over so fast that there was no time for rational evaluation and any uptight victim would have felt the king's fool to broach the subject anew.

191

On off hours I would drive my father around Palm Beach which, in itself, is a decorator's dream: Phipp's Plaza, Worth Avenue, Via Mizner, and scores of other abscesses of terminal affluence abound within minutes of one another. One is just as likely to jostle a shoeshine boy as Nina Dodge or Dee Kellogg. Many of the large homes toward the south have private tunnels leading under the manicured public road to their private beach. Decadent, yes, reminiscent of the last years of Rome, yes. But how could I count myself other than practically chosen to have been raised there?

3

By the way, who am I? Somebody out there must be interested in the answer to that question by now. So permit me to digress for a few minutes by way of introducing myself and my family.

(Light, color, and buzzing confusion. Yes color, doctor, on July 21, 1947 in Conroe, Texas, 4:10 A.M. Born without consent or consultation.)

My mother must have been a remarkable woman. During the entire course of my fetal development, she consumed enough Benzedrine daily to kill Lester Maddox outright while Big Bill, my father took three bangs of H a day to keep up with her in his own ivied and contemplative way. I was born to conversation and in seconds flat onto an alfalfa farm in the Rio Grande valley. The main crop, marijuana, grew between the rows. My father had hired a guy name of José to tend the fields, and a couple of times a week he'd go down there and nudge him in the ribs. "Hey José, what's that growing in my alfalfa? Haw, haw, heh, heh."

We split for Mexico City almost upon the moment I was born and all I can remember of the valley is the hot droning of locusts in the distance as seen, yes, seen, through gasoline fumes and the net over my crib (under a flat tree near a flat white house) to keep out the scorpions, beastly black things that danced and capered together between the blasted gnarled roots of trees until one was dead and only flexing spasmodically and the other crooked and haywire.

I have no memory of our flat in the native quarter for reasons soon to become evident, but the spiral staircase that led down from our top floor was banked with cool blue walls that kept out the heat. Perhaps I was just young enough then to feel the temperature of the color. At the bottom of the stairs, in poncho and sunlight was my little Mexican friend, Micco, who was the proud possessor of a white rabbit named Chili. I had never worn shoes in my life until one day Chili thumped up to one of my brown and bare toes and bit me like a Gila monster. I went crying to my mother wah!, who was soft and warm and pulsing, and not only got a set of shoes, but also a fresh can of beans.

I had a half sister named Julie, full of smiles—a tiny naked dancer who was my mother's daughter. She was only two years older than I, and the first hint of disaster that I can recall was an impossibly mad drive along whimsically sudden changing mountain roads, terrifying glimpses of death rusting wreckage far below and hearing my mother saying, "Ha *ha,* how fast can this old heap go?" Julie and I spent the trip on the floor of the back in the intimacy of fear as Allen pleaded with the driver to slow down. Finally we hit something and there was a little blood, but not much. The driver was not my father and Allen tells me that for a long time there was some doubt as to whose child I actually was. (If they only knew.) But I have my father's chin and I have his heart and spend no time in the forest licking imaginary wounds.

Again, my mother (Joan was her name) was not one of reason and she had soft brown hair and heart-shaped calves seen from behind. Some time later, my grandmother spoke to me in a failing voice about how timid Joan had been in "correct" company (meaning herself, poor doll), and how she spoke only to Bill.

The Allen I refer to is Howl Ginsberg, and he told me one New York cold Chinatown night that my mother was also a death freak as is anyone who makes a habit of speed. He said he had the morgue photograph if I wanted to see it, but I chuckled chilly uneasy and said something to the effect of "maybe later." It *was* a cold night after all and the photo was overtown. Besides . . .

So mama was tempestuous to say the least, and one night at a party in our home where everyone was plastered or stoned, she placed an apple or an apricot or a grape or myself on her head and challenged my father to shoot. Bill, usually an excellent marksman, missed. (Accidental homicide. Cause of death: Cerebral Hemorrhage (at least) Weapon: Colt .45.) So I can remember no details of the apartment or my mother. Is there a Scientologist in the house?

"The past is fiction," my father says, and I tend to agree with him. In any event, these memories or reconstructed memories are flashes, strobelike and fitful, easily rewritten. Only as much of me as I allow, as much of me as I care to dispatch, is there, and now, these. I am very sick in a rich woman's house where I am given brutal cold baths and Julie led me up a long winding staircase to a tower where I was dizzy with the view and illness, but she taught me the best way to wash my hands, which made me feel glad. What the hell a sink was doing up there, I'll never know.

Then, with incredible suddenness, my father was there, pale and haunted. He took me to a park all agreen with dusty Mexican trees futilely waving away the wind from a cloudless blue sky, like widows with their memories. I was nauseous but happy as we stood by a fountain, a big one that touched my face with spray in points of light. By the water, he unveiled his gift: a red boat that ran on alcohol-soaked cotton ignited in the stern. An awesome machine with real fire. "We have to be careful now," he said with the utmost gravity as he shakily lit the cotton and then the little boat chugged crazy circles on the water. But my eyes were on three teen-agers with greasy hair who were watching us from the other side of the water. They were snickering and I was afraid of them.

At this time, Bill was looking straight into the abyss. The rock he'd built upon was rattling and crumbling and echoing down from beneath his feet and he was pale and thin. I was his main concern there by the fountain, but over the yearning and pain that he felt for me hung something heavier. Like lead, but molten and smelling of gunpowder and burnt copper. The Burroughs Curse. I don't know when it was first visited upon us, but I felt it then and the chug, chug, snicker, snicker painted a very lasting picture.

So Julie went to New Orleans never to be seen by me again. Allen was not allowed to see her and it was clear that Bill would have been dried and cured on sight. As to myself, my father made the wisest choice available and took me to live with my grandparents in St. Louis. I remember arriving at their house on a hill all afeard with a piece of paper crumpled in my hand and asking, "Where's the wastebasket?" My father had always been a stickler about litter. "Now Billy, there's enough crap around, huh?" And then he was gone to suffer in abominable ways and to write or more accurately transcribe *Naked Lunch*. No shit man, he stayed not upon the order of his going but went at once. "Wouldn't you?"

I was taken in without reticence and with great compassion. My grandmother was Laura Lee Burroughs, aristocratic, proud, possessed of great strength and a great disgust for all things pertaining to bodily functions. Wielding *enormous* power, she had once been extraordinarily beautiful.

My grandfather was Mortimer P. Burroughs, known as "Mote," a name picked up in the south. He was kind and gentle, and while largely under Laura's thumb, still provided most of the merriment in the house. "Oh-h Mote!" she would say as he'd slip into his favorite story fraudulently aweep about the time he ate a robin for Christmas dinner. During that fifth year he would take me out in the twilight, laughing and dropping dimes from his pockets and saying that the angels were dropping them for me. I'd see him drop them and I always gave them back, but I didn't care a whit. I knew that somehow the angels had dropped them and they fairly shone with stardust. I remember how concerned he was and how he chuckled to himself when he found me crying at the bottom of our steep driveway in winter. I couldn't get up the drive because it was iced over and I didn't think to walk in the snow.

I slept in the same room as my grandparents in the house in St. Louis. It was unspeakably horrible to be alone in the dark. Laura would reach from her bed to mine and hold my hand until I fell asleep. There was something that waited for me in the dark. Not some long-legged beastie, but something real. When it rained, we'd all sit on the back porch. I was welcome on any lap and we'd watch the cars make the water spray on the thruway a mile away.

My grandparents took me to Palm Beach so I could grow up properly. Mote was a dealer in antique furniture and we lived in a house on Sanford Avenue surrounded by relics of the fictional past. The house smelled of dust and imported wood. There were expensive vases full of expensive wrought-metal flowers languishing under glass domes. Everything came slowly to be forbidden as I got older, unless it was wholesome.

I saw my father three times in the next ten years. And what times those were! Driving to his hotel—he never stayed with us and favored the less expensive places at the beach end of Worth Avenue—the air was always soft and salty in the evening. Body temperature air. I remember that it was difficult to tell where my body left off and the air began. He always seemed to be standing in the hallway and locking his room the moment I arrived, me running to meet him, doors flashing past, into his arms and he smelled of cigarette smoke.

He would come over for dinner, though, and I would emulate his European style of eating, fork upside down. There was a general conspiracy in the family to convince me that Bill was an explorer, probably because of his South American Sortie for Yage, and on these two occasions, Bill took me for a walk after dinner and would show me how fast he walked through the jungle. I'd have to run to keep up and he'd turn about suddenly and snatch me in the air, then he'd be very quiet and we'd walk on as he lit a cigarette. (And right here I must digress for a moment. You see it used to be that people involved with hard drugs, that is people in the predominately white middle class, tried to keep their usage a secret. And if their people found out, *they'd* try to keep the lid on. But today, whole gangs of kids are shooting up together. No secret, no realization of the cop out. By God, they think they're doing a *good* thing and one kid with dope and a needle can infect ten others. Do you see the mathematics there? It's like a chain letter, this thing is really getting serious. Now it's no secret that hard drugs have been funneled into ghettos for years by white power groupies. Maybe you haven't noticed Mr. and Mrs. America, but that's because there is nothing as politically inactive, or as *satisfied* as a stoned junkie. But surprise! Nobody's safe. It's not just the niggers, spics, chicanos, and nasty old Indians anymore. It's Billy and Susie and

Johnnie and that nice professor down the block and at the risk of sounding like a crank, it's for the same reason. Satisfied people don't complain. They may be poor, unhealthy, lonely, alienated, spiritually stamped VOID, but by God, if they're *satisfied*, we won't have any trouble offa *them*, anyway. Ain't that right mister? Yeah, you! The one in the suit behind that desk. I leave you to form your own opinions of this kind of shit, but please read what I just said one more time, you have no idea what's at stake.)

And then the third time my father came to see us, I met him at the door with a ready embrace, but encountered an uncertain handshake, probably because I was twelve by then. That evening we all went to Stouffer's restaurant overlooking Lake Worth. I vividly recall Bill becoming involved in telling us a story about some "little monsters" who lived downstairs from him in Paris. It, uh, seems they'd cut off their cat's head with garden shears. Bill found this most amusing and came on with a tooth-clenched parody of the little monster in question snapping his fists together in front of his face over the gratin to demonstrate the action of the shears. Whenever he laughs at all, which is seldom, one gets the impression that he's restraining a boisterous guffaw and I noticed his grin to be very toothy and rather carnivorous. And this was in Stouffer's. I mean for some of the surrounding tables it was a Naked Lunch indeed. "You could have heard a soufflé drop." I seemed to have been the only one who knew what was happening. My grandparents were appalled, Bill was totally involved in his story and the people nearby were nauseous. My father spends so much of his time thinking about other people and what's to be done for them that he is almost totally unaware of what other people may think of him. He left the next day and that evening, Laura corrected me on European use of the fork. She said that Bill's manners left something to be desired.

But in the years between his visits I was well brought up and well cared for. I went to the Palm Beach Private School with Kelloggs and Dodges and Posts, etc. I once knocked Winnie Rockefeller on his fat little ass and me knuckles are still agilt.

Then, two years after his last visit, I was fourteen, and my father wanted me back.

Tangier, Morocco. My grandparents stood at the airport gate in Miami and waved good-bye to the wrong window of the plane as I, square, pink, fourteen, and American, settled into my seat to watch them. Riffling through my science-fiction anthology, I watched them slide away as the big jet wallowed down the runway-bare ribbon devoid of foxprints. A blast of power, for some reason planes didn't bother me then, and there I was a few hours later waving to an odd-looking man on the other side of Lisbon customs. Fifteen minutes before it was time to board the next plane, a strangely accented voice came over the PA system to announce that it was imperative for a mister somebody to report to the customs desk immediately. I wouldn't have noticed the name sounded like ours if Bill hadn't tensed instantly and very slightly. He'd already relaxed by the time I caught the resemblance. "Is that us?" I asked. "Nope. We're cool, man." He chuckled as he settled back to digest a canary. The words seemed strangely incongruous coming from a man who could have passed as an English bank clerk. He took a long deep drag on a Players Medium cigarette and I noticed that his fingers were stained a very un-British dark nicotine yellow.

Moroccan customs officials were bored and indifferent (who would smuggle anything *into* Morocco?) and waved us past their lidded eyes into a tiny run-down taxi driven by a stoned-out hashhead who scared the daylights out of me. Tangier at that time had no traffic lights at all and the cabbies would careen through intersections playing an eternal game of chicken that *was* a game of chicken, and every time we would avoid a hair-breadth apocalypse, my father would mutter a word of appreciation like a calm bullfight aficionado. "Bueno"—even though the language spoken was French.

But finally we pulled up to the curb by the Parade Bar. Just off the European section, and out of nowhere one of the people who shared our house on the Marshan appeared to shake my hand: It was Michael Paltman. "Michael, this is my son."

An unaccustomed attempt at fatherly pride and

then we were in the bar and I was apart, being accosted by an aging fag. "I know I'm old, but I really *haven't* lost my figure, dear. You know, half the old Tangerines knew you were coming and wondered what you looked like. Well Baby! I mean if you ever want your nuts blowed???" I was a little nervous, but I told him if it ever came to that I'd let him know. He looked overly hurt and gave me one of those pitying looks, like perhaps someday the poor child will see the light, as he slid off the stool caressing my thigh. "Bad medicine," I thought, and I mean to say the old fart was definitely not my type.

After something to eat and a small glass of rum (the Parade is the only place in Tangier where you can get a decent hamburger. "You needn't *insist* you're fresh from Amercah," says Michael later.), we took another Kamikaze cab to the Marshan. Most of the Tangerine cabbies speak French and my father's French is abominable. He has a very respectable working vocabulary but his accent is enough to instigate a riot. When we got to the number of our house on Calle Larache, he went to say *"ici"* but it came out southern Texas style, "eechee." The driver, understandably did not understand and drove on. Bill was livid. "EECHEE! GODDAMN IT! EECHEE!" His tone of voice got through and the driver backed up to stop.

Inside: total disorganization. Bill had known I was coming but he had to search the house to find a place for me to sleep. With a flashlight because something had happened to the electricity. "Wait for Ian," he said, another tenant, who came home later and fixed the electricity by going outside and striking a power pole with a broomstick.

I didn't sleep well that night. I beg you to remember that the last time I had slept was in Palm Beach on a mahogany dragon bed from the seventeenth century. And now here I lay listening to strange sounds and Arabic mutterings outside the window.

But I slept nonetheless and awoke the next morning to find Ian sitting on my bed looking at me like a loving mother. We talked for a few minutes and then he took my hand gently, ever so gently, and tried to draw it to his groin. But the attempt was premature and I pulled away. He didn't take it as hard as the old swish in the Parade though, and we were all friends that evening as he, my father, and Michael lit up their pipes. Very long pipes with clay bowls. I was curious about their contents. . . . "Kif." I remembered the word from *Naked Lunch* and asked if I could try it out. "All in good time, Billy," said Ian. But the next day the good times rolled when Bill said, "Ian, take Billy down the Grande Socco and help him pick out a pipe."

That night, I took my first draw on the celebrated medicinal herb. Problem is, that in Morocco so many people smoke dope that it has become a social thing. So they mix it with a cruel and unusual tobacco that makes Gauloises taste like ambulance oxygen. "Goddamn!" I thought. "This is worse than

205

whiskey." But as it happened, my father had some tasty little hashish candies on hand of which I consumed quite a number not knowing what they were, and then dipped into a Mason jar of homemade *majoun*, which is grass fixed up to eat and will stone you into the middle of next week my friend.

Off the subject for a moment, *majoun* can be dangerous if prepared stupidly. I understand that about a month before I arrived in Tangier, Gregory Corso had dropped by for a visit. And that he, Bill, Ian, and Mike had all got together after a few drinks and rather drunkenly decided to consume a bit of *majoun*. So Michael went out to buy some tea, and damned if he didn't buy the tobacco-infiltrated variety. When he got back he just went ahead and cooked it all up replete with raisins and honey. About twenty minutes after ingestion, my father sensed something amiss and immediately repaired to the bathroom to vomit up the entire dose. Everyone else followed suit except Mr. Corso who stubbornly refused to believe there was anything wrong with the stuff, or that he couldn't handle it, if there was. So about an hour later he quietly excuses himself from the room and rushes back in red-eyed as a charging ostrich, flailing at Michael and shrieking, "Poisonerrr! Poisoner-r-r!" He chased him out of the house and all the way to the medina before he calmed down, a distance of some two and a half miles, but never caught him because he had to stop every few minutes to vomit. Dynamite cat.

You will hear people say that one never gets stoned the first time but I was so far gone that I couldn't even remember the onset. Only visions of the entire course of human history, from the ape-man all asteam on the hostile plains on through the blessed virgin and plunging into the abyss of technology. After two million years, Ian nudged me gently and said that he'd like to go to sleep. "Oh! Sure man," I said and went downstairs to sleep very well.

Hash dream under the influence of earphones: I see two ruined buildings, their backs blown away; naked girders grope in a smoking twilit sky. On the tenth floor of each building, leaning out the window, is a pale man with a sheet of metal. They are playing a dreadful and hyenic game of Ping-Pong with something dark and indiscernible, perhaps a human head. Below them, as far as the eye can see, is a multitude of people on their knees, some with flaming hair. They rock from side to side, hands clasped, and follow the indiscernible object; and their wailing merges with the crashing of the sheet metal to shake the girders that grind and sway as technical fingers in the darkening sky. I have the feeling that the man who misses the object first, loses and no matter who loses all the people die. . . . Michael Portman stirred me from this dream with a look of concern on his face. When I told him what I had seen, he went and told Bill about it. Bill was at work, and when Michael was through he stopped typing long enough to say "very accurate" without looking up and then resumed business.

Our house in the Marshan was very fine. Two stories and consumed by mosaics. My father's room was austere to say the least. Spotlessly clean with an army-type bunk and a cabinet and that was all besides an incredibly haunting picture of a brooding moon done by his good friend Brion Gyson. I might mention that Mr. Gyson invented the cut/up method as applied to words or at least he was one of the first to take it seriously. The cut/up method enables the writer to achieve the same effect as the artist can with picture montage. The effect can be and often is shattering to the receptive reader because words are images in a much more personalized and internal sense than pictures. I recollect one mind-blowing ditty that my father had on his tape recorder. It was a word montage by Brion Gyson and consisted of one phrase: "I come to free the words." repeated over and over in different order. That is, "The words are free to come, I come freely to the words, The free come to the words . . ." And while the words were repeated, the speed of the tape was increased gradually until it became a supersonic whine. But because of the rhythm, and after the cartoon laughter stage, some part of the listener would keep pace until he was virtually transported. To where, I don't know, or cannot report.

There was also an orgone box in the upstairs hall in which my father would sit for hours at a time smoking kif and then rush out and attack his type-writer without warning.

The rooftops, by custom, are the women's province in Tangier because that's where they do all the washing and gossiping and whatnot. I made the mistake once of going up there during the day and the Arabs threw little pieces of mud at our door for the next week. But Bill would be on the roof every night to watch the colors in the sky as soon as the sun was starting to set. I would stumble to the roof occasionally, stoned out of my squash and would see him transfixed in his favorite spot. Transfixed and absolutely motionless, right hand holding the perpetual cigarette, lips parting to the sun, and himself stirring only to drop it when it burned his fingers. When it was finally, absolutely night, again, the sudden rush to the typewriter.

I tell you one thing though, he and everybody in that house had an appetite. Bunch of goddamn hashheads and I recollect one time I came back from the main part of time (stoned obviously) with an apple pie and a roasted chicken intent upon retiring to my room and plumbing the joys of the taste. But I was met at the door by the entire population. Zapo! One piece of pie left over and I went to my room to scarf up my angry piece of apple. Old Bill used the leftover chicken bones, scant and gnawed as they were, to make a soup that he cooked for two days using such an incredible amount of pepper that the stuff went down like whiskey. But he was so proud of the finished product that any visitor, including myself, was instantly overcome with compassion and "enjoyed" a cup and sometimes two under his imploring eyes. It would sometimes take a few minutes before the victim was able to express his appreciation.

Tangier was still pretty wild then. There was a café on a cliff called the Dancing Boy that Ian took me to my first time. Smells of hashish, kif, and mint tea. Beautiful music. The violinist sat cross-legged and played his violin upright before him like a cello. As we came in some European existentialist-type hippies whispered among themselves. They looked as if they hadn't seen daylight for years and were dressed entirely in black. They all had dark hair, underbelly skin, and black circles under their eyes.

The dancer wore long robes and a cork inner-tube affair with tassels around his hips, and did swirling routines with trays of water-filled glasses or with lit candles, which he somehow managed not to extinguish. Something to see.

The café closed about three A.M. and sometimes Ian and I or a fellow named Peter would laugh down the street with the musicians and dart into a strange house there to continue clapping and dancing and listening and smoking until everyone dropped. Pick ourselves up at dawn and rush to the bakery to catch the boy wheeling out the new loaves in a barrow on his way to deliver to the shops. Buy a huge round loaf too hot to handle without wrapping it in a shirt and stop before home for a pound of fresh butter from a clay urn at the neighborhood 7–11.

These were pleasant times, but I couldn't make it; I was too young and found it difficult to get involved. I took to wandering the ocean cliffs with my pipe and quarter pound of unadulterated grass that Michael had very kindly gone out and got when he saw me choking one night on the other shit. I'd sit on trees that grew sideways out of the cliffs and smoke until I was unable or unwilling to make the climb back. Wait a while and then walk through the alleys admiring the colored broken glass placed on top of the rich folks' walls to keep out the riffraff. I went to cafés, movies (try watching a French movie dubbed into Arabic sometime), beaches, but I couldn't figure out what was wrong until one night Ian came to my room and told me I wanted to go home. He was on the verge of tears when he said that I didn't want to live with a houseful of "fags." The quotation marks were in his tone of voice and I wondered how my father felt. He was in his room. Was he trying to read?

So I went home, went to school, and while I was there Mote died on a windy day and the palmettos trembled. From that time on, Laura's mind began to go and after I graduated, I'd play the guitar for her in the sunniest window of our house on Sanford Avenue. "Billy," she'd say, "sometimes I think that Mote is right here and I can almost talk to him." He was too, I think.

I left home in confusion, looking for adventure and went to New York, which glittered with sex and romance, but succeeded only in getting busted twice on drug charges, developing a rampant case of paranoia, and leaving five months later in an emaciated shambles.

Back in Palm Beach, busted again and thence back to my story now, but that you know well enough. Henry's drugstore vs. William Burroughs, Jr. (This was no New York Bust where the freedom fee simply rises with the charge.) I was to be made an example of and my father flew over from London to keep me out of prison.

Offstage, while you've been getting the background, my father had been jumping through legal hoops of fire back here in Palm Beach, trying to keep my fool ass out of prison. The cops had been playing all their not-so-silly games with him but were frustrated at every turn. Documents were already notarized, papers were signed, and so on through that legal shit, ad infinitum.

Back at home, the strain finally got to him and he cornered me in the kitchen one night to say, in effect: "Billy, for one thing, this damn house is haunted. It's obvious as a cop. I can't get a decent night's sleep in that back room and when I do, it's all again in nightmares. And mother is driving me *right* around the *bend*! She calls me by Mort's name, she asks me to move things that aren't there, she calls me by any name that comes to mind. All this, on top of those stupid cops is frustrating, I tell you. And finally, *you're* no help at all." He was right on all counts, of course, but I came right out and asked him what in God's name he expected me to do, wave a wand? I wasn't having any more fun than he, and besides, I was starting to get symptoms whenever I went too long without a shot. We both apologized wordlessly and shook hands.

I can back up the house's being haunted, though. I remember one night I was reading some book and was under the influence of nothing but silence, when a sudden soft voice whispered in my ear, "I won't bother *you*." I was not at all reassured and glanced around the room to find that all the furniture had gone about two degrees awry at different angles that working together were positively alien. Then, I remembered my grandmother when she knocked on my door one three A.M. to say, "Billy! What *were* you doing flying down the hall all bloody? And with the wings of a bat!" Seeing what was happening now and remembering what she had said then was pushing this tit a little too far, and I broke the smaller bedroom window and bloodied my arm in the process of escape, landing in the front yard with a visual scream from the window glass glittering around me like diamonds lit from the window beam. My stakeout must have been astonished.

It was some two weeks now until my trial, and I noticed an odd change in the general public's attitude toward me. I found myself being on a short but almost (friendly?) first-name basis with people I hadn't approached or been approached by for years. After my much publicized bust, I picked up feelings of relief especially from my own age group. As if something unknown and, therefore, disliked had come into the open.

I even got into conversations with some of my old school buddies. Seven years no see. I recollect one night in particular. I was sitting in the back of their car, a couple of "males," oldies but time-killers. Somehow the conversation got around to "scoring" with girls. I started to say something about the built-in failure implicit in treating a woman like . . . like . . . well, the mind boggled. Not the least reason for which was the sudden vulturelike and *rapt* attention I was receiving. Now, I've fucked here and in a different way and for different reasons there, sometimes just with an old friend who wanted to try out some new tricks. And don't peg me for one of those little runts who uses the act to get back at God knows what. And there have been beautiful mergings, wherein the two of us were no longer nouns, but verbs. Just as we always try to place ourselves in time and space, between here and there, now and then, the phrase "doing its thing" is actually a marvelously simple and satoric statement. Tables are not *tables*. If you will agree that everything is constantly changing, then you must agree that tables cannot be such a narrow simplification. I realize the convenience, but will retain my right to think in terms of "tabling." Remember that kit I mentioned? This only because I threw away their kit long ago and make my own, a new one whenever necessary. But that is neither here nor there. The point is the stupidity of trying to explain to these two hot young studs with their fast car and stereo tape deck that "fucking" is the most accessible human process of verbalization, a most necessary process. The above is perfectly clear to anyone that I would have in my home for dinner, if I had either, but I had to excuse myself beneath their coallike eyes. For two reasons. So, they were square. So what? That's not so bad. What was bad was that I, at least, had the good sense to go insane during adolescence.* Untouchable, you understand? Dangerous, yes, but far better than to have a childhood sense of self suddenly wrenched away and being forced into a type. Wham! Bam! Thank you kindly, Uncle Sam! At least, I can be whatever I wish. And the other reasons, sad though they were, I wouldn't wish 'em on a yak. Or even on.

Short conversations like these with people I hadn't seen, hardly, for close to seven years, made me realize how unspeakably far I had come away. I knew too much now. During the two weeks before my trial one phrase kept going over and over

* Never quit either.

through my mind like a mantra, "If they only knew." Until the answer came. The shock would be so great it would have to be me or them. But, oh, Hell! If they only did.

4

The day came, though somehow I thought it never would, and I stood before the judge decked out in my Sunday-go-to-meeting clothcs and a little junk sick, which I had rather listlessly tried to hide from my father. But he can smell it at fifty yards . . . it does have a distinct odor, you know, something like paranoid perspiration. But I could have been wearing a gorilla suit for all the bench noticed. Judge Makintosh—the bastard had a reputation for never looking at the defendant, only just to study his shining transparent papers one matchstick away from meaninglessness and to deliver maximum sentence. But by some fluke of justice or perhaps because of my father's legal gymnastics, I pulled a mere four years probation (tantamount to saying: "Long enough for you to foul up again and then we *really* got you, you little monster."). Along with a cure to be taken at the Federal Narcotics Farm at Lexington, Kentucky. And all without being adjudged guilty of a felony. That was our worst probability. A great many fringe benefits come along grinning with a felony conviction. Like no passport. Jesus.

When the judge said "four years," many of the blacks in the room shook their heads in pity and as we walked out of the courtroom, a photographer flashed my picture onto the front page of the Palm Beach *Times*, there to be preserved for some prurient posterity. Namely me. I tried to find the picture in the library a couple of years later because it made me look so innocent, but I never had any luck.

Now I don't know if the following sketch will remain intact but in the mood of the moment, I feel like chronicling a caper of a lighter nature, though it hurt like Hell at the time. So . . . the night before I left, Al Oliver and I decided to go down in the sewers and kill offa few them nasty rats. So armed with crowbars, superstitions, flashlights, a dark street, and warnings not to smoke, "I seen a cat light a fart once, man. Can you imagine if you lit a cigarette in a fart pocket?" we attacked a likely-looking manhole. Manhole covers are very heavy. Al got the crowbar wedged in and lifted the damn thing a couple of inches giving me a finger-hold before he

slipped and the cover fell with a beautifully resonant
Ommmmmm as it ripped the fingernails away from
four fingers. But I was not "shown the way" and we
repaired immediately to the nearest "juke joint"
where I stuck my hand in a "coke please, lots of ice."
Manhole covers should all be busted down to BB's.
Incidentally, I quote juke joint because it was spe-
cifically stated in the articles of my probation that I
was not to frequent such establishments. Can you
imagine that? "No jukebox, that's cool. Jukebox: we
got you if we want you." But I reckoned quite
rightly, that they didn't want me *that* badly. I shall
have to be more careful from now on, however.

I was driving gingerly somewhat later, my hand
wrapped in a bloody towel when we passed a grave-
yard. As we slowed for a stoplight, it was late and
ours was the only car on the street, Al grabbed his
crowbar and leaped from the car hissing, "Follow
me." Then he was gone over the fence. I parked the
car and walked in calling his name, but I found
nothing but a lit cigarette in the fingers of one of the
statues. I never saw him again either . . .

Airplanes terrify me. I won't go into the usual
routine, but a team of wild women couldn't get me
on one. My father did, however, by coaxing me with
stories of the first shot you get at the hospital. "The
first shot'll probably knock you on your ass." O,
sweet blow. But we had to change planes somewhere
up the line and not even the thought of a good jolt of
morphine could get me on the next flight. After

219

mucho appealing to reason on his part and some borderline psychotic blockbusters on mine, Bill finally bought me a ticket for a fast train. I tried to hustle him into renting me a car thinking I might pick up on some P.G. (that's paragoric-opium base) by the wayside, but it was no go. He probably thought I'd try to take it on the lam, and thinking back, I might have done just that. I wasn't looking forward to the hospital at *all*, I'm sure you understand.

So he went the high way and I went the low there by the train window and feeling as rotted out as the ass end of the nighttime towns we snaked through all amoan with the whistle and clatter. I remembered the words: "Longest train that ever run." And it occurred to me that Romanticism must be a reflex/side effect of moderate paranoia. But I can't help it and when I was only about this big I wondered where all those people sitting up like dolls in those trains were going. And it eased my heart some, if not my guts, to know that somewhere there was a little kid, namely me, hearing the whistle and thinking indirectly about myself. That's time travel.

The hours clacked by. Sleep was just a word I'd picked up somewhere maybe in third-grade geography? I wasn't thinking right and along about dawn, I wistfully threw my syringe to the rails. Maybe it would be found and used by some bum as a Bull Durham cigarette holder. God's fuzzy sun-warm peach to Woody Guthrie.

Lexington station was cold and dismal my God, and for some reason there was a foul-up that made it impossible to call a cab. The man behind the screen directed me to a windy doorway across the street where I could wait for one to come by. People drove past through the snow on their way to work and some of them shook their heads with a pity-the-object-smile when they saw my Florida clothes and purplish lips. Perhaps a junkie freezing at the station is not an uncommon sight in the Lexington winter.

When I finally got to Bill's hotel, I spotted at least three plainclothesmen and a couple of doubtfuls lounging around the lobby as if to satisfy a lazy curiosity as to what I looked like. But it probably wasn't me; half the town of Lexington is made up of narcotics people. God but I'd hate to be busted there. Let me tell you man, there is nothing more exasperating than a bored flatfoot who has finally got *you* to entertain himself with.

Bill's room was phantom gray and dawnish from the snow outside the window. The Old Man was already packing. There was a definite and heretofore unencountered air about him. It was obvious that he wanted the whole scene shut down and stored away as soon as possible. I stood by the heater as he gathered up what was left to be taken and he taught me a simple code referring to places and things because all mail leaving the hospital is censored. (Side thought: All the mail that comes out of Argentina is censored.) I never saw that room again. Never wanted to much either, and then we were packed and taking the elevator to the lobby. Rusting, dusty rectangle where the inspection sticker should have been.

I was colder than ever in the cab as my father said with the utmost politeness, "U.S. Public Health Service Hospital, please." The ham-necked driver picked up his mike to call in and grunted, "Got two for Narco," and as we started off through the snow, I wondered for the hundredth time how I got myself into situations like this.

We passed the Coca-Cola signs, Eddie's Grill, The Kit Kat Klub, and a tiny cemetery between some buildings. Greasy clowns caressing gas pumps. As we drove I was wishing that the cab would crash by some miracle and that everyone but me would be incapacitated. Then I could shiver on up to New York and they'd never find me there. I knew a fella split probation on the West Side and evaded the "science-fiction groping arm of the law" for nine months simply by moving to the other side of town. I was with him when they got him during one of his rare sorties to the West Side (Fred! Don't make me shoot!) and sort of inherited everything he owned. . . .

Eventually Lexington thinned out and we entered on a long road lined by trees on one side and an endless snow-gray meadow behind barbed wire on the other. I'd been watching this meadow for about ten minutes, and that's a long time—try counting it out some time—when a huge old fortish thing heaved into view on the horizon with a silent groan. Even from more than a mile away on the grayish white, I could see that it was enormous. There was nothing pleasant about it, not even the customary solidarity. But it was *solid,* Jack, and don't ask me to explain that, because I can't. "Whoee!" I thought to myself. "I hope that ain't the place. Maybe it's a factory or something." But sure enough we pulled into a little welcome station by the side of the road. It was very warm inside. A heavy final outpost sort of atmosphere. "Which one of you is checking in here?" says a very old man. My father told him quick and the radiator creaked, accompanying the reaching of the housekeeper's arm; snowy claw reaching for my luggage, such as it was. He said that I'd receive hospital clothing and that I could get my guitar back through channels. I suppose it had to be X-rayed, rattled, and flashlighted. My father and I shook hands and he left.

After the cab backed out, turned, and diminished down the road, the old man told me that if I had any drugs on my person I could turn them over and it would be all right. (I could have broken his stringy neck with my left hand and a knife in my back.) But if any were found later I would be "prosecuted to the fullest extent of the law." He had long since forgotten what the words meant, it was obvious, and I said, "No, no, haven't any." So he picked up the phone to call way up there to the hospital for a pearly white station wagon. I saw it coming for me down a long winding road, standing out like a broken tooth on a black dragon's tongue.

In the car I listened to the driver's reassuring patter, which was entirely too pat and all in a day's work. "Feel sick?" My God, what a question. No, I feel like Jack Lalanne. "Well, we'll help you. You're gonna see a doctor you know." I liked that sound; all five senses were primed for that first shot of morphine, but it didn't work out that way. "You volunteer or prisoner?" I shivered. "You look like a volunteer to me." I had volunteered under court orders, a technicality.

And there we were alongside the hospital. The patient's entrance. I was to find that the parking lot and the glass doors for the doctors were on the other side of the ex-prison. The wall strutted against the scudding clouds and the wintering wind about forty feet above and perhaps a thousand beyond all sides of a tiny iron riveted phone booth that the driver opened for me with a key that could knock out your teeth. "Good luck, son. Come out on top!" KA-CH-UNNNG! The door slammed or rather replaced itself. I tried to open it again and it was *solid* solid. Not a rattle, and I thought for a moment of a grain in my room in Palm Beach and of my earphones before I pushed through a swinging door into a waiting room.

A waiting room. Here I was in one of the only two federal hospitals in the United States that allegedly cures junkies by treating them "not as criminals, but as persons personally afflicted." I don't know where I got that one but I know it's a quote. The room was only about ten by fifteen feet and painted a soul-depressing institutional green. If there was any reading matter around, I can't for the life of me remember it. And for the *life* of me, I'd damn near remember anything. But I mean to say that this was a waiting room *extrodinaire;* I waited three hours after I rang a bell in a corner with an enormous arrow pointing to it and a nurse brought me a form to fill out: How big is your habit? . . . What's your favorite drug? . . . (That was a tough one). Do you like girls? Boys? . . . Love yer mutha? And the inevitable and meaningless question obviously devised by the CIA to drive my type around the bend. "What were the dates (entrance and exit) of the last two schools you attended?" A variation on this one is the same question applied to jobs. Now you aren't a hardened, vicious criminal like me, are you? Right. What were the last two schools you attended along with the dates of attendance? Five'll get you ten you don't know. And yet here I am sicker than you'd wish on a dog and they ask me such a thing.

There were two ugly, big city guys in there with me who looked a Hell of a lot worse off than me though they were probably thinking the same thing. But there was obviously no style to them and I was feeling too ornery myself by then to try for any conversation.

Finally the nurse came back from the movies and took both the guys inside within two or three minutes of each other. There was a mirror in the room and I had a not so insane notion that I was being watched, so I spent the time trying to look sicker than I actually was. (I just had to stop typing to clobber a tarantula with a sandal. God I hate those things. Can you imagine if one crawled into your half-full glass of beer when you weren't looking?)

Inside, finally, they had to go over my whole questionnaire and they just would not believe that I didn't steal to support my habit. I told them that I was a relatively rich kid and that I didn't really have a habit, which, strictly speaking, was true. The extent of my discomfort was similar to a very bad cold with staccato chills and fever. But while the three spinster nurses seemed to like me, they'd heard all that before and just kept typing. This went on for some time (my sense of time had gone all to flinders in the waiting room). Perhaps twenty minutes.

The next step in my admission obtained of more waiting in a little green room that actually bore some resemblance to one of those you wait for the doctor in when you come mewling around to the emergency entrance of a big city hospital. You know the scene: "Is there anything you can give me for the pain *arr-rgh!*, doctor?" "Well, I think this antibiotic should take care of that; just stay quiet for a couple of days." "O.O.K." Useless prescription thrown and skittering across a windy late-night street, past a bum sleeping on a subway grating under tucked-in newspapers.

It was under an hour I think before the doctor came in, and to my surprise he looked just like any dumb croaker despite his goatish face and long sideburns. What I was expecting, I don't know; somehow I just felt like the government ought to be able to do better. He proceeds to search me for dope in no uncertain terms. "Run your fingers through your hair." Then, "Open your mouth." Gag, retch. Then he says, "Take the pants off and bend over. Noo, facing *away* from me," he says as he puts on his little rubber glove like it don't mean anything to him. But it was humiliating I tell you and he says, "Spread the cheeks," as he slops an inordinate amount of Vaseline around my paranoid American asshole. And Ram! Wiggle! Zip! the search was complete. "Heh, heh," said the doctor. "You look a bit nervous." "Well . . . " I started, but he was heading out the door. I was desperate. "Uh, doctor?" He turned and said, "Oh, Hell yes. I'm sorry," and handed me two or three European-type Kleenex to wipe my ass and pointed to some ragged blue pajamas hanging forlornly in the corner. "Get into those, I'll be right back." "Yeah, right back," I said. "Ha, ha," as the Kleenex slid around accomplishing nothing.

Finally I gave up and climbed into my hospital P.J.'s greasy-assed and wanting to go home; somehow thinking it was still possible. The outside couldn't have been more than a hundred yards away and some part of me was waiting for an authority figure to walk in and say, "It's all been a mistake. It was yer twin bruthuh and you are free to go." Fat chance. You see I go slightly nuts every time I get locked up or abstain from anything I like. Paranoid delusions and (by the way) there are nothing *but* political prisoners. Chew on that one for awhile friend, it has a strange taste but true.

This time, blessed relief, I found an old tattered *Life* mag lying lonely under what the dictionary would describe as a "basic table," and read something about them shameful demonstrations on college campi, which I love to hear about the more the better. In my father's words, "There should be more riots and more violence." Street fighting aside, I have a word of advice for campus radicals, if there are any left. Don't it piss you off when a fine and concerned professor is dismissed? Don't it piss you off when land is misappropriated? Ain't it just terrible when a playground is canceled? Wake up. What about the *secret research* being done for the government on almost every college campus? You must realize that it is secret because *they don't want you to know what they are doing.* A pox on burning R.O.T.C., they'll just build another one. Get those *papers.* They can't rebuild the truth once it's out. And the next time you get caught in a riot, start yelling (from a safe place preferably; I may be crazy but I'm no fool) at *everybody.* "Are you gonna take that shit offa *him*?" Lotta people going to put me down for that remark but don't worry, Jack, I get my licks in when I can, and after all, riots are just roughhousing and I don't like getting my head busted for merely fomenting temporary unrest. Sometimes they go for the collarbone, too, and I can just imagine how that feels. Besides, collarbones are sexy. By the way, motorcycle gangs are marvelous in such scenes but have a tendency to become indiscriminate in their choice of targets. I seen a bunch of them cats corner a cop in an alley once and it was just esculent like a new penny left in a steak overnight and placed under the tongue. Don't ask me how I know how *that* tastes, wow.

I was savoring said penny when the good doctor came back with a trustee to take me up to the shooting gallery. Ivan was the trustee's name and he was a prisoner. In all fairness, prisoners were eligible for the pleasanter jobs at Lexington. Simply because they had to do them longer. Working at the shooting gallery was Ivan's job and was considered one of the best because it involved no moving of heavy objects and he was always the first to know who was back, when celebrities were admitted, and who had kicked themselves to death. The morgue at the hospital is an integral part of the setup. What a sad dreary way to go. It has the irony and silliness of ricocheting off a turtle on your motorcycle.

Ivan was a magnificently tense kid with rotten teeth and a white suit. "Do I get some of those?" I asked, because I like the clothes. "Huh? Oh. No man, you gettin' gray unless you get a hospital-section job. And listen, if you got a skill, start screaming about it now or they'll stick you in the kitchen. Sure as shit."

As I say, I was acting a Hell of a lot sicker than I was, hoping for some wild-eyed doctor to come rushing up out of nowhere with a grain of morphine in a glittering horse syringe, and Ivan stuck around a while saying, "Is it that bad? Yeh. Well, *I* know. But you won't see a doctor until tomorrow. And they get pissed as Hell if you're faking it, man. They can tell." I asked him was this a bad place and he said Hell no. It was a country club by prison standards. The best prison and the worst hospital in the country.

We were sitting at one of a number of W WI card tables and in an effort to take my mind off myself he told me that he'd been in and out of prisons and jails for the last seven years; mostly in. I could see he wanted to tell me some kind of story so I asked him, "What was your horrible crime?" And may I drop my beer if he didn't tense up to high C to tell me that when he was twelve, some cop had grabbed him on the street wanting to find his big brother who had done something illegal at least. Now at twelve, a kid, especially a street kid, is usually pretty snotty anyway, so Ivan said the wrong thing and the Heat started slapping him around. "Well, I hollered at him to stop it, you understand, but he just wouldn't, so what could I do? The next time I hit the pavement I come up with a piece of pipe and beat his fucking brains right out on the sidewalk. He wasn't ready for a little kid to come up like that." Then he winked, grinning multicolored and rotten teeth. I really dug the story but I didn't believe it until later when I asked a prisoner who had access to check it out for me and he said it was all there in Ivan's file. Ivan hadn't told me that when they caught him he'd gone from the precinct to the hospital for three months because he "fell down some marble stairs."

He had to leave then to keep up with his time-table, and left me at the card table trembling slightly and looking around at a bunch of junkies who were sniffling, whining, and playing whist. They all looked as interesting as five intimate minutes with an aardvark. As a matter of fact I was soon to find that the junkie who is not a one-track-minded bore is rare indeed.

So I sat there, absently staring about the room for some minutes, spotting an unhosted spider's web in a ceiling corner. . . . Something sad about that; I wasn't thinking at all properly, and the only sign on the wall began "In the event of nuclear attack . . ." That was all I needed so I shuffled over to the out-of-character nurse's station, my tatters a-tattering. I asked the nurse, a real caricature, about "medication," as Ivan had told me dope was called on the gallery. Incidentally, the shooting gallery got its name from the good old days when patients were taken off their habits with slowly reduced injections of morphine. The nurse clicked her little beak to the effect that the doctors would see to that, young man, and I didn't feel like pursuing the matter any further than sinking my teeth in her throat in view of what Ivan had told me about the croakers pegging frauds. So I asked her if there were any books or magazines around. She looked at me as if I was criminally insane as no doubt some of you out there already believe, and said, "The *book* cart won't be up until tomorrow, but the TV room is down that way." Vaguely indicating the direction.

I walked down the ugly green hall. Institutional; smelling of the morning's ammonia and hot dust on the radiators. Lexington is nothing *but* a labyrinth of tunnellike halls. Leading to the interrupting of a fag servicing her current boyfriend, or a dead wicker chair to sit on with a scrap of paper to look out a window. Picture the highway and Buicks away off in the distance as in a silkscreen rainy painting.

The television room was big. From way over here in the left-hand corner where I am in my pajamas and worried old blue bathrobe. Seven-foot windows hung through the walls on either side above huge radiators, which might as well have been absent and clank/clunked beneath them. And the television room was dark. Nobody at Lexington can stand light in a TV room. Don't know why. Way over in the flickering, silver-lighted corner sat a group of about a dozen junkies watching a Kentucky Kountry Music Show. There were three or four other people sitting alone at card tables in the dark (this was a *huge* room), away from the radiators. I've felt that way before myself but 'tis better to describe than analyze. Start analyzing shit and you get all screwed up and never finish, it's impossible. Goddamn scientists and head shrinkers think they got X-ray eyes.

So over in the corner where the action was really hot there was this show going on which was alright as far as country music goes what with spangled guitars, ugly women, and silly "WHEE-HAW's." I felt like a compost heap, high grade but compost nonetheless, and anyplace was good enough to rot so I squeezed in by the TV waiting to meet my maker.

Just as the next show, something like a pauper's Ted Mack, got started, something that might have been human croaked from the back of the room that it was time for dinner. So a dozen junkies get up sniffling and groaning, strictly from Dante, but I stayed behind to watch a tap dancer of all things. When he was finished, Mr. Interlocutor mentioned that the dancer made about $220 a week at his "trade," and dig this. That I was so fucked around and vulnerable that I thought, and I quote indirectly, "Oh, Jeezuz! Looka Him. He, just about my age and he's making all that bread and he don't stink like I do and he's prolly in good shape gonna marry Cherly and here I am all locked up and shot up and Cherly woo'n even look at me. . . ." I really felt the guy had something over me. And he was wearing a bow tie and could have clapped with his ears, it was terrible, I tell you.

Back up at the end of the hall, I caught up just in time, almost upsetting a sand ashtray as the guard opened up the door to lead us down a hall of brutally and, it seemed to me, *purposely* white tile. Around this corner and into an elevator. There is a couple of guys in here that are doing their jobs. I glanced at them casually, but secretly I stand in awe. They've already been through the gallery and through orientation where I'm going next. Now they're in "Population." What's it like over there? Is there some kind of initiatory flaying? But I knew that whatever it was, like anything else, was ready or not. By the way, if a junkie ever looks at you "casually" you can be damn sure you're being sized up to a T in three seconds. 'Tis a necessary mechanism.

After being served enormous quantities of food cafeteria style onto heavy metal trays, we were taken to one of nine dining rooms off a huge hall, each with a capacity of perhaps one hundred. I later discovered that there is a large influx of junkies during the winter and that in all probability at least 25 percent of these are bums there for the food and warm beds. Looks like no matter where you're at, somebody would give his right arm to be in your shoes. A volunteer patient can check out on twenty-four hours notice, so if you're ever down and out in the

Lexington area check right in. The trick is to drink a couple of bottles of P.G. before you arrive so when they take a blood test there's dope in it. Technically the only way one is supposed to get into the hospital is to write ahead and get the "papers" stating that they have a place for you. But if you come reeling out of the bushes on the other side of the road and come vibrating up to the welcome house looking like you're gonna throw a withdrawal on the front lawn, they'll very likely take you in. That sort of thing would look terrible in the papers.

The lights in the serving area hurt my eyes. *Everything* seemed to be chromeplated or made of stainless steel. And the nameless rumblings and screeches from the kitchen! In a bin of cottage cheese before me I saw before my very eyes Fafnir going down all torn and fanged before the A train; adripping rivets and bolts from his noble jaws dere, as the screeching became momentarily more agitated. "Hey! Boy! Maybe you sick, but don't get wiggy. Let's go now!" Slop! Navy beans. Slop! Barbecued pig. Slopety-slopslop. Spinach, salad, and Jello. Good eats as they say in preferable company, but I wasn't hungry; my guts felt to be a gray desolation of jagged peaks and dusty crags. I tried to eat some beans but a crazy Puerto Rican was tossing lots of thin red sauce on his, which made them look better. I did the same and burned the living bejeezis out of my mouth. When our time was up we all piled our half-filled trays on a wheel deal and left by a different door, again opened by a key that could relieve you of consciousness.

Back on the gallery, amid sounds of vomiting from the bathrooms, I was given a tiny cupful of a sweet syrup that made me feel drunk so I did the natural thing and went to sleep, glad of the chance to be no more, if only for a few hours. When I mentioned it to Ivan later, he slapped his forehead and said, "Shit man! Wow, I'm sorry. I forgot to tell you." It seems I had missed a trick.

To explain: Narcotics withdrawal and barbiturate withdrawal are two completely different conditions and must be treated differently! And lots, even most of your poor street junkies have whopping big barbiturate habits along with the other because of unscrupulous merchants who cut. Barbiturate withdrawal (screams of protest) can, if pozzible, be more dangerous to der subjeck here (poke poke) than narcotic withdrawal. So one of the first things they do at Lexington by way of medical antics, is to give a good jolt of barbiturate. *Then,* you understand, the accepted thing to do is fight it and stay awake like it don't faze yer. So then they have to give you more and more to find your tolerance. One cat fell right off his chair in the TV room one night. Just kind of went "whew!" and he was down and out much to the amusement of the surrounding junkies, some of whom were laughing with admiration at the fight he'd put up. Junkies have a tendency to laugh when they appreciate something. Endearing, eh? So, then starting from the point where the curee finally fell on his teeth and had to be helped to bed, he goes through a regular barbiturate reduction cure. But I, poor innocent, went right to bed and didn't get any, though it would have been a blessing in the next few days. Trouble with lockups and crazy wards is you got to know the ropes before you even get there or things are pretty hectic for a while to say the least.

I woke up the next morning looking into a ball of flaming magnesium as a fiendish intern pried my gummy right eye open to his twelve-gauge flashlight. This barbarism has, I think, something to do with ascertaining whether or not the patient needs methadone, which is the morphine substitute currently in use on the gallery. It is administered orally since these are no longer the good old days. I think that if one's pupils dilate and don't contract when brutally bushwhacked first thing in the morning, they figure you need *some*thing. All I wanted at that moment was the intern's life's blood; he didn't even have the decency to *say* anything. He just let me fall back rather rubber-faced and walked out. I'da thrown something but when you're in a place like that under court orders and a grumpy report could mean three to five years in Raiford Penitentiary, you're in a terrible fucking position. That clown could have come in with a syringe full of Novocaine and left with my earlobes. Lemme tell you man, once they got you, they *got* you, you don't even exist anymore.

Anyway, evidently, my eyes betrayed me and I was flat ignored from then on. But goddamn, I really did need something during the next few days and I don't think a Valium or even a blasted Miltown would have particularly wounded their Hippo-blah Oath.

That morning after breakfast, which I couldn't eat either for picking away at it and thinking of poor old Fafnir in there, Ivan came up to the gallery and told me to my extreme joy that a man named Bob Vaughan was in the hospital. Bob was an ancient acquaintance of mine from Miami and Ivan told me he worked in the library and would be bringing up the book cart later. I'd forgotten all about the book cart. Double joy!

Later that afternoon I was talking to a Georgia cracker in his favorite spot, one of Lexington's many forgotten rooms, where someone had left an old mattress crumpled against a wall. It was very comfortable and you know that image of "dope fiend" that's been fed to you? Well I'd fallen for that myself, spike in hand, more than I care to admit. Among many other discrepancies, it seems that almost a fourth of the hospital's patients are freckled-faced deep south saltines trying to cool paregoric habits. The way it looks to me is that on all levels of society, if you put something pleasant in front of people and they take it just once, they're gonna take it again. I mean what happened the first time you got laid, hah? Like monkeys yanking the pleasure switch until they starve to death.

So this old fart was a nice guy, the type you spend an afternoon talking to in a run-down marina, rotten wood everywhere as he tinkers with an outboard motor. Flies and perspiration. He was telling me how he and some friends had gone through four sets of tires in one year driving from town to town alternately hitting up all the drugstores for P.G. "Dee Pree's the best," he said. He was a volunteer also and he didn't have "pressure" (to stay) like I did, so he was planning on checking out the next day. Infected with the manufactured determination that characterizes the shooting gallery, I suggested that he stay and clean himself up once and for all. He looked at me from the other side of the moldy old mattress and he said this: "Son, I gave up my wife (wives are always the first to go. Usually an attempt to clean up is made at their insistence, but when that fails, the rest is quick to follow.), my home, my job, my self-respect, and the respect of my kids. All for that stuff. Now *where* would I be if I gave that up, too?" Man, I didn't say a word. That fella needed a shot and no value judgments allowed. Poor fucker was about fifty. Build a new life, shit; then the book cart went by.

Please excuse these digressions, but I must remember to clean under my desk while I am thinking of it. I had to murder a tarantula with spray last night, which is like cruel and unusual but I clouted him first with a sandal so he shouldn't have felt much. Big mother, too. I understand they are very affectionate and make nice pets, what a drag. I hope you don't object to my taking notes along the way, they might be useful sometime. See, I'm writing this in a Godforsaken little room in Yucatan, swatting at mosquitoes. Evasive little bastards. My wife had some sense and split back to Savannah to fix up the dysentery. Aw, go ahead man. Drink the water, and make sure there's a beauteous wench about to soothe us in our delirium what we can ham up and go out for a beer after the obvious occurs. I think maybe an occasional break from the hospital might be refreshing like I bop across the street to this strip joint when the takka takka of this damn machine gets me wall-eyed. But I shall try to keep close, if not upon the story track. But the book cart . . . "Bob!" "Billy!" We shook hands, felt silly and embraced. You just can't shake hands with an unexpected old friend in the lockup. There's nothing on this earth like belly-to with a woman, but also nothing like the slap whomp and gorilla stomp with old friends.

Oh, but old Bob was far out. He is or was (I have it by hearsay that he has since drunk himself to death) about forty, looking sixty, a tall tall ecto-morph poet wearing a glass eye or a black patch as the mood struck him. When he lay on a bed, it seemed he was not so much in danger of ill health as of disappearance. Four and a half inches thick with a marvelously deep resonant reading voice resulting from years of reading his poetry in seedy Miami studios. He had never been one for needles when I'd known him back in Miami. I remembered the last time I had seen him when he was sliding wide brim black hatted into a studio with an enormous sheaf of papers under his arm. Bob was not one for skinny steel in the main so I asked him, "What are you doing here if not for dope?" He said, "What am I doing here?" and went into a ten-minute spiel about how he had just come up from Key West where the scene was marvelous, the boats floated as if in midair, the water was so clear they just floated in midair with strange creatures beneath them beyond the beaches better than beds and it was all *behind* you! The whole United States! And the bars at night with the fishermen, and the *bar*maids! Gasp! "But what are you doing *here*?" "Here?" "Yeah, here." And he bottled the general picture. Seemed he drank too much. And one night he blacked out, which was not unusual. What was odd about this one was that when he woke up on the beach the next morning, he found he had given everything away. His home, his car, a wallet with his papers, his watch and ring and a fossilized whale's tooth. He could have gotten his house and some of his effects back of course, excluding the car, which was probably in Georgia by then, but the idea of blacking out in such a way bothered him a little. So thinking the time had come, he stepped off the train into the Lexington snow drinking down two ounces of paregoric in his short-sleeved shirt and, winking in the guardhouse, checked into the hospital. The tiny guardhouse, gunless, warm and forlorn. As soon as he got into Population he haunted the library until they gave him a job there so he wouldn't languish.

He told me in his yearning voice that the books he had on the cart were pretty poor but I took three anyway and then he had to "Carry on for God's sake." He left then, wrestling with the cart, which creaked and veered into walls because the wheels were almost rusted fast.

So now it was better. I had something to read and the promise of someone to hang out with when I got to Population. Population is the largest section of the hospital where the curee winds up after a month on the gallery and on orientation. Until I arrived Population always strobe/blended in my mind with images of brutal guards and animalistic inmates. I was scared to death that some two-hundred-pound slobbering moron was going straight up my ass, mama.

But I just had to wait and see and spent the rest of my time on the gallery reading crummy books. I remember one by some newsman about his experiences in Europe during WWII, and how he was always sprinting out of town just ahead of them Nazis. It was a good story; chicken-heart that I am I think I would have fought in that war. "Well ya wouldn't have fought in any outfit of *mine*, ya damn dope fiend!"

It was a strange as Hell place for anything aesthetically pleasing, but for about ten minutes every day at sundown the TV room on the gallery was really quite beautiful. The windows looked out on one side at a vast expanse of bluish gray snow, and on the other side, in at Narco. And there is something wonderful about the way the sun reaches across the reddening snow and hits the windows, filling the room with a reddish gold haze. It was rare meat for the senses, and because of the dull institutional construction of the place, people were always the most interesting objects present. I watched the toothless and suffering faces of three-legged cane bearing old men disappearing into the gold at the end of the room, it was that thick. And the long-lost royalty retaining faces of the slightly silvered black men before the television also tinged with gold them stony statues with their jungle vine veins. *My* veins know what's up, diving almost snakelike for the bone the minute I pick up an outfit (syringe). But I got so I'd quit reading a minute ahead of time and sit back to watch with my thumb in my book, it was that definite. If it was cloudy out and the sun didn't show, I was downright driven to frustration; didn't seem like asking much.

There were new curees coming in every day; myriads of exotic and erotic anxieties, much shuffling and groaning—again Dante comes to mind; perfect physical specimens driven wild and an occasional misshapen monster. Some of these cats was obviously to be avoided, all they wanted was their knuckles skinned. "I hear you gonna work in the kitchen, boy. You gonna bring me eggs? You better bring me eggs." or "What the hell you doing changing the station nigger?" Wham! A chair flies across the room and the security force *sweeps* the room. But one batch brought in a guy named Sammy whose knuckles always remained as white as snow. Sammy was another cracker, oh, six feet tall with another nine inches tacked on for good nature. Hopelessly good-natured. It was a good thing he was so big because people would have walked all over him. I once mentioned to him that the idea of getting my ass raped worried me and he said, "Billy, I'm shamed a you. You look pretty quick to me. You ain't so weak. Get it on boy, you're alright." Made me feel better. He could shovel more coal than any four men in the furnace room and not think twice or even at all. His whole problem was that he couldn't get into it, didn't *have* that rat race gear like you and I do. All he wanted out of life was a little dope and a lot of women. The women were no problem, but for the dope? Did he learn how to wheedle doctors? No. Did he get hip to making connections, even buying P.G.? No. Did he receive dope from charitable buddies? Sometimes. What he would do, and I mean with his *peculiar* directness of purpose, was go out and buy a cheap third-hand junker. Then in the small hours, he and a friend would just drive through the front door of any drugstore that came handy. And while his friend flopped on the sidewalk like a basket case, Sammy would lope for the dope. And if the police arrived before they could get lost, why he was just looking for a phone to call them. My own reaction was that it was a likely damn story, but perhaps I was only thinking of what would be reasonable within my own framework.

We got to be pretty good friends up there and he was always telling me what a great team we'd make and how we should get together on the outside. And then he'd laugh and come up with ideas for armed robbery, banks, drugs, and a few people he had it in for; didn't want to really hurt them just "fix it so they don't look right." Do you remember how to blow air between your teeth and cheek, like to imitate Donald Duck? (Jesus Christ, what *is* this?) Well, that's how Sammy laughed, but much louder.

There is very little to do on the gallery. A man can read just so much after all; put down yer book, play cards, and watch television and that's about it. The doctors of Lexington Hospital, however, had therapeutically provided a daily break in the monotony. My second day there I was sitting around procrastinatin' on entropy when I was horrified to hear somebody whine, "Aw-w-w SHIT! It's time to go to the goddamn gym!" Now really, in your mind's eye, picture this: For two weeks, fifty moaning anguishing junkies drag themselves daily down, down to the damp gymnasium smell of withdrawal and exertion sweat, to toss medicine balls around and play trip and fall basketball. A couple of side rooms had some half-inflated punching bags, one with dried blood all over it, and a stinking molding mat to break one's neck upon. On the court: "Throw it to him! To Him! No man, not me! What's the score? Fuck!" There was surely a sound medical reason for all this but no one seemed to know what it was.

At intervals during the day, the medication cart is wheeled through the gallery, bright and shining. A big stainless-steel table with holes in it to hold the little cups of methadone. The interns call out names at the huddled mass in tattered blue. Combat mail call was never like this. "Jimenez!" "Here mon!" grabgulrp! "Lippertt!" " 'Rot chere perfesser!" schlurp! After the patients get their dope they go to the water fountain and rinse their cup so as not to lose a drop, a most pathetic sight. There is a pseudo-legend on the gallery about four guys who actually did what everyone always thought about and ripped off the entire cart by force, slopping methadone right and left. They were volunteers and all that happened to them was their expulsion from the hospital, nodding and reeling. That was in the early days of methadone when junkies traveled hundreds of miles expecting morphine and got mad.

So since I had nothing whatever to do with the big deal of the day, I was impatient to move on to orientation. I had an insane notion that I should be allowed to work at "My own speed," and get out early. But that freedom seemed to belong to previous days and my requests to be moved were met with those kinds of explanations that disappear from your mind when you try to remember them. And I went to orientation with everybody else.

Orientation is where the patient is told what a wonderful place he's in—its boring history—and is shown slides of the hospital taken from every unimaginative angle by the "photo boys." We even got to see slides of the prisoners' Christmas party a few years back. And as if this sort of thing wasn't enough, every other day we were obliged to spend two hours sitting in the day room listening to representatives of various volunteer patient groups rail on about the virtues of their specific organization. No one, absolutely no one, not even the speakers, gave a damn about any of it.

The only good thing about orientation was the private rooms. (Sometimes it was three to a room on the gallery.) Rather than an act of kindness on the part of the hospital administration, it was rather more probably an effort to curb homosexual gymnastics. Because this was that irresistible time when junk was fading from everybody's immediate metabolism and we were all getting memories of cunt and come. Ah, weren't those the days, when there were really women in our lives? It hit me as hard as the others and every night I was coaxing it up and out in the pale window moon. Outside, slow snow fell in blue halos past lights on distant fields. Inside, in all the rooms the radiators clunked sadly and faint sounds of satisfaction drifted in from down the hall. (Poooo-Ta-a-ah!) Some Puerto Rican.

Bob would stop by and rap whenever he ran his literary rickshaw through and I would always quiz him about Population still having a feeling that I was about to be thrown to the lions over there. Innocent blood, but I only got vague generalizations from him and a feeling that I should just wait and see. Perhaps he thought I was just being childish as I probably was. I had never yet seen him wearing his eye patch and one day in what struck me as an attempt to observe my reaction to the bizarre, he just plucked out his right eye and tossed it in his mouth to see would I wig. It was obviously shock tactics of some kind because he didn't say, "This is a glass eye and I'm gonna take it out now to clean it." It was just "Schlup! Gulp!" But who knows? Maybe he just wasn't up on his post and really wanted to clean the damn thing. But at any rate, I asked him if I could hold it and then just to scare him a little, I fumbled like I was going to drop it. When I gave it back to him at his insistence, he jammed it back in his head without even dusting it off. He grumbled something about $350.

But Bob only came by twice a week and that was four times while I was on orientation, so I read, listened to obscure meandering lectures, and tended to the practical matters imposed upon me like getting standard clothing from the hospital laundry. Gray pants, gray shirt, keep your own shoes and for a pack of cigarettes, a cap. That bit about the shoes looked awfully funny sometimes because you'd pass some cat in the hall all decked out in prison gray but with these weird pointed alligator shoes gleaming undercuff with buckles and chrome. I found out in the laundry that my name was 75598 and I'd better not forget.

On orientation, in order to prepare the client for the hard-working life ahead in Population, silly little fifteen-minute jobs are assigned every day. Like mopping the hall after the "sweeper" has done his bit. Again, no one gave a damn how well it was done.

It was after my job of hall mopping, which I had done with my characteristic gusto, that I came back to the first floor day room one day to find Charlie being intellectually accosted. Poor Charlie, the dumbest and the most talkative black man I've ever known. He told me himself much later that he'd found out his IQ was 60 and I had to hold his hand. Literally. All right, all right, IQ's don't mean much anyway you look at them, but when you get down below 70 it is, at least, a reflection on your school and your parents.

Charlie was being grilled about religion in a friendly sort of way, but was visibly agitated. His inquisitor was a fellow about my height (5'8") with blondish hair in sort of a side top. He was built like a bear, very powerful, and had a big head. In fact that was the moniker he was eventually tagged with in Population: "Hey! Bighead!"

I liked Charlie so I sat down at the table just as

Bighead was saying, "Well, I personally follow a religion called Zen Buddhism." I immediately thought "ugh" remembering a vast panorama of occidental Zen Buddhists whining in my nightmares, "I just couldn't *tell* you how much Zen has done for me . . . mannn!" However, in the next few days I got to talking to Dennis Bighead more and more and finally decided that luck was with me when I met him. He was all wool and a yard wide, the genuine article. And he knew his Orient; sutras, mantras, Upanishads, Ramayana, Gita, mutatis, mutandis, ad infinitum.

Now, let me tell you something about this Federal Narcotics Farm at Lexington, Kentucky. Aside from the bums, a lot of other nonjunkie types wind up there. Dennis, for example, had been arrested for possession and I think sale of LSD. And since acid is a drug of sorts and owing to the unspeakable ignorance of the narcotics people, Dennis was able to cop an article nine. Make that *Article Nine* and look for it pal.

Don't ask me where you can find an article nine. All I know is that it's legal and states in essence: "Oh, pleez Massah!! I'm jus' a po' sick junkie. Sick and not really responsible for that holdup because I'm sick, so pleez don' throw me in that Kentuck briar patch." What I'm saying is that Lexington is a country club as prisons go, and anyone who takes too much aspirin can have an armed robbery charge transferred to the hospital if his lawyer is very sharp as Dennis's was. An extremely beneficial confusion. Probably, you'd have to be white, too. My God but this country has got itself screwed up. Who's in charge here? Who's . . . never mind.

And while we're giving away trade secrets, let me tell you something else about this hospital at Lexington. I wasn't in Population two weeks before I made a connection for Dilaudid. That's synthetic morphine, very fine, and with all the money they're spending on the damn moon, you'd think they'd be able to keep junk out of Narco. One carton of cigarettes, one fix, works were on Uncle Sam, they came from the labs. You see, even though the government puts up a big front with two narcotics hospitals, the other in Dallas, no one really wants the junkies to clean up except the people that love them, and believe it or not, dope fiends are deserving of love as much as you are. The Narcotics Bureau just wants to keep them sick enough to keep their jobs. And dig: After a while it becomes easy to tell the difference between one batch of dope in town and one that came from someplace else. Just ask your next door junkie. It is no secret that most of the dope confiscated in raids finds its way back onto the street. A bit incinerated here and there for the camera and Bam! I have tasted it on the rebound myself.

Anyway, Dennis had come to Narco on an article nine, which tickled him pink and he'd never touched a needle. I even had to explain to him what makeshift syringes made with eyedroppers and pacifiers were all about. He was reverent about his body at the time, but his term at the hospital gave him the *orientation* all right. I have called him in Detroit since and he is addicted to morphine. That's Lex. for you in a nutshell, but there's more to come.

I got my first letter from the outside while I was on orientation, and suddenly mail was very important to me. Every day from then until I left, I'd be loitering around the mail area about that time. I'd be overjoyed when I'd get a letter from Tina, languishing at the Institute of Living in Hartford (I'd tell you *her* story, the bastards, but doubt if she'd want me to after what they did to her) or from Michelle who was in Florida. Or Nancy. Matter of fact, Dennis and I would both be up there, eying and circling each other in a manner calculated to keep the security force on their toes.

But Dennis came to orientation almost a week after I did, so when my time came up, I very trembly and afeared went to Population without him. . . .

5

It was a long way from orientation to Population, perhaps a third of a mile along one hall. In Population, I lived on the fourth floor of Block E Designated E4. Windows looked out on the doctors' parking lot that emptied slowly every afternoon going home to pot roasts and warm breasts . . . and were it not for some bars, our day room would have adjoined the prisoners' section. Some of the volunteer patients had prisoner friends and would pow wow with them at the end of the room, but for the most part the two groups disliked each other. I could see the reason actually; how would you like to be doing five years and have to watch eighteen separate groups of volunteers come and go?

As soon as I got my bed made and went to the day room, Bob introduced me to Ricky Pierce who was from Boca Raton, practically my own stomping grounds and I was supposed to know him but memory wouldn't serve. I also met Johnny, a cool, sloe-eyed fag who played jazz guitar, and a crazy-ass LSD freak that Bob had brutally branded the Zen Moron. Ricky was always plaguing Johnny with *Playboy* foldouts that he'd stick on the walls of the room they shared with several other people. "Goddamnit! Man, I mean *really!*"

So now I had a permanent place to sleep. Sleeping arrangements were as follows: On each floor as you come out of the elevator the guards' station is in front of you. Windows are on the left. This is just Block E now, I don't know about the others. And a short hall on the right leads to the day room, lots of light in there through the windows and Ping-Pong tables, another and longer hall files away perpendicular.

There were twelve doors on the longer hall. Each one opened on a dormitory-type room that adjoined another on the other side of a bathroom. At night the guards came to the doors every thirty minutes and would flick their lights over the beds to see was everybody home. Click, they'd go. Click, click down the hall not noticing that the me in my bed was usually a pile of clothes because the real me would be in the bathroom reading.

I read in the bathroom every night until I couldn't focus, but I usually couldn't sleep when I went back to bed because the next guy over snored like a hog-caller. For the most part, I think that thing is true about if you sleep on your back you'll snore if you can, but if you lay on your stomach you won't. But what this bastard would do was, he'd fall asleep on his stomach, and with his hand, so help me God, under his chin twisting his head up so he could snore. Now some people snore in a way that I like. You know the old cartoon snort/whistle. Regular. Put you to sleep. But this monster would snort and hiss for a minute and then just as I was about to drift off, he'd cut loose with a "GRO-O-NK!" that would damn near give me nosebleed. I used to lie awake at night thinking, "That bastard's so-o-o nice in the daytime. He must have a lot of hate stored up to act like this at night." I really took it personally and I'd have the most realistic visions of working a broken broomstick up and down his bloody throat as he lay there, and then copping an article nine.

In Population, all patients and prisoners have a job of some kind to keep them off the streets, and by now mine was kitchen cleanup just as Ivan had said. What was good about this otherwise awful job was that there were two shifts, and I had the afternoon to evening one so I could sleep till noon if I didn't feel like getting up for breakfast, which I never do. They'd tried me out on various jobs but I was either too weak, slow, or little so I eventually wound up on general cleanup. By the way many commonplace things are weird when multiplied by a thousand. Try climbing up a vat and staring a quarter ton of spaghetti in the face some time.

General cleanup consisted of taking the garbage down to the garbage room (there was always at least a hundred pounds of perfectly edible good wastage), cleaning all the serving carts and counters, taking leftover trays and silver to their places, and then mopping the floor twice. I did all these things daily with a passive fag named Bones Gilliland, who was famous for the saying, "People who live in glass houses shouldn't get stoned."

Bones and I made a lot of mistakes in that kitchen. If you want something done right, never, under any circumstances, turn the job over to a junkie. We submerged the back of the kitchen with suds from using too much soap in the dishwasher, just as slapstick as you please. We accidentally dumped a bucket of mop water into a vat of hot grease thereby precipitating a violent eruption, which took us four hours to clean up. The list is endless; I also slung a mop over my shoulder into a pan of chicken pot pie and got yelled at. The mops at Lex. were six feet long.

Adjoining the main one there was a cute little kitchen about right for a mansion that catered to those inmates with dietary problems. They served the food with little numbered flags stuck in it. The patients' numbers. The man who ran the dietary kitchen was a good-natured, powder-brained speed freak in his late thirties who gave me fruit and other leftovers. He was a dead-end victim of "amphetA-meenz," as he called them, and when he learned that I'd had a sweet tooth before I came, he was always grinning and asking me with bulging eyes, "You gonna shoot up any more that stuff Billy? When you get out Billy? Them amphetAmeenz?" And his eyes would glimmer for a second but you could never see who or what was left inside. He told me his best friend had carved off his right bicep in the throes of wig, thinking he'd ax-murdered his mother and father, which he hadn't. "Boy, *I'll* tell you." He'd say two or three times a night. "Speed is *the* nastiest shit." I was inclined to agree with him.

Mopping his kitchen was part of our job, me and Bones, and I'd always say I'd take care of it alone because there was a radio in there, and I'd mop, talk to the good freak, and hum to myself as the sun went down.

And I'd also take care of the garbage room down in the hospital bowels, dumping half-full cans into each other and cleaning out the empty ones with a monstrous steam-belching hose. It was cool and damp and private and I had two controls, one for steam and one for water. Sometimes I'd turn on the steam alone and stand there as it screamed out hotter until I could hardly see my feet. Then I'd kill the steam and chase it off with cold water, washing down the walls and chasing banana peels across the brick floor.

This last was the end of our job, and then Bones and I would split up because he was a prisoner and off he'd go, his clothes all lumpy with stolen food to peddle on his block. I never robbed any leftovers because I didn't think the rewards were worth the penalties. Food robbing is punishable by an unspecified number of hours in the Hole, wherein the relapsee is deprived of all clothing except a pair of shorts (invariably too large), is fed crap, and is obliged to sleep without a mattress. All in all, not worth a pack of cigarettes, I thought.

So back on E4 to sit in the day room watching television, rapping, or playing whist. If I had misguidedly attached any sophistication to the use of narcotics, it was swiftly dispelled by the fact that half of E4 was up at seven o'clock every Saturday morning to watch the cartoons. I noticed a number of guys who were so dumb that when a good-legged girl would come on the screen they'd hunker down and try to look up under her dress.

That's the weirdest damn thing about junkies, how they can be so ignorant and so cunning at the same time. I once passed three black guys in the hall progressing with the typical Lexington tunnel junkie walk: changing sides of the hall every forty feet in a curious sliding half-drunken bopping motion. Tacking would sum it up, I think. As if to say, "I don't give two shits. I got the whole *hall* to walk in." But still walking against an imaginary wind. At least it looks that way, and it is true that junkies *thrive* on adversity. *No* adversity, no junkie. More on that when we get to group therapy.

So I passed them with my own "keep to the wall and keep your eyes open" walk, which must look rather funny, too. A crab? And I heard one of them say, "Man, there ain't *nothing* a junkie don't know!" He meant, of course, there ain't nothing a junkie don't know about being a junkie. Righto, it's the fastest learned occupation in the world and perhaps the just plain fastest, stoned-out periods excluded. Lightning calculations every day. Is this cat cool? Is this shit good? You don't like it, you can . . . Ooops! Here comes the man! Out this way rounds the corner make the cop whose got some works? Shit! Works, works, whose got some works? All the way to so and so's share the works, sharpen the needle, bang! Nod. . . . Is this cat cool??? and so on and on.

You can take the laziest dumbest son of a bitch you can find as long as he can count past a hundred dollars with no trouble, can talk and walk. Give him a habit and Kabambo! He'll be out on the street raking in that ten grand a year. I know of no other occupation that incites such initiative. For obvious reasons, but the increase in competence remains. As long as it has bearing on the deal. Buncha fanatics man. Anything for the cause. Why junkies? *Because.*

Be-cause. And a junkie is his very own. The incorrigible fanatic. Every junkie knows this, if unable to say it and yet here these clowns are looking up the television. Beats me man. I just work here.

Maybe these guys just acted that way while they were locked up, I don't know. But at any rate, I was relatively secure in my family of fellows. We were all sitting around being pleasantly sarcastic to each other one night when Bob mentioned that the editor of the volunteer patients' newspaper was leaving soon and why didn't I try to get the job? I did and eventually wound up with a private room, the use of a typewriter, and all the paper I wanted. Stranger things than ever reached the paper slid out of that machine. Oh, Paganini, where are you now? Oh well.

Now, previously, the paper had always been along the lines of "How I found God at the bottom of the spoon and began the long descent back to decency." But that kind of copy is enough to send a man spinning into the drugstore out of sheer boredom, so we started out with a mess of innovations. The name of the paper was the *Drummer* (you know, like marching to a different drummer? Jesus.), and Dennis, who was the art editor, did a wild drawing of a naked chick holding up a drum for the first cover. Then Bob suggested that for the premier we print an interview with old Clarence. Clarence was the oldest junkie in the hospital and had been a dope fiend long before narcotics were illegalized. He was well over eighty and his arms were in such condition that the doctors took propaganda pictures of them for textbooks. Those doctors did a lot of strange shit to inmates, especially prisoners. They had a thing going where they'd take prisoner volunteers, and hook them and kick them and hook them again until they didn't know which way was high. This was in the name of research, but those poor clods; I mean I don't know what kind of deals they made with them. One prisoner was telling me about his last session and he said, "That doctor came at me with a hit so big that I told him 'Man, don't give me that. I can't take it,' you understand, and he said, 'Just relax, we know what you can take.'" They'd dissect junkies if they could get away with it. Buncha fascists and God knows what goes on in the morgue.

Anyway, I interviewed Clarence sitting in his wheelchair (he and another old coot used to race their wheelchairs down the corridor to see who could get to the milk machine first) and he was talking about how he used to do up a kilo of pure heroin every thirty-six weeks. "A shot of real stuff would kill one of these kids." He gestured with a snowy claw to the guys playing cards around us. I asked him if he enjoyed sex and he said that's how he'd like to die. "Underneath heroin and on top of a woman." Ecstasy sandwich, though I didn't see how he could do it. Maybe they don't make junkies like him anymore. "What's your favorite color?" I asked. (We had to keep these things simple for our readers.) And

261

son of a bitch said, "Brown. I don't like white girls."

So we livened up the paper somewhat, throwing out all the testimonials, and we used it to organize handball tourneys and bingo games on Saturdays to which we maliciously invited the psychologists who then had to come to show they were interested in patient activities. And to lead up to something, let me tell you that the women were fanatically guarded on the other side of the hospital. You'd have thought the doctors wanted them all for themselves, were hoarding them. If you happened to be in the same hall when they were on their way to a meal, you had to go down some stairs, into a hallway, hide your face in your hands, anything, but it was against regulations to look at them. The one notable exception was the movies.

In the theater, which doubled as bomb shelter because it was under the hospital, the men sat downstairs while the women occupied the balcony. Once a week, seven hundred and fifty men turned in their seats toward the balcony as the girls filed in waving and mewing. Rows and rows of teeth in the near dark, as the nodding, smirking guards scratched their crotches. To see those junkies, you'd have thought that, given the chance, they'd have had Margaret Mead flat on her back in seconds. And to hear them talk! Why, every other fiend at Lexington claimed he was a pimp. "My women buys me clothes, keeps me in a fine place, and I don't eat nothing but *steak*." Sad, eh?

Along in here somewhere, the *Drummer* got together with a couple of other groups and started pulling for a dance to be held in the gymnasium, or rather a series of dances so the groups wouldn't be too large. At first the administration was horrified. "Why, we'll have an orgy on our hands! You've heard them, they're all pimps." But after a while the news got around that there might be a dance and that was all anybody could think about, so finally the doctors agreed to try it out.

I went to the first one to "cover" it for the *Drummer*. It was on a Saturday, and you should have seen the famous hundred-woman pimps. The poor bastards were petrified and so were the girls. It took well over half an hour before anybody got up the guts to dance. Tall skinny girls, short fat balding junkies, and they couldn't really dance because all the band knew how to play was listening jazz. I didn't dance at all, like most of the pimps who grouped up at one end of the room and waited for the girls to come get them. Old Clarence and his racing partner couldn't dance, of course, but they had fun sitting around sipping punch and talking about dance fads in the twenties. All in all though, the sheer monotony-breaking novelty of the thing made it a glowing success, and the paper raved about it in the next issue, thanking doctors and decorating crews and commending everybody on their gentlemanly deportment.

So the *Drummer*'s new image succeeded for the

most part. A few of the junkies didn't like it because they couldn't understand some of the words. I remember when Dennis and I got a letter of commendation from the head shrinker and all we'd done was print in the margin, "Are mental health laws archaic?" Something for everybody.

Remember Charlie, the black man that Dennis was grilling when I met him? Well, he was starting to get on my nerves. He had a job over in the mental section where the government hides all the wiggy soldiers and such (I wonder how many "missing in actions" are over there) and he was always cornering me to explain his simpleton diagnoseez. He'd go, "Bee-ul? Na, Ah believe that a man has got to think what he wants and not have to think what other folks do. You know what I meeen?" All my life I've been an easy prey for bores because I'm such a nice guy, and I don't know how many hours I spent listening to Charlie drone on about the nuts. He considered most of them his patients.

So I'd listen to him for a while damn near every night when he saw me first, but occasionally Dennis or Ricky would come and rescue me before the lecture was over, saying, "Let's go to the gym," or "Let's go get some ice cream." You could even get a strawberry sundae at Lexington if you had money in your name. You'd get a little coupon book with five-, ten-, and twenty-five-cent tickets that could buy anything from candy to record players. Kool cigarettes were the biggest sellers in the hospital because the junkies liked to bop in and say, "Gimme a pack a *Kools*, man!" They even sold lipstick to the fags.

And I remember just how to get to the gymnasium through a labyrinth of tunnels and past the tiny watch shop that had been set up for an old fag doing twenty years. He sits in there all day tinkering with mainsprings and trying to coax boys inside. Leaving him behind, we'd pass an enormous vault with a six-foot golden eagle painted on the black door. "That's where they keep the dope," everybody figures, but nobody really knows. Past the morgue quickly and Bam! There it is. "The Blue Room for Strength and Health." Inside, there are always fifteen or twenty musclemen tempting fate with huge weights. "Hey man!" they'd say. "Look at that arm! When I get back on the street . . . huh! They won't even recognize me when I get back on the street!" So six months later a disease-ridden bag of bones checks in again and totters back to the Blue Room.

Beyond the Blue Room is a basketball court and several rooms with half-deflated punching bags as mentioned before, and up some littered stairs is a two-lane bowling alley, which has an old velvet couch to sit on while you wait your turn. Red. Bowling is not usually my style, but I got awfully bored at Lexington. Lexington is pretty small as federal institutions and prisons go, not like some of the big joints where you can even get a degree. You know what

265

they give the poor bastards in Florida's Raiford Penitentiary to do? Make license plates. I went on a sociology tour through there one time, feeling decadent, and their school is just about that big compared to the machine shop. I still wake up sweating sometimes, thinking how close I came to four years of that place.

Anyway, we were bored, and this was about the time that banana smoking fraud sailed across the country. Bob was the first to hear of it. Good old Bob always had a damp finger in the winds of change. Stranger things have proved to be true, so one day he explained the theory and curing procedure to me and the next found me roasting up banana in the oven next to the barbecue. We smoked it later and I felt nothing. Bob swore, though, that there was something there but it was "subtle, subtle." "Too damn subtle for me," I thought and laid off banana as the word spread that here was something to get high on. It was debatable whether it worked or not, but sooner or later, a lot of the patients tried it. In fact, it reached epidemic proportions, was discovered by the guards and doctors, and bananas were removed from the menu pending lab tests to see if they could really have any effect. When that happened, we had a field day. Some of the things they served were vile, you understand, and we started taking everything we hated like Brussels sprouts, drying it, and sticking it in our pipes to smoke it. For about a week, before they caught on, the lab and the dietitians were in a frenzy.

One day, about a month after I got to Population, I got to feeling artistic and went to get my guitar back. They were keeping it over by the main entrance to the hospital where the doctors came in. I crossed an enormous half-heartedly Gothic courtyard with a large social worker and went through a little door like the one to the first waiting room. And there was a hospital lobby on the other side! These people were really trying to convince themselves that they were running a regular hospital. A little stage play set up in one of the black outer walls. There were the swinging glass doors, there the copies of *McCall's* and *Legion*, even a nurses' station, cute and starchy. Several people looked at me with curious distaste as I snuck through with my social worker, me unwelcome splash of gray. "Ugh! A patient!"

So I got my guitar out of the storeroom, and once back in the secure section, the social worker directed me to the music department. It seemed at least half a mile past the Blue Room. I went there through more gray tunnels, the paint peeling in these, and past great piles of old musical instruments rusting behind heavy screens, as if they could ever sing another note if anyone let them out again. Through high colonnades of rusted steel girders with mandala dust-beam light bulbs, and finally the hall swung right. There on the corner was the music room, occupied by a featureless fat man. An unidentifiable opening in his face told me where the practice rooms were and between which hours I could use them.

They were off down the hall some more past a splintered and dusty basketball court, long unused. I later learned, by hearsay you understand, that that was where all the practicing fags service their boyfriends. Bubbles and Fifi. I used to wake up at dawn sometimes to the prettiest feminine voice singing alone in the day room and it would be two-hundred-forty-pound black Bubbles. If she ever sees this, she'll bitch her head off, but she looked like two forty to me.

At any rate, peering into the gloom, I didn't feel like starting off for the practice rooms without a canteen, so I just sat on a bench around the corner from the office and tried to play. But my fingers had gotten stiff and I sounded terrible so I put the thing away vowing that while I was in the hospital I would learn music notation and embark on a serious study of the instrument.

That same night while playing whist with the boys in the day room, I asked if anybody knew how to read music. Dennis chuckled in his two-hundred-pound chipmunk way and asked what the Hell I wanted to learn to read music for. I told him and he said that he'd played bass for about four years and could probably get guitar notation across to me.

So the next day we sat on the bench by the office

and I promptly lost interest. I hate fumbling with somebody's artistic specialty in front of them. Dennis, I found, was a musician. He'd never touched a guitar before and he put me to shame. I was suspicious. "You mean to tell me you've only played the bass for just four years?" Finally I got it out of him that well, he had played the violin since he was three and that well, he had been a soloist for some Royal Canadian Symphony Orchestra when he was eight. Everybody's a goddamn prodigy but me. Dennis had already sent for his violin and when it arrived, we made the long trek to the practice rooms, which were metal-lined cubicles with wild orgones. Any doubts I might have had about his musical ability flew off somewhere. His thick fingers worked the skinny neck to flames. He could play *Scheherazade*, could pluck the strings like in *Danse Macabre*, and play things I couldn't even follow.

But Dennis spoke of his fiddling disparagingly, saying that what he really wanted to do was learn to play jazz guitar. And every Sunday morning we'd go down to the movie theater where the musicians would be jamming and putting shows together. Lots of the musicians at Lexington were very good and some of them were spectacular. One guy did a number with tenor and alto sax that was rather appropriately called "Elephant Stampede."

One Sunday when Johnny, the fag, was playing the guitar, I got up the nerve to ask him if I could see it for a minute. It was a fine two hundred horsepower job owned by the government, and Johnny handed it to me with arched fey eyebrow. Now I guess you've heard of Sandy Bull from some years back, and I know you've heard of Ravi Shankar who made everybody crazy at Monterey. Well, if you put a guitar in D tuning and if you fill your ears with solder, you can pretend that it sounds like a sitar. I did this and what I want you to know is that I'm a poor guitarist. My ragas go like, "Thoom! ping! Thoom! ping! dum dum dum!" But to these guys who could really play it was a new sound and they thought it was great. Somehow, I guess they didn't understand that jazz *is* music after all, and that music is bigger than just jazz alone.

The guy who did "Elephant Stampede" was overjoyed, and he started telling me how this Wednesday night the drums would do this thing, then he'd come in blowing that thing along with the piano, then they'd all stop for thirty seconds while I did my thing, then everybody would come back strong and we'd knock 'em dead man, we really would! I was pleased and humbled out of my mind and sat there like an idiot, sweating and going "Yeah, yeah." But I defected later behind visions of shearing off a fingernail on the E string in front of nine hundred people. Stampede was disgusted when I told him I couldn't make it. *He* couldn't make it, he just couldn't believe that anyone wouldn't get up there and play if they had a chance. So ended what could have been the start of a jazz legend and that

Wednesday I sat listening in the audience and I wasn't sorry at all. Personally, I like to be safely out of sight before anyone gets any message of mine.

Sometimes, after shows or movies, Bob and I would go up to his dormish room to talk over what had happened. Ricky would usually come along and we'd all sit and talk while Bob would roll up some of his subtle banana. Occasionally, the Zen Moron would drop in to say, after every factual statement, "Man, that's just it! Don't you see!?", but Bob could usually calm him down without hurting his feelings.

Bob was an incredibly sensitive man. For example, one night when he came in the day room, I waved to him and said, "Over here, Bob!" and I don't know if you're acquainted with that evil/useful part of yourself that knows when someone is off guard or vulnerable without benefit of external sign. Well I could see that his psychic flank was unguarded, which made me smile. From clear across the room in the half-light, I could see that he was instantly uptight. To tell the truth, it was awfully funny the way Bob would tense up, like a root pulling in its tendrils, and Ricky laughed. Bob turned right around and left, avoiding me for the next three days until I cornered him to apologize in the library's mystery section.

But for the most part, we treated him with kid gloves because we liked him and we liked to hear him talk about Fidel Castro and Che Guevara whom he had known briefly. He had a story about a

271

bar fight in some Argentinian cattle town, where a gaucho got slashed across the belly and said "Enough!" Then he stood at the bar holding his guts in with a bloody napkin while he finished his beer, after which he got on his horse, pointed a dripping finger at his adversary, and said, "You haven't heard the last of this!" before galloping off into the night.

Bob had a great rich reading voice; he was a disciplined poet and a scholar of Pound, and when he talked about the Cuban revolution and the mountain wounded and the hunger and vermin, his voice would gain deeper resonance and his one eye would wink and twitch. But he'd sink in on himself at those times and look even skinnier and weaker, and if I could have given one gift to the poor bastard it would have been 150 pounds of muscle.

By now the snow had melted away. The boys who had worked in the furnace rooms all winter were getting their well-earned rest, and a young junkie naturally turned to thoughts of getting the Hell outside for awhile. At least farther than the courtyard or the crab grass baseball field.

Always in the vanguard of reform, the volunteer patient's newspaper began whining and holding its breath for the doctors to take select patients just over the hill for a picnic. That may seem like asking the impossible, but it was reasonable. We weren't asking them to take prisoners out and the few volunteers who had pressure, like me, and might possibly take off, where would they go? Two-thirds of the population of Lexington, Kentucky, is cops. They can smell junkies; buy a bottle of cough syrup and they're on you like metal shavings to a magnet. By virtue of obscure legal proceedings, people have been known to be back in the hospital the same day they left, but on the prisoners side.

So a few psychologists volunteered, but not many. I could see their point actually. Who wants to sit on a hill in brisk spring weather and watch a bunch of freaks gum sandwiches? I say gum because few street junkies keep their teeth for long. People have so much trouble that the dentist shop at Narco will pull out all your teeth free of charge, if you so desire. But they won't put any in. I remember back on orientation, a Pittsburgh dope fiend I talked to a lot returned to the day room one afternoon without any teeth. We played cards for a while, but I excused myself because I couldn't stand his new mushy voice and the way the blood crept up the Lucky Strike cigarette that he kept in the corner of his mouth.

Once, a long time ago, I hear that some doctor had a cosmic vibration and decided to show a junkie kindness, like there is no such thing as a bad boy. With the permission of the hospital authorities, he went so far as to take dat fiend home with him and give him a job around the house. In all, he treated him like a member of the family. So one day he comes home to find his wife raped and hogtied and the whole house neatly ransacked. Old Chinese proverb: Never trust a psychologist to have any sense. Now before certain parties jump on this as a confession of corruption from within the ranks, I must say that this junkie was wildly untypical. But it is true that if a doctor ever did such a thing, he would be naïve.

But flip the coin and if anything is more lost on an addict than fatherly kindness, it's a tough-guy attitude. Nothing has less effect on dosage thinking than a tough guy. (Of course, Americans think of everything in terms of doses: money, love, sex, sunshine.) You see, things are rough all over, that's what *maintains* (*not* creates) a junkie. The tougher the better for the junkie paying his dues and more rough stuff only reenforces him.

Our psychologist in group therapy often came on with a tough, condescending, loving father attitude that was too horrible, just too horrible to relate to. Time and again, I've seen some poor guy just about to blurt out some desperate honesty that had been rankling him only to be steered back to that tired old wheeze about trying to be in with the group. What these people can't get out of their minds is the idea that everybody has to be *led* astray. By older kids, by Communist pederast pushers, somebody. It never occurs to them that some people burst from the fold with shrieks of joy. No! No, we're always dragged, shit-faced and pleading into the murky depths of depravity. Until we get to be the bad guys. Then we haven't been led astray, we've always been rotten as hell, and just waiting to get at your daughter. Now really, does that sound reasonable to you? Fact remains, most of us love it out here. Wish you were with us.

I always thought of the shrink in group therapy as *my* shrink, because I had him convinced that I was cured and headed for a new life just for giving out with the things he wanted to hear. He thought I was one of the rewards he got for his weary toil. And you know, I used to wake up in the *Drummer* office sweating from dreams of Raiford and wanting a shot so bad I could hardly stand it. Old parking lot light would be shining through my window lighting up the ceiling with grotesque crosses and I'd be just about to lose my mind.

A man could get high in the hospital, as I said. Not many people knew about the Dilaudid, but there was always nutmeg, mace, and of course banana for the borderline psychotics. I wasn't about to mess with that Dilaudid deal and the rest were absurd, so I stayed straight. Banana was frowned upon and condoned because we might have hit the pork chops next, but the guards would really go, uh, bananas over a little mace. One time, I recall, somebody finked on a guy for mace. (The fink was caught later in the shower and bloodied up something awful.) Mace and nutmeg were available to the guys who worked in the bakery, and our boy was just strolling by the security desk where they sometimes searched you as you came out of the kitchen. Never bothered old Bones for some reason. . . . Casual as you please and all of a sudden the "sunshine boys" of the security force were all over him. Ricky thought up that name for them in the *Drummer* and they didn't like it one bit.

So four of them grabbed this poor clown as if they expected him to fight with the superhuman strength of the stoned. One of them even had his hand over the guy's mouth as if he would call for help. He got five days in the Hole, which was no mean punishment. There weren't too many things they'd put you in the Hole for, just getting high, robbing food, refusing to work, fighting, and come to think of it, you could get a day or two for repeated untidiness at inspection.

Maybe it was because spring was in the air, but there was general racial unrest festering between the Puerto Ricans and the "crackers." And especially between four or five Puerto Ricans and one blond-headed kid from Georgia who was built like a swimmer. He was tall and quick and about nineteen. Dennis and I had taken a liking to him for his good looks and innocence, and because all he could talk about was rumbles back home in Atlanta. He had a score of incredibly gruesome fight stories, but he told them in a proud dumb way that was refreshing to hear.

Now for the last two inspections he'd gotten marked down for not being straight. But he'd been there a while and knew he was doing everything right, so he went to the guard and asked him what was wrong. "Dirt under the bed." And George knew damn well he'd not only cleaned under the bed, but mopped as well.

That afternoon in the day room of E1, where he lived downstairs from us, he noticed those Puerto Ricans eying him in a satisfied way. He never explained to me exactly how it got started, but pretty soon, an enormous guy, the Ricans' champ, was swearing he was a karate expert and chopping air, so they all went out into the courtyard.

Each block, like Block E or Block D had its own courtyard about two hundred feet by fifty feet. In the middle of the yard, there was always a twenty-foot brick wall for handball. George went around behind that wall with the Puerto Ricans, so if any guards came into the day room they wouldn't see the fight. Of course, news of a fistfight had traveled like electricity, and Bob and I watched him disappear from upstairs thinking, "Oh Jesus is he gonna get it." We couldn't see what was going on for about three minutes; then the noise of people rooting from the windows along the sides brought a crowd of bullies bopping in, bearing billies and running low. But they didn't get a chance to use them because the fight was just about over. They led George back in with mangled knuckles, but they had to help two of the other guys in, and a stretcher was called for the big karate expert. We didn't see George again for about two weeks. When he got out of the Hole, nobody bothered him anymore. That fight was a major occurrence and everybody talked about it for days. "Whap! Bap! Shee-IT!"

Another big break in the monotony that sticks in my mind were the very rare field trips that high schools in the area would send through the hospital. The break was in the girls. They walked right past you in the halls and for some reason we were allowed to look at these people. Probably would have given a bad impression to make everybody face the wall as they passed.

They'd come to see how things were run. . . . And Baby, if you're a girl that's reading this, and if you ever go on one of those tours or pass a road gang, do something kind and smile. Nobody'll come after you, they'd get shot or clobbered. I know, and others, at least among my friends, told me it was the same for them, that when some chick caught my eye and maybe turned up a corner of her mouth, my nights were clean again. All the visions of kicking and raping, all the visions of hurting flapped out the window like some grisly great bird and I'd come in the dark just thinking of her face because I never saw her body. The only guys who never looked for a sign from the girls were the long-term prisoners. Moy, the Chinese cook who really was a karate pro, would go right on stirring soup. I suppose it would have been painful to them.

So one day one of those tours went through and an absolute angel of a little girl smiled at me and even pulled her shoulders back in a barely perceptible promise that she'd meet me in some fantasy of hers, too. I smiled back and then she was gone, heading for the laundry room. Those split-second encounters have a way of exploding into infinite implication and leaving me paralyzed in the center of a universe of possibilities, each one just slightly different like the mirrors in a barbershop. I was absolutely overjoyed. She was such a pretty innocent-seeming little creature. "Going around smiling at dope addicks! What's become of our daughter?"

That night, there was a show to be put on by the female patients. It was a big deal. Of course, I was there and after a couple of songs by an ex-Miss America (I wonder what happened to her?), the mistress of ceremonies came on to say that here was the moment we'd all been waiting for. Some brassy jazz came up and the curtain parted on two girls, one black and one white. The white girl was a little fat, but the black one was okay with a big sexy ass.

So they stroked around the floor awhile, almost, but not quite bumping and grinding, but mewing and making little yelps. The audience was going "YEAH!" and "RAWW!" and I'd seen them all at the dance and the whole thing was such a drag that I left to go to bed with that little doll on the tour.

And an odd thing happened that night. The oxygen movie of the high school girl kept fluctuating with images of ramming it to those two in the leotards like they were pretending they wanted, shifting faster and faster with strobelike intensity until I wound up vomiting ambiguously in the bathroom down the hall from the man who snored.

Every evening now I watched the doctors get into their cars below my window and sometimes I'd gesture obscenely just to show I cared. A final word about the doctors. Those doctors were so incredibly inept, so totally ill-equipped to deal with drug addicts, that my eyes roll back in my head just thinking about them. The group therapy sessions I mentioned to you were held only twice a week and were often led by some fuzzy-cheeked little shrimp who'd never seen a junkie before he arrived. Just doing his internship. Imagine eight or ten ghetto dope fiends all scarred up, some toothless and muscular, some with silver bullet blotches on them listening to this pink little creature saying, "Well, we have found, of course, that many of you begin taking drugs . . . well, because (you recall that because is where the explaining stops) you want to be 'cool,' you want to be 'hip,' you want to be 'in.'" Now the guys don't even know what he's talking about. Some of them had been dealing stuff at fifteen, had been junkies since they were twelve and thirteen. Been on the receiving end and lived with death and mayhem all their lives. "Yes, that's it doctor. You hit it right on the head. I want to be 'in' so bad I can taste it."

It's obvious that the value of group therapy is questionable to begin with, but given only twice a week for a few months expecting to cure a heavy habit lugged around for years, it borders on insanity. And you couldn't even get a good confrontation going without the doctor pushing a button to summon a bunch of guards and saying (I quote), "I can't cope with this!"

Heroin is an entity to the street junkies at Lexington. Pronounced "Heron." They draw pictures of him in black shrouds riding camels from Turkey. "God's own medicine, if he made anything better, he kept it for himself." And when I asked Clarence what was the best way to cure a junkie, he said to "Put in a new brain." And I think he was right. The final and only decisive step in drug release is a massive change of consciousness that affects the whole identity and all its sensory capacities. Narcotics become so much a part of the body/mind that escape must result in temporary madness because an entire identity and way of perceiving the world must be traded for another. It's called giving up everything for nothing. I think this last step can occur years after the physical cure. *"Put in a new brain, son."* That's the only way.

So as far as presenting any alternative to a dosage-oriented lifestyle was concerned, Narco was a bust and I knew it. I was impatiently trying to clip enough tape to get myself transferred to a commune-style treatment center for wiggy kids in Florida that was run in a perceptive and semihip way. I was getting somewhere but it was sap dripping slow.

Every time I went to group therapy now, I would

wait behind afterward and ask my social worker what was happening with my transfer. Finally, one Friday, he told me that some nebulous board of experts had agreed in their vast compassion to transfer me to Florida if they received a letter from the center stating that they were willing to have me. And if they received written permission from my grandmother who had signed my original admittance papers.

The letter from the center came promptly, but my grandmother wrote back saying that I had to stick this thing out once and for all, and besides, how did she know I was cured, and besides, she simply couldn't afford the fee at the treatment center. I wrote to the center and explained the hang-up to the superintendent who very reasonably wrote to my father and hit him up for the money. My father agreed; I wrote back to my grandmother. . . . But to shorten the long, what finally happened was that my grandmother, who was suddenly shoved into senility by introspection and myself, sent her permission to my social worker care of Lexington Hospital, and it went to damn near every hospital in the area before it got to him. I wasn't transferred until fifteen days before I would have gotten out anyway.

But now I was justified in thinking that I'd be out any day. Ricky had left about a week ago saying that he was going to Boston to stay with his sister. He showed me his walking papers, which consisted of a list of things you had to do before you left. Each item was checked off by the head of that department. Laundry: return clothes, Library: return books. I walked with him as far as the security desk and watched one of the sunshine boys take him away to the world. "Be Careful!" But I have seen him since.

I was now "short" as it's called when your time is nearly up. I met another guy about that time who was also short and he was going through a thing that was very painful to watch. You see, I knew where I was going when I left, to that treatment center, and knew the place and liked the people. But this guy Gary, he was going back on the street. He was one of the Blue Room nuts and was always flexing proudly, but you could see he was scared. It's awful to see the desperate look in the eyes of some guy who would like to stay clean, who really would. Who'd like to get a job and one of those clean chicks if she had enough brains, but who knows it's going to be impossible. And *some* people don't *get* the breaks. It's just like that. They hit the street with a past record as a junkie. They can't get a job. Old enemy fuzz frisk them down. Chicks won't touch them with someone else's hand. And they know right where they can score. (Music of a merry-go-round running down.) Sometimes it's impossible to stay straight and when people start getting short, they start thinking. If they're going to have to climb back on the rack, they know it and show it.

Gary was very much in this condition, and I

talked to him about it a lot before he left, and about maybe even going home to his parents for a while if only for a clean bed. I even went down to the Blue Room with him once and almost killed myself.

Then he left and it was just me, Bob, and Dennis. I don't know what happened to the Zen Moron, maybe he had a wrathful vision and just melted away.

I was so eager to get away that the paper was suffering, but I was leaving soon and had lost all interest in anything that had anything to do with the hospital. The place is useless by its own standards.

My day came. They had my ticket to fly to Florida. Bob signed my papers on behalf of the library. They took our group over to the lobby; we were going out the real doors. They took us to a dressing room to give us the street clothes we had worn in and my joy faded. I had a black sport coat, black slacks, a black and gold paisley shirt with a black tie and vest, and buckle shoes. The pants were too damn tight and there was a marijuana seed in my coat pocket that spoke ill of the future or past, or both.

But there I was, apprehensive as we passed out into the sunlight and got into the station wagon. The guy next to me had just finished fifteen years. He didn't look back and I did as we drove away in the heat. No one spoke; and all you could hear was the tires husking on the road and the chirping of an occasional bird. It was an exceptionally quiet day.

6

I was seen onto a slow, four-engine prop plane that took me from Lexington to Louisville. We didn't pass over the hospital. Slow planes don't bother me so much and I made the trip with little more than schizophrenically acute awareness of changes in the engine sounds. But in Louisville I was slated for one of those beasts that are able to "climb 35 percent faster" than other jets. I thought bloody murder, but got on anyway. Now here's the scene: It was Memorial Day and the plane was packed with soldiers. There were no empty seats, and as the jet started wallowing down the runway, I started getting scared. I remembered all the catastrophic headlines

I'd read and I could just see this one. "Memorial Day Disaster! 197 Soldiers Killed! . . . one body as yet unidentified. . . ." I had to do something fast so I said to the stewardess, "Listen, I have to get off! It's very important!" She looked at me, perceiving that I was some kind of nut, and then went to get the captain. Thoroughly annoyed, he came back to ask what this was all about. "It's my mother, she's dying of cancer in Louisville," I said. "I was going to, but I can't leave her." The captain made an exasperated noise, but went and got the copilot, I presume, to stop the plane. I ran down a narrow staircase out of the jet's ass with the engines screaming in my ears and right into the arms of some airport cops. They quizzed me about bombs for a while and then let me go, evidently deciding that I was just shit scared of them flying machines. So I stayed in Louisville that night and got drunk but didn't get laid. The next day I was petrified on the plane but was enough ashamed of fleeing the last flight to smile cadaverously at the stewardess whenever she walked by.

Okay. Bam. Orlando airport. That's another thing about airplanes: no time to get ready. I took a plane to Tangier once and the culture shock almost killed me. Anyway, Orlando's McCoy Field is a crumby little port; I think the terminal used to be a huge hangar and I sat in there for two hours waiting for my ride. I was watching a cooking show on a television that had kindly been set up for the public when I spotted my pickup before he spotted me. I don't know what, but there's something, an *air* about people that are looking for me.

I'd never met the gentleman before and he introduced himself as Sumner Black. A short, hand-crushing, muscular type with a superior attitude. Unwontedly so. All the way to the school I tried to engage him in conversation but with no response save a few short, decidedly ugly chuckles. It was hot and I was sweating but didn't feel like wrestling out of my vest. I began to wonder what I'd gotten myself into. At one point as we passed a lake on the other side of the thruway, I saw a canoe capsize and two people were thrown into the water, one floundering. "Hey man," I said. "Looks like those people got trouble." "Snark, snark!" says Sumner Black. I gave up.

When we got to the school, he took me to my assigned room and lo and behold, as I live and breathe, perdition if I'm not searched again, right down to the skin. It was later explained to me that if I'd flown straight through, there'd have been no problem, but since I'd had time to cop, they had to check. Reasonable enough, but this clown Sumner was really enjoying himself. I couldn't see why he was being so nasty about it. He got me so mad that I finally bent over and demanded to be searched anally. But he cleared his throat and said that that wasn't necessary.

After he left, I cleaned and set up my room rather angrily, but my mind was on pleasanter things than

Sumner Black. Do you remember Michelle? I mentioned her earlier on orientation as one of my hospital correspondents. I'd received eight letters from her while I was at Narco, all of them clearly intimating that now that she was at the school, she'd be waiting for me; waiting to take up where we'd left off. She lived in New York and I'd left her there about a year previous because it had been either get out of town or die of speed.

So I went to find her at twilight, happy as you might imagine after being locked up for four months and returned in the dark whistling blues. "Sumner Black! Son of a bitch! So that's why he smirked at everything I said!" I went back to my room, insane and angry. The night had turned an ugly brooding purple and I'm sure I frightened Michelle because she locked her door instantly behind me as I left. But at least I had pencil and paper, and I've managed to find what follows; an exorcism of that evening's mood:

Everything was going along more or less according to plan. He lived his own life and minded his own business. Until one day something happened to his hearing. His ears became sensitive to the highest and lowest of frequencies, which was a very annoying affliction indeed. After that, things began to happen very quickly; he had absolutely no say in the matter, nor would he have *known* what to say. He began to feel that he led a very silly life actually, with people laughing outside his window in the night and dogs barking in the distance.

The snarl of the present would wrest him, cracking, back from nowhere on the end of a psychic leash, fast to land in pain and shock and suddenly reaware of the ugly rumbles of buses and motorcycles across the night.

He'd get up from his window on these darkling evenings not knowing how he got there (the last thing he usually remembered, was sitting down to read a book. He had thought the lights were on and he knew he wasn't by the window. . . . No, that wasn't . . .). And he'd make himself a drink while his ears pulsed with the small sounds of his home.

He became a man of coincidence and strange happenings. His matches had a tendency to reignite and one weary dusk an owl walked in his front door with the strangest of gaits and asked him who. "Jesus Christ!" he said. The owl removed his whirlpool eyes and walked out, a feathered metronome.

He was subject to sudden attacks of urgency as when he was fitting keys into locks and the whole of existence would narrow to his hand and the key and the clinking of metal would fill the sky and his hand would seem some bird of Bosch pecking faster and harder trying to get in and time was running out . . . faster . . . sometimes he had to rest for a few minutes after opening his own front door.

Things were getting difficult. His knotty pine paneled den crawled with vermin, he was sure, but they always scattered just before he opened the door. All but one big roach that was always weaving air on top of an ugly African demon mask. He began to take a shoe with him to throw at the roach whenever he went into the den. But one night he broke the nose of the mask and it was so very ugly, then, that he had to burn it. He was very careful not to inhale the smoke.

His girl friend had long since left him, taking her body with her because he no longer paid much attention to amenities and would jump her on sight. In her absence, he studied his penis and learned that he could make it rise or fall by will alone, without fantasy or sensation. In fact, he shaved his pubic hair, the better to observe.

Other things had been happening. He was now surrounded by an ammoniac mist. . . . But he still functioned; he even went to work at his gas station, but when strangers asked him for directions and he had to point the way, he had a tendency to feel like a windmill and would begin to flail his arms. Business dropped off.

Shaving in the morning became an agony and he was often moved to tears to see his whiskers lying lonely and desolate on the whiteness of the sink, like, "Like my own black soul in the purity of the world. Everything is God but me, oh Damnation." It was clear that this man was developing some kind of complex.

He would have survived all this, however, if his sense of hearing hadn't moved in for the kill. Forced as he was to listen and listen and listen, he began to understand what he heard. He even listened to the news and his friends and that was entirely too much.

Truck driver: "I dunno, this nut was hanging by his legs from the overpass! I was going too fast and as he went through the head-

lights, he looked right at me and
laughed, so help me! This here was in a
cigar container that got stuck in his
side."

I have every right to be afraid.
Why, planes are crashing all the time.
Just the other day I read about a woman who was
Be-
Headed
By a meteorite
While knitting in her living room.
On thruways, trucks have been
Known to rumble
Across the midway just to get you.
I mean every day thousands of people jump into their
                                        cars
And drive into each other
Smiling like idiots.
Radiators and pressure cookers and washing machines
Explode.
Ball lightning rolls into houses killing pets and people.
Guitar strings snap out people's eyes.
I'm not trying to be funny.
The continent is sinking, for Christ's sake.
And the squid is waiting in the sea.
By the way, do you realize that for every organ in your
                                        body
There exists
A germ
OR virus
Whose sole function is to destroy it?
I realize it. I've thought about it.
And the bomb.

And the policeman standing on the earth always ready
to forget himself.
And the sick and wheezing man on the street
Lost beneath his last load.
I have every right to be afraid of Paranoid Governors
Infantile and petulant.
I fear that time is running out.
The troopers are getting restless.
They are about to let the dogs loose.
Somebody spilled the beans!
Nixon is going to get scared and slap us all into camps
Where we can concentrate.
And learn to be good down-home folks.
Everyday a treaty broken . . . marching . . . wailing.
Is there no ground called sanctuary?
I felt better and was very tired after that; it took a lot
out of me, so I went to sleep.

A word about the treatment center/school I had
arrived in. Nestled in the fragrant farmlands of central Florida, home of the mockingbird and balmy
with the sun, there is an old monastery one mile
from Orange City, the "Home of Pure Water" because nothing could live in all that chlorine.

Some years ago, the monastery was purchased by
the Reverend George Von Hilsheimer, a man of
some foresight, who started a Summerhillian community on the property. The community has since
degenerated to something of a mental ward as so
often happens to communal experiments, but the
transition was made smoothly, so the place still re-

tains a lot of the old spirit. Part of that spirit is the abiding feeling that there is nothing intrinsically groovy about a junkie. On the contrary. I had some friends there already, though, and made others easily enough, but sex, which I needed most, seemed out of the question.

This was in late winter and as the days got longer and longer, I got hornier and hornier; I was well in rut, eying the goats and such. Now, as in most schools, fucking was against de regulations, but they couldn't guard everyone all the time so in spite of the efforts of the administration, there were a number of liaisons on campus. There were lots of girls there, groovy girls, and lots of couples. But me? No. Uh uh, forget it, brother. Two months and my back was beginning to hurt. I know my eyes had acquired a glaze and perhaps I had developed a wolfish look, but I seemed to scare girls away. It was "National Let's Keep Burroughs Horny Week" *all* the time.

So to keep my mind occupied, I spent my time wandering around fixing things with a friend named David Jones. Things dragged along bearably, albeit asexually, until Jane came up from Miami to join the staff. Tall and blond, with long legs, she seemed to like me. But you know how things go, I'm sure you can understand; I'd gone cowardly in the face of my many rejections. Rejections my ass, before I'd given up, I got into some situations too disastrous to relate. Sorry.

Anyway, for almost a month, I'd been trembling

on the verge of making a move at her. David was constantly egging me on, and one night he and I were in my room when she came up to visit with a guy named Blakely. She would come up to sit around fairly often, and this also I took as a sign that we could gravitate if I ever lifted my palsied hand. "Tonight's the night if she comes around," I'd been thinking. David noticed a naturely gleam in my eye and excused himself with admirable tact saying he was going to the other end of the campus where the girls were. This was it, so I set my teeth and nugget and was just getting ready to ask Blakely to leave when suddenly Jane went to the door, looked over her shoulder, and asked him to go with her. Now, talking to her was the closest I'd gotten to a little touching in well over nine months. I mean my hand was getting callused, so I was furious. Cursing the gods in an insane bristling huff, I caught up to David halfway across a field that we used for soccer. I was railing on to him about my bad luck when, about a hundred feet from the woods on the other side, it all got to be too much for me and I started screaming and jumping up and down. The third time I touched ground, white fire exploded under my kneecaps. Somehow, I had put all my weight into attempting to bend my knees backward and it didn't work. I sat cross-legged on the ground, holding my knees like an Indian with gallstones while David alternated between hysterics and concern. Finally I struggled up and hobbled on with him. I gimped around that end of the campus for a while before my right leg got worse. I found that I had torn something very important and eventually it had to be amputated just above the knee. No, that's not true, what happened was I maliciously tracked down some guy who was having fun with his girl and asked him to help me through the woods and across the field to my room. I really did need help and he couldn't very well refuse because his old lady was of the bovine altruistic type.

The next night, after seeing a doctor in Orlando, I was lying in bed all taped up tapping the floor with my crutch and grumbling when Jane came by and made the first move herself. She said she'd left with Blakely to ask his advice on how to get through to me. "I've been after you for a long time," she said. Damn if I didn't drop my crutch and it was awkward and painful with my leg, but everything worked out all right.

Old Clarence had said that the best way to cure a junkie was to put in a new brain. The Rev. G.V.H. took the behavioral approach, being a psychologist subscribing to that school and said, "Kill the parents and move the kid 3,000 miles." He specializes in adolescence.

So it seemed as if Jane and I had been together a matter of minutes when good old George gave me a long therapeutic look in the dining room one day and said, "Willy, I think I'll send you to Alaska to fish crab with Lee Ricketts. Lee Ricketts had built his house in Alaska—Halibut Cove, believe it or not. The kind of tall wiry fisherman tourists take pictures of, he spent his winters at the school and fished crab commercially during the summer. Brown and veined, Lee stood behind the reverend, complimented that George would turn a wreck like me over to him, confident of some kind of rehabilitation. I felt like a building in need of repair, which takes some doing as I found out in the next few weeks, helping Lee out around the place.

Lee simply could not accept the fact that some people weren't born with tools in their hands. Like he'd hand me some iron contraption that I'd never seen before except in nightmares of the Inquisition and say, "Go fribidah the roof." And I'd go and start tearing the fucker apart and get yelled at.

I'd seen some of Lee's pictures of his house in Halibut Cove across from Homer, and I'd even read a few books and travel folders on Alaska. The folders spoke of the Alcan Highway as "picturesque" and "laden with breathtaking scenery." When I spoke to Lee about it, he said the "highway" consisted of 1,500 miles of dusty dirt road. This was going to be quite a trip; from Orange City to Homer, over 4,000 miles. And all the way in a Land Rover, the kind of vehicle that John Wayne drives through herds of giraffes.

I was spending all my spare time with Jane now, and some that wasn't spare. I'd been made junior staff by then, and every so often, the reverend would corner me and yelp about my responsibilities. I suppose he was right, but I couldn't help it and the last night Jane and I bought some wine, which was nothing unusual, and tried to make the time last. But it didn't work and there I was the next early May morning, cutting down the road in the Rover and leaving Jane behind crying in a white sheet. Maybe you left yours in San Francisco.

One hundred yards, two hundred. A mile, past Orange City's pure water fountain (office type, under a canopy), ten miles, one hundred and we were in Gainsville to pick up B.J., the only girl going aside from Lee's little daughter, Coral. I had hoped we could spin through Gainsville express, picking up B.J. like a mailbag, but first we got lost looking for her house and then were obliged to have coffee and dry cookies with her parents. Uncomfortable amid small talk, as usual, I sat in a corner for an hour, eying a painting of young Jack Kerouac that hung smoldering on the wall. "Moose hunting? Oh really, B.J., don't you think that's fascinating?" When we were finally ready to leave after ten minutes of preparatory standing up and going "Well . . . ," I was the first one out the door and into the Rover. The kissing and waving was so overdone that I took the liberty of waving my hanky as we drove off but nobody took offense because it fit right in.

We had some food from the school and stopped a few hours later to make sandwiches from canned pork that we were doomed to see a lot of from then

297

on. Lee had to build a fire to make coffee and Coral and B.J. had to pick wild flowers. I leaned on an obscure monument that stood next to the Rover, wanting to go back and knowing the only thing for it was to keep moving. But we did make good time that day and camped in the dark at Red Top Mountain in northern Georgia. I slept under a concrete picnic table, which everyone thought was fearfully amusing but I enjoyed the dancing reflection of the fire over my head.

Stiff and full of knots, I woke the next morning at dawn and walked down to the rest rooms to pull myself together. B.J. was on her way back, not an unpleasant sight she, so I smiled brightly as I passed her. Her gaze passed over my head to a distant point in the treetops as she stepped woodenly by; I couldn't understand it. But when I got a good look at myself in the mirror, I could see her point. For the last few months I'd been sleeping well and regularly and showering daily, but this first morning out, I mean to tell you that I looked like a tale told by an idiot. My eyes were glazed bloodshot, my skin looked as though I'd slept in it, and my hair was laced with clods of unidentifiable foresty debris. Ah, vanity; I did the best I could to look human, but I was soon to give that up in favor of efficiency. Lee's feelings may differ with that statement, but a woodsman I never was.

I believe we reached St. Louis late that night in a driving rain. I remember crossing a bridge through flashing girders and seeing tear-streaked neon lights ahead to the accompanying thud/squeak of the wipers. We were to stay at Lee's mother's house this night and the next; I would have time to see my grandmother.

The next day on my way to the rest home, I stopped and sat on a bench across from the Holy Jewish Hospital, 216 Kings Highway, St. Louis, 10, Missouri. Letters of fire as I watched the occasional people passing windows in the mental ward seven stories above. Years ago . . .

Palm Beach. For reasons never made quite clear to me: "How would you like to take a sort of vacation with some people mostly your age, dear?" School was a bore and I was nothing loath, so, to St. Louis . . . Kachun-ng! The door slammed shut. A black man in a white coat on either arm. "Here's your room for now." Everything was bolted down inside and there was heavy screen on the window. No belt, suitcase ransacked, and the door opened out unblockable with a small window in it for faces to watch me at intervals all through the first night. The next morning: "No, you can't make any calls, you'll have to take that up with Dr. Gretetzer." Not even a phone call. A week later, deciding I wasn't dangerous, they moved me to a better section. No smells of diarrhea and midnight screaming here. It seems to be SOP on mental wards to put the patients in the worst area first, just in case. No justice in these institutions for psychological rehabilitation, not that there's much anywhere, but in the bin, a man is insane until *he* proves *other*wise. A tall order since the actions and explanations of an already "seriously disturbed" individual are twisted by definition. If seemingly reasonable, the nut is up to something.

I met Tom there, a brilliant Afro-haired Jew, and his friend Marianne, ten years older than I. She later said she loved me and burst into tears saying it was humiliating to love a kid. And there was Bill Kapnick, a huge bull manic-depressive who loved Marianne. Loaded down with phobias, for days at a time he'd be the picture of cooperation, then he'd suddenly lunge for Marianne's throat in the hall, shrieking, "I love, I love YEEEW-W-W!" Then the orderlies would tote him off for a good bang of Thorazine, him going, "This isn't me! I'm not like this! Arrgg-h!"

This was a classy joint as such places go. Nothing but the best lockups for yours truly. Palm Beach County Jail, etc., darling, and at the beginning of each week, menus were brought to the ward. We were supposed to check our choices of what was offered for each meal of each day. Now the guy in charge of collecting the menus was a fat, greasy staff goon named Scotty. Scotty and I had hit it off at first sight, we hated each other and made no bones about it. So one week, he simply tore up four days of my food. When I complained to the head nurse, who could have stepped right out of Kesey's *Cuckoo's Nest*, I was met with the most maddening of the frequently used administrative statements. "That's *your* fantasy, take it up with Dr. Gretetzer." And when I told the good doctor, all he did was cross his eyes ever so slightly and change the subject as he always did when faced with anything definite. But I was hungry and this was a bit much, so I asked him straight how long he thought I'd have to stay. This time his eyes crossed definitely and stayed there as he said, "Well . . . I would estimate between two and three years." That ended the session as far as I was concerned and I left knowing that I'd have to elope. (Elope: nut slang for escape.)

There was an honor group of sorts on the ward. If a patient's behavior met this and that requirement, and presuming that he knew himself from a coffee table, he was eventually allowed out of the hospital in a group with one of the strong-arm boys. So for two weeks I did everything right out of the book. Tom and I would quietly watch television in the evenings and I would go to sleep early. "Breaking Point," a show with a psychiatrist hero, was popular on the ward and I never missed it because more often than not some nut would wig halfway through and fall off his chair, a mild diversion.

My first time out, I was ready to split but, as luck would have it, our chaperon was a fellow named Clarence. He was a thin, good-natured cat, and I didn't think it fair to elope on him and endanger his job. We were supposed to go to a movie but he took us to a ladies' wrestling match instead.

Back on the ward I got an idea, nothing earthshaking, just how to kill two birds with one elopement, and it took me three weeks to make friends with old Scotty Greaseball. Finally I got him to include me when he was next scheduled to take a group out. So on a Tuesday, we were five blocks from the hospital on our way to a bus stop, and Constance, a religious nut with a thing about her mutt, was filling my ear: "I love my dog Axle, and God loves my dog Axle. If I brought my dog to you, would you love him as much as God and . . . Oh, are you leaving us?" "Damn right Connie!" and I cut up an alley behind some houses. Scotty was fat and I knew he could never catch me, but I hadn't counted on what he did next. Behind me, I heard him yell, "Kapnick! Get him!" I thought, "Jesus Christ! That goddamn *idiot*!" It was impossible to tell how Kapnick would react when he got his adrenaline going and my worst fears were realized when his bellowing to the rear changed from "Bill! You're making a mistake!" to "AAA! Ima *get*chew!" I cut off the alley over a fence into a backyard, and there on the lawn was divine intervention in the form of a little white poodle. Kapnick felt about dogs the way I feel about the hydrogen bomb. I grabbed up the poodle just as Kapnick was hauling over the fence and threw the poor animal smack in his face. An old lady tilted out on her porch and started screeching feebly, "Who are you? Stop it! Stop it!" as I went over the other fence, and the last I heard was Kapnick's shrieking in a voice that ended in a peculiar shrill whine, "Arrrgh! Dogadogadogdogdog!"

It took me fifteen minutes to catch my breath and then I went to a phone booth to call my grandparents in Florida. I told them to call the hospital and sign me out or I'd have to send them postcards from wherever I wound up. They did, and "Sukiyaki" was playing on the day room radio when I went to gather up my belongings. I shook hands with a sad Tom, and Dr. Gretetzer called me later at my uncle's house to tell me that I had "difficulty forming lasting interpersonal relationships." I told him he needed glasses, hung up the phone, and I was home in time for my fourteenth birthday . . . years ago.

I came back to myself with a start and realized I'd been sitting on the bench over an hour, and continued on to the death house, which was on a dirt road behind a Piggly Wiggly supermarket. "Today only! Center cut pig chops, 69¢ lb.!"

The home was a nice looking place planted with trees and grass and bushes, smell of artificial life in the flower beds like the whole scene had been dropped by helicopter. Old eyes watched my progress from rocking chairs, nodding and smiling benevolently. At the entrance was an ancient woman of flexible ivory, tugging feebly at a glass door. I opened it for her, horrified at my own strength, and saw that on the other side, facing the door, a fat nurse sat in a plush chair chewing gum and reading a movie magazine. As I passed, I stepped on her foot heel first, as hard as I could without being obvious, and apologized profusely.

The desk told me where Laura's room was after consulting a file and asking how "the name" was spelled. I went to the room and a young nurse was waiting for me at the door. "Whadda they have around here, walkie-talkies?" I thought. "She may not know you," the nurse said as I glanced at her breasts leaning myself against the wall, unshaven and smelling of wood smoke against the alcohol. I said, "*Yeah*. Yeah, well she'll know me," and pushed open the door.

Laura had lost weight. She wore a pink robe and was strapped to a chair. "She removes her clothing," the nurse whispered in obscene confidence. "Get out!" She made an astonished little noise and left hurriedly. Don't misunderstand me. I felt no mercy, only pain. In a better world, my father and I would have taken her to ourselves but we had more important things to do. Her wrists were thin and pale, laced with blue veins like some artisan's threads. Tina gave me that image, and I thank her. (You.)

She knew me as I knew she would. She said repeatedly that she didn't like it here and in the course of our talk, she called me by many other names but it was only the names she got confused, I could see that. God help me, I'm going to spend some good time in purgatory, because I even asked her for money, thinking about the thousands of miles to Alaska without cigarettes and about maybe signing some papers at the nurses' desk. "My purse," she said, "my purse, it's in the dresser." There *was* no dresser. "There isn't a dresser *here*, Mama." "My purse, it's in the top drawer."

I spent the next ten minutes telling her that I didn't really need any money and then the nurse came in without knocking. "Your time is up." She left and I mumbled, "No lady, not mine," and I couldn't keep from starting to cry. A pale, transparent shadow of my old strong mother looked at me from her strait-jacketed bones and said, "Billy! What's wrong, lamb?" I started to say I couldn't stand to see her there, but then remembered that I had no home to take her to and said nothing. She sighed, looked vacantly out the window, and went back to picking at her robe.

Then I had to go. I got up to do it and she breathed, "Ohhh, you're not *going?*" She knew I was and I knew I was, and we both knew it was probably the last time we would meet, as indeed it was. She died a little time ago after three years spent mostly in the same chair, waiting. Her thin arms faltering after me above the straps as I shut the door, I will never forget.

I wigged a little and went to the nurses' desk on my way out to tell them they'd better take damn good care of her or I'd have this place into a lawsuit they wouldn't believe. They looked at me open-mouthed as I stomped out the door shedding dirt from my boots onto the glassy floor.

I bought a pint of hundred-proof and a bottle of paregoric and went down to the zoo because bandicoots and wombats send me on laughing jags every time. Watch out for those sad-eyed lemurs, though.

We picked up Mike and Charlie at the big Omaha airport. Lee, Coral, and B.J. hiked to the terminal through a glittering prairie of flashing cars. The sun caught them just right; I was on top of the Rover making room for Mike and Charlie's gear.

Only in America can you see a sight like those jewely cars of all colors flashing in the afternoon sun as far as the eye can see and where's my goddamn passport.

THE CREW

Charlie, the youngest, was the best natured of our three, which was a good thing because he could have killed Mike and I with no difficulty whatsoever. We all got to hate each other at times. He was approximately five feet tall and eight feet wide, solid muscle, fifteen and bearded with a wide space between his two front teeth. Worth millions also, but not a presumptuous bone in his body.

Mike was a farmer's son, his old man had a helicopter-sized ranch. That sounds odd, doesn't it, but it *was* big and Michael had learned a little bit about work and work-related subjects there before he came to Alaska. He was a tall, thin, precociously serious kid. Wonderful to work with and kept his cool like a pressure cooker. When he did blow it, he came on like a cross between Steve McQueen and Olive Oyl.

Having done his best to put the other two in an unfavorable light, there was left only your crafty narrator who you should know by now anyway. Eyes of piercing green; yes Lord.

THE CAPTAIN

Lee Ricketts, previously mentioned. Very tall coffee addict. Very craggy and veiny, he could have whupped the whole crew easily. Half blinded by a driving determination to "get it done," Lee always "got it done." But nuts? Wow. The best man in the world to work with. Charlie always seemed to get his elbow in your nose.

THE "WIMMIN FOLK" (they called themselves that)

Coral, Lee's daughter, who was possessed of the occasional ability to assume the form of Satan. That's true. She was only about this big, but when she felt like it, she had a way about her that would have you ready to pull out your teeth, throw her over a cliff, anything to be left alone. Voice like a red-hot darning needle.

And B.J., the last of the gang, was a very attractive tall brunette with panic-stricken eyes and an oddly appealing smile. She believed in the myth of "feminine wisdom" and was alla time quoting Mae West enough to turn your stomach. "Is that a gun in your pocket, or are you glad to see me?"

So now that we've got everybody straight and know what's happening, let's put Lee at the helm of the Rover, me glorying in "shotgun," scatter everybody else around the car, and skip the prairies from Omaha to scene next; nothing ever happens on the prairies.

DEAD COW

Except for a dead cow that we found one afternoon. We'd stopped to stretch our legs and make sandwiches out of that wretched canned pig again. We wandered, exploring, over a windy hill covered with rippling grass all the same color. I remember it as gray. Coral found the cow in a gully where there wasn't any wind and old Bossy was pretty far gone. The inside of her skull was dark; I couldn't see in there. Didn't want to much either, there might have been an old cow thought inside that didn't die, might fly up to the eye and scare me on my ass. It looked as if Bossy had somehow managed to die kicking. Two legs stuck straight out into the air. Charlie had a camera with him and I said, "Take a picture, man. It isn't every day you see *this*. Take a picture. Think of it, 'Bossy's Dead' hanging on a wall." Charlie said he didn't have enough film as I grabbed one of the projecting legs and shook the carcass. The skull spoke but it was only the buzzing of its fly brain as they all flew out the eyes. A few of them went too high and were whisked away in the wind above the gully, tiny black streaks through the waving gray grass. I do recall that one of them got a terrible lick on the head from off a twig that was in his way.

That was just about enough for us all and we went back to where Lee was smoking his pipe in the wind by the Rover. At the top of the hill I looked back, but already I couldn't tell Bossy's gully from any others. I don't know why I remember that tattered old cow so well. Perhaps because it really *was* the only thing that happened on the prairie.

Mount Something National Park in Oregon. Very majestic and absolutely silent. No leaves in the forest yet and Mount Something looming over my head the whole time made me tiptoe for firewood. Twilight getting darker, that icy-cold wood burned after all, and Mount Something slowly disappeared, leaving its white head behind for a while to keep watch. Michael got into his goddamn warm eiderdown sleeping bag.

Charlie and I didn't like Mike's sleeping bag at all. First night away from Omaha . . . no, it must have been the second; the first night we all got rained out of a picnic shed on top of a barren hill overlooking a heartbroken lake by miserably cold fast-moving rain. The wind whistled and the rain stung and the lake wept silly rippled tears as we cursed off down the highway. It was too dark to notice equipment when we camped that night and stacked up picnic tables to keep out the wind almost killing Lee with a big one that fell, so it must have been the second when Michael dug out his sleeping bag and Charlie and I chuckled at the compact size of it. Charlie had a big double deal from Sears, a real monster, and I had a beat-up old army surplus bag I'd bought in Orlando that Lee said would be "fine." So Mike slept like a kitten and Charlie and I froze nightly.

So this was Canada. Hmmm. Damn. So what? The Crew felt that the minute we crossed the Canadian boarder (oops, sorry fella, border) that we were immediately entitled to at least a bear cub playfully chasing a porcupine and just about to learn a painful but necessary lesson about life in the forest, or a moose, or even a goddamn Mountie. But no, just more flattish land and American Gothic farms. Mount Something was a lonely mountain all out there by himself.

Because of a possible paucity of supplies on the Alcan, we stopped at a grocery store in Dawson Creek to stock up on beans and whatnot. We had well over a thousand miles of wilderness road ahead of us, so Charlie and I each bought a can of something to break out when culinary monotony became unbearable. He had spaghetti and I was soul-warm over my can of tuna macaroni salad.

The second day on the highway I broke out my stash but Charlie said, "No man, save it until Lee feeds us something horrible." I did and it was that canned rotten pork again. I wonder why none of us ever disputed Lee's right to declare meals. But eventually, through my own subversive machinations, the damn stuff got lost in the snow while I was packing it.

So Charlie did in his Heinz pasta and I ate my can of macaroni tuna. I thought it was marvelous at the time, it had been sitting over the axle and was kind of warm. Two hours later I felt a little sick. Four hours later I had the runs, and that night I was vomiting steaming holes into the snow. How can I possibly express the abysmal misery of nausea and

diarrhea on the vibrating gravelly Alcan? I can't.
But even that wouldn't have been so bad without
the insult of the belching. You see, once every five
minutes or so, I'd bring up a messenger that would
choke a buzzard. I won't try to describe the smell
other than to say that I covertly blew on each one
trying to disperse the green cloud before anyone got
wind of it. I thought I was keeping it reasonably
cool, but Charlie told me later that he was watching
me out of the corner of his eye and wondered what
the fuck I was doing there, blowing into my lap at
regular intervals.

Many, many miles. I saw a porcupine up in a tree
and everybody said it must have been a clump of
pine needles. Mucho coffee, Lee percolating at the
wheel. We longed for the occasional lodgings as we
drove by, but Lee was always able to locate a spot
where the trees kept the snow off the frozen ground.
Every time we stopped, I'd go off and explode from
both ends. I was ashamed to admit I was sick, oh
agony, and not a great deal else happened. I did,
however, drive us into a snowbank to keep from
going over a cliff and Mike told me all the ways I
could have avoided the incident, him being a professional snow driver. But I didn't know the methods at
the time and was convinced that considering my
limited knowledge, I had saved the lives of all concerned. Not much gratitude though and just to
make the chamber of commerce happy, the scenery

was fantastic. "What more can you tell us about the Alcan, son?" "Nothing man, I'd rather forget it." It's that kind of a road.

The highway ends at Fairbanks, but the gravel is replaced by pavement some eighty miles south in a neat little political promo—smack on the U.S.–Canadian border. The blacktop begins by a big sign that says, "Welcome to Alaska, The Big Land." Underneath it, someone has painted, "Wow! We made it, baby!"

Homer, Alaska is very small. Moose amble by the laundromat that advertises a shower for a dollar—bring your own soap and towels. The movie house is closed, the ticket booth full of cobwebs. Out on the mile-long spit where the fishing boats tie up, there's a hotel, "The Land's End," and a restaurant that's open for the tourists during the summer months. I don't care where you are on the face of the earth, sooner or later, some clown will be sniffing around with his family and a camera.

Lee pointed out two mountains that were part of a range rising out of the water away over yonder. "That's where we're going." And out there on the dock, I suddenly couldn't believe any of it. Here I was, just a few months out of the Federal Narcotics Hospital, me and my tracks 4,000 miles from familiar ground and staring out over Cook Inlet. I knew I was lucky, just one in a thousand and I wondered what was happening to Gary, or rather *how* it was

312

happening. Was a momentary vision of Kamerad-
erly arm bindings in bare bulb rooms desperation
and relaxation with the hiss of a radiator and I fell
down on some duffel bags to experiment with a recorder, tenement paint peeling in my ears and the
smell of urine and paranoid sweat.

Slim came out to pick us up in a small funny-
looking boat. A tall skinny man with a knifelike
Adam's apple and a passion for gizzards. He came
over for dinner once, a real feed where we'd roasted
up two turkeys and he stabbed one of the gizzards
right off. Now I got a thing for gizzards, too, so when
I saw him eying the other one, I got to it quick. And
the look of sorrow in his eyes, the look of real an-
guish like he'd just lost the Holy Grail down a storm
drain, made me so sorry I couldn't believe it. But not
enough to give up the gizzard. Because there's only
one thing I love more than a gizzard and that's a
train ride.

Slim never said much or even did much for that
matter. But he was a genius of a welder and could
have done a fine business but he was lazy and set up
his tool shop over in Halibut Cove where nobody
could get at him. He did sometimes work for the col-
onizers. His wife weighed, well Hell, I don't know.
She was fat as the earth herself, she just didn't know
how to stop talking or eating. Because she ran the
Cove post office and read all the new magazines she
thought she had the world figured out from the soul
on through the Chicanos to the president. Two-Ton

Tessie from the Yukon she called herself and Slim never said a word. They had a couple of Eskimo kids they'd adopted and looking at the parents I could see why. There wasn't no way I could picture them in bed, why, Slim would never have been seen again.

At intervals during the trip up, Lee had impressed on the Crew the fact that we were on the wrong train if we expected to be "catered to." So I, for one, had steeled myself for practically anything. But we were all set back a yard when we found the bunkhouse we were supposed to live in for a while. It was nothing more than a dirt-roofed cave hacked out of a hill behind Lee's house. And we all three of us crowded in, fallaciously good-natured with tears in our eyes, eating cobwebs and saying, "Well! This isn't so bad!" There were only two filthy, shelflike things that could serve as bunks but we decided we could take turns sleeping on the floor. So when we told Lee what we planned to do to make the hole habitable, he near laughed his ass off because what we'd found was his root cellar, but I suppose he realized we weren't cowards.

There in the Cove, we worked on Lee's house for a few days, connecting up the water that came from a high stream through a hose by the grace of gravity— there wasn't any hot water, which went without saying—and putting in new windows where the old ones had been blasted out by winter. The real bunkhouse was alright. It had a heater and two and a half bunks. Lacking seniority, Charlie had to use a barrel at the end of his bed to hold up his feet. So we stayed there a couple of weeks getting acclimated before we went back to the mainland to get to work on the boat.

The dry dock was about an hour back up the road from Homer, with the Crew ajitter all the way to see the boat and whoops down a hill through some mud and there she was. The "Dewdrop."

THE SHIP

Thirty-five feet long. Solid wood, she was an old boat with a big hold and cramped sleeping quarters in the bow. Didn't amount to much more than I've said. Her name bothered Lee as much as it did the Crew, but not enough to overcome his frugality. It costs twenty-five dollars to change a boat's name. And I mean to say Lee was *frugal*. Tight mother is what he was; I'll tell you more about that later.

So the "Dewdrop" was up on beams twenty-five feet off the ground and after we all got up there by homemade ladder, Lee started ripping corrugated aluminum off the deck like there was no tomorrow. And later, after we had time to talk about it, Mike and Charlie told me that they felt just as screwed as I did like we *all* just wanted to pack up and go home. We'd come prepared to work, but goddamn! we thought to ourselves, this old tub looks like it needs a complete overhaul. Which it did. All the old paint had to be removed, everything beneath had to be sanded, the hull had to be completely recaulked, which is sticking the worst glue you can imagine between all the boards to keep out the water after we'd wangled the old caulking loose, painted twice, once with lead paint and then regular. Two new ribs had to be put inside, which was a day's work in itself what with steaming the wood so it'd bend, and a new stove hadda be put in. The old one . . . well, the Crew just couldn't believe it was even there it was so rusted out.

It took us almost a month of getting up at dawn and working until Lee gave the word to fix that boat. And like I say, Lee's existence was based on "getting it done." Sometimes before he blew the whistle, the Crew was downright punchy and mild hysteria was setting in. This was *work*, this wasn't exertion, and the three of us young fellers went a little crazy. Mike and I started remembering old songs and singing them at the top of our lungs to pass the time. What became our favorite was "Teen Angel."

Matter of fact, most of our songs centered around teen death for some reason, and old violence ditties like "Liberty Valance."

Charlie was weird though. He didn't join in our musical recall; he just talked to "Samson," his electric sander, and made up his own songs. One of them went:

> Hot dogs and mustard, ginger ale, too.
> French fries and onions, walking with yew.
> (Repeat 60 times)

316

Looking back, I can understand why Lee would sometimes vault over the side of the boat and hit the ground in full stride up the hill toward the yard owner's house who was a friend of his, hollering over his shoulder, "Gonnagetsomecoffee!" Funny thing in close quarters like we were; nobody seems to know why anybody else does anything. No perspective.

Working like that every day gets up an appetite and a half, so I took over the cooking right at the outset and made breakfast and dinner from then on until we left. Mike couldn't cook very well though he thought he could, it didn't seem proper for the Captain, and Charlie made sandwiches so lopsided the bread fell off. And I was damned if I was going to work all day and then have somebody ruin dinner. Lee's friend, the guy who had the coffee, frequently made us gifts of moose meat and caribou sausage, which, much to the Crew's surprise, was better meat than we'd ever come across.

Incidentally, a funny thing happened the first day we got to work on the "Dewdrop." The Crew was sitting on the insanely disordered deck taking a cigarette break when Lee came out of the cabin with an ashtray, the picture of propriety. He held it out toward us and said, "Ashtray?" The deck was in such a shambles that it honestly did not occur to any of us that he was offering it for use. We thought that perhaps he'd cracked up just a little, nothing serious, and we smiled and rather cautiously humored him. "Yeah, uh-huh, *ash*tray."

The moon was starting a new phase by the night we put the "Dewdrop" on the tracks and ran it down to high tide. Running after it, I slipped in some mud and almost dislocated my jaw, much to everyone's apelike amusement. The tide was too low that first night, but we got the old tub afloat a couple of evenings later as Lee revved the engine in reverse and Mike and Charlie ran from port to starboard to get her rocking in the bottom mud while the yard owner and I stood in the water pushing with poles, and the "Dewdrop" was like some great frantic sea monster bellowing in the shallows. It was a great moment for the Crew when she finally slid out on the water. Lee just said, "Finally got it done, for Chrissake!" and I didn't get to go along because I had to drive the Rover back and meet them at the Homer spit. . . .

Right now I can see Fuji steaming over there about twenty miles away. It's an active volcano and its real name is Mt. Augustine, but Fuji's handier and less formal. We're hanging out in the lee of an island a good twelve water hours from anywhere. Steering at night taking extra time, Lee showing me the rocks up ahead on the map. We're lurking, actually, lying in wait for a run of salmon that Lee expects right soon. They're due back anytime to this desolate, my God, coastline. Massive cliffs like one of them solid rock and fifty stories high fringed with scrub and cut with little cold rivers winding down to the water. I'm sitting here in the net at the stern thinking what it would be like to be left alone over there at night and watch the warm lights from the boat diminish across the icy water, a morbid thrill. Marooned! Jesus what a situation and there ain't no native girls or coconuts around here.

On my left is our little island that the Crew explored yesterday, we rowed the skiff onto a squat, rock beach and climbed the rocks to a grassy plateau on top. In the center of the island, there was a wind-blown pond fifty yards across and we chased what looked like a wild turkey all over Hell and gone without getting near it. So we gave up and set on to where near the cliffs on the other side we were suddenly smack in the middle of a nursery. We stepped as carefully as we could over the eggs and the baby gulls that kept their eyes shut tight so we couldn't see them as their parents wheeled over our heads shrieking, "Don't hurt my baby! Don't hurt my baby!" as clear as day.

We tiptoed past the children with apologies to a soft, tufty spot beyond where we sat for a time watching the gulls and wishing Fuji would do something epic. On the way back, we came across a shed with a sign that read: "Geofribidah Expedition. If you are lost or in need of food, welcome. If not, please leave this for someone who may need it later." So we did, albeit a little reluctantly. There was some good stuff in there.

Everybody's taking it easy today waiting for the

salmon. Maybe I'll take the skiff over later to jerk off in privacy and see what I can do about that turkey.

"Jumper!" That's what you holler when a salmon flips out of the water and gives himself and his buddies away. Lee stands up with the pinpoint eyes of a primal hunter blowing his image with his crazy-ass red baseball cap askew on his head, and we're off. Lee made it very clear that this wasn't fun but serious business and he maneuvers to a position a little ways ahead of the school. Mike is in the skiff astern and at Lee's wigged-out flailing signal, he starts the outboard and takes off around the fish. Actually, he just holds his own, pulling the net off the stern while the stalwart "Dewdrop" does the most circling. Charlie's up on the bow waiting to get the far end of the net from Mike when we come around. I'm half in the water holding onto the stern and trying to keep out of the propeller because I got my fool foot caught in the net. I'm not about to yell to Lee because he hates like Hell to lose a set and I mean to say he has a terrible way about him when he's angry.

But it's all right cause I manage to get back on board by the time Charlie's getting the line from Mike who takes the skiff round the other side as Charlie and I tie the line all along the edge of the boat. Now the salmon are encircled, you understand, and the only open place in the net is right by the stern where it angles down from the deck. So Charlie's jamming bubbles in this spot with a

twelve-foot aluminum-cupped toilet plunger because he's the strongest. I tried that part of the operation once and was nearly crippled. Some minutes
later, the winch tightens the circle pulling in the net
(Mike and I are separating lead and cork lines as
the net comes in) and then Charlie can let up gasping because we purse. That is, we bring the lead line
up under the fish so there is finally no escape, nyah,
haha. Then we got this mammoth pet store scoop
net to dump them in the hold. We were rather inept
with that net, though, and never got more than a
few per scoop. And the first ones in the run were
handsome fish, too. Real strong and solid colors.

Yes indeed. We worked like I never did at Lexington. One day we ran through this routine six
(count'em, six) times before breakfast, which came
to four skillet-size pancakes sourdough type, one-
half pound of rare beef sausage, five eggs, and what
was left of the coffee, after Lee finished, for everybody but me. I use the stuff as a purgative.

We didn't seine very long. That's what that frantic shit I just told you about is called. Seining. Besides we weren't very good at it what with the Crew
being a bunch of city kids and we didn't particularly
relish competing with another boat that had shown
up. They were from the Cove also and were a
smaller boat that could follow the fish where we'd
have grounded. Not only that, but their crew was
downright professional and, to add insult to injury,
they'd brought along a barge in tow that they non-

chalantly proceeded to fill up with fish. Now, *our* luck, on the other hand, wasn't so good, you understand. Hell, we made every dumbness known to the industry. We ran aground hauling after some fish we thought we could *just* head off and had to take the embarrassment of being pushed off by the other boat. And we got our net caught in the propeller horror of horrors, and Mike and I stayed up all night and went blind mending the damn thing. And it was Lee's fault, son of a bitch, he left the engine idling while we were pulling in a set. So there. I can only say in our defense that the other crew killed time by going to *our* island and shooting *our* birds.

But the worst happened one afternoon when we were loading our fish onto a tender. (Tenders are like floating canneries that come out after your catch to save time, they count the number and type [reds are worth more that humpies and so forth] and lay a receipt on you that's redeemable later.) So we just get through unloading when the captain says to Lee, who's looking through his binoculars, the picture of grizzled Alaskan, "There's Hell of a lotta jumpers over there, Lee. Ten or twelve at a time." That's a lot of jumpers and Lee pins them through the glasses and we're off as fast as the "Dewdrop" can wallow. Seemed like two knots once the Crew spotted all them jumpers. This was one fantastic concentration of fish/money.

So we made our set and we used all 1,200 feet of net. It was like a dream; we had this perfect circle on glassy water clean around four separate schools of fish, which almost never happens. "Well," you may ask. "What's so bad about that?" And I'll tell you, man. Nothing. Nothing at all but what happened next was that the lead line got caught on a goddamn rock. We couldn't pull it in and Mike flashed over in the skiff to pull it loose. It cost him five minutes and as many fingernails before he finally ripped it free. And then Godamighty, the winch broke down. This is unheard of bad luck and let me tell you that there's no way you can pull in 1,200 feet of net and lead line by hand. "We'll pull it by hand! We'll get it done!" bellows Lee. After ten minutes and ten feet gained the fish are getting nervous, Lee lurches inside and finally gets the winch going. Somebody up there didn't like us though, and by this time a current had come up out of a calm sea and the net was collapsing. That is, drawing together and the salmon, who usually swim near the surface, were confronted with netting fore and aft, so they got hip and went under the lead line.

We took exactly twelve fish out of that fiasco and nobody said a word. Lee said later that we had a good 5,000 salmon inside the net when we first set and they were all "dogs" worth near a buck apiece or half a good season right there. I mean, we weren't frustrated, we were *sad,* and went back to the Cove a couple of days later to change gear.

Now we had a big old oil heater in the bunkhouse and I set fire to my eyebrows lighting it once. It groaned and rumbled. Lee once forgot that I was at large, and taking me for stable, told me that a man can hear a heavy earthquake coming before it hits. So I scared Mike and Charlie near to death one night when I mistook the heater for apocalypse.

I sat and watched and waited sometimes for hours when I had the time, but I never saw it. It was some beautiful bird that was always audible from the bunkhouse. It had a call like the clearest cut glass and I remember that one night since I couldn't spot it, I whipped up a vision of the bird in a dream. When I woke up, I couldn't remember what it looked like, but I was left with a feeling of satisfaction and completion, knowing that the image *had* been accurate.

This rowboat is the smallest one we've got. It's only about just past my feet is as far as the front reaches, you couldn't call it a bow, and I'm on my way down the Cove to fill a bucket with sand so I can grit the deck. The water is dark and very cold— I just touched it and for some reason I don't like the looks of it at all. O Holy Christ! A fivefoot finI'mgonnadie! I made it by the shore in minus time and followed the banks for the rest of the whale, I mean, way. Lee said it must have been a killer whale and alerted the Cove and whew! your poor ex-junkie narrator was one jittery kid. Those things belong on "Sea Hunt" in black and white.

An old fella named Rosie was more or less recognized as the Cove's master brewer. Everybody there made their own beer, but he was just about an artist to hear people talk. . . . He lived just across the water from us and made three different kinds of brew in his little house with the inside absolutely covered in girlie photos. When B.J. or Coral would come to visit, he'd yelp "yoost a meenoot!" and take ten hiding all the pictures so he wouldn't offend and then he'd let them in and give them a cup of his special "ladies' brew." He always left up a picture of a standard army review with his own writing under it. "Democracy? Phooey!" This guy was old, I don't remember exactly how old, but he used to tell us how he got caught and caned jumping ship as a cabin boy in 1892.

With lots of chuckles about the patience that was necessary, Rosie told us how he made his beer so the Crew promptly went and started a ten-gallon batch of its own in the bunkhouse. Every evening after dinner we'd hustle back to the shed and take the towel off the barrel to smell the yeast. But aside from a few impatient swigs and subsequent runs we didn't get any until our first break during drifting. It takes a while to get worked up right.

Speaking of that, our base for drifting was a few hours from Homer at a little town called Ninilchick. There must have been fifty boats there with us in the narrow harbor; we were all sizes and colors docked side by side. Husbands, wives, kids, hippies, beer, radios, and I smelled a bit of reefer down the dock a ways. There was a romantic Russian Orthodox church on the hill with bulging towers, and joyous wander-mad hippies that were passing through took whoop-and-holler ice cold showers down at the public bathhouse without soap.

Drift fishing is allowed by Fish and Game, which is like Alaska's FBI, only every other twenty-four hours, and the operation is simple. A long net attached to a reel at the stern is set "adrift" behind the boat. That net, now, is a fiendish thing called a gill net with holes just large enough for a naïve fish to get his head in and then get hung up by the gills trying to back out. Must be an abysmal drag. God-awful things we do for food on this planet, but who am I to argue.

Everybody's glued to their radios five in the morning, nobody wants to miss a minute and F&G gives the word, it's like a carnival scene as everybody runs out on the inlet waving to their buddies and constantly yammering over their radio sets about where the fish might be. That's a funny thing: your drift fishers aren't greedy. If one guy sets in an area that crawls with salmon, he sure as shit gets on the air and tells everybody this's where the money is.

After the net's out, all there is to do is sit and rap and watch the net to see it don't foul up with somebody else's, which is the worst thing in the world that can happen—a terrible tangle and, of course, it happened to us but I'll spare you the scene. Every so often the water'll splash and foam up by the cork line where a salmon hit near the top. (For those people who haven't figured it out, the cork line keeps the net floating and the lead line, which isn't the "leed" line, keeps the net hanging down to hang up the fish.)

And when the fish hit all up and down the cork, your line is "smoking," but that never happened to us.

Sooner or later, when he figures it's time, Lee steps up to the reel and onto a pedal to start pulling the net in and for the next forty-five minutes we all crack gills inside out and thump the aliens on the deck as they arrive. That pedal was an important safety feature. You see, when a man lifts his foot, the reel stops turning, which is a damn good thing because it's easy to get your hand caught in the net while yer messing round with the fish and lots of people got horribly maimed before somebody thought up the safety gear. Can you imagine getting wrapped up on a reel that don't fit at all? It'd be like snap crackle pop.

At night, the show must go on because we only have limited time, so the net stays out and we sleep in shifts to keep a weather eye out. Whoever's on watch has to sit up on the bridge in the wind and absolutely freezes his balls off. I tried every time-passing trick I knew up there, but I got so cold that nothing worked. I couldn't talk to myself, I couldn't sing, I couldn't make insane methods work . . . nothing. I never loved an object in my life like I loved my ratty old sleeping bag after my watch. Lee always said, "We're at the mercy of inanimate objects." And that's a lifetime's realization right there. So the next day, we're all double-sighted, bleary, and sick of sea reaping when F&G comes on the air and extends the period for twelve hours. Old Crew never bargained for that kinda thing but we were learning.

On Charlie's birthday the Crew got drunk back in Halibut Cove. We all dipped into our poorly-made laxative home-brew, and shades of timing, right on the day, some Vodka arrived from Charlie's brother. Withal, Mike and I were happily plowed and talking nonsense, but Charlie went right around the bend walking or rather dancing on a plank thirty feet over the nastiest looking rocks you ever saw. And he had another one of his crazy-ass songs going, sounded like a leaking bass boiler. It had something to do with a crazy motorcyclists' lame odyssey and how he had to repeatedly explain the difference between a two-cycle and a four-cycle engine. There was no discernible tune and the chorus went:

A two cycle go boom boom Booom!
Ana fore cycle go boom boom boom BOOOOOM!

But everything worked out cause Michael and I got him off the plank and back to the bunkhouse where we lit up the heater and lay around calming-down smoking and feeling mellow.

There's no probation officer in Homer, but I met the local state cop. He's doubling as my proby and he's a good six-foot-seven and has two dogs as big as me. He shook my hand and stuck my fingers together in a roomful of guns and said that he didn't expect any trouble and that's right; he'll not get any from me.

The same day I met the cop and after Lee and I got back from Homer, Lee brought up octopi at lunch and why don't we catch one and eat it they're delicious. "We shall!" said the Flopsy, Mopsy, and Cottontail Crew in unison. And soon enough we got a pole with a cloth sack full of blue crystals tied to the end of it. These crystals dissolve in water with what must be a tear-gas effect on octopuses. See, they hang out under rocks and sometimes when the tide goes out, they'll stay under there with a little water. That is, until we come around and shove our pole in there with them and make conditions intolerable. Then he comes boiling and bug-eyed out from under that rock and heads for the water, but Mike, who will risk his life at the drop of a hat, gets a grip on him or vice versa, couldn't tell which.

So when we get back to the house, Lee says to douse Otto (I'm not liking those intelligent eyes) in boiling water and then the skin'll come right off. Maybe we dunked him too long, I don't know, but two hours later we're still picking scabs of skin off the tentacles. The tentacles are tough muscle and feel like a hard-on and Charlie says, "Any minute now, Lee's gonna come in here and say 'Ha, ha, it's all a joke. *Yew can't* skin an octopus.'" Eventually, though, we pronounce it skinned and proceed to bash it tender for dinner. We put so much work into it that we all hypnotized ourselves into enjoying it, but the leftovers went to the birds.

An old guy who lived on our side of the Cove told us this story.

"Fifty years ago, there was a miserably cold winter in Homer and a man in the Cove died. He came down with pneumonia and he died. Of course, everybody did everything they could for him—the women brought him soup and the men kept his fire going, but he didn't care and he died anyway. Somebody radioed over to Homer for an undertaker or a mortician or whoever's necessary at such a time, but Homer said the water was froze up all the way between and nobody was about to try walking across, so some of us concerned parties got together and decided that Zeb would have to be buried in the Cove. One of the boys went down and measured his body laying there on the cot and the reason Zeb was on a cot was because everything else in his place had been cleared out for use by the living. After the measuring, we just left the windows and doors open so Zeb wouldn't start to you know, spoil, and he froze solid in a few hours.

330

"We found a nice spot to bury him, up on a hill where you could see most of the Cove, and three days later when the box was ready, we got some whiskey and some shovels and Zeb, of course, and everybody climbed up the hill boozing and complaining it was just like him to die in this weather. Then the first problem was the ground was froze like a rock and after an emergency meeting with the whiskey among the men, everybody decided to put him down a well that had gone dry. So that was fine, but when we went to put him in the coffin, you see, he just wouldn't fit. That was because we didn't account for the sag in the cot when he got measured, and the box wasn't deep enough. So there wasn't but one thing we could do. The women didn't like it, but some of us had to get up on top of him and sort of break him down in there. It took a while and I'd tell you a couple of other things except that Coral and B.J. are here, but finally we nailed him up and set the whole bunch of him down to rest. And, oh yes, our proxy preacher was late because he had to pick his way across the ice from the end of the Cove and he was madder than Hell that he'd missed everything, especially the whiskey."

We're putting a new fiberglass fuel tank in the "Dewdrop." Everybody's knuckles are skinned and Lee's nose is running again. He's bent over his work and his nose is running. A large drop has gathered on the tip of his nose and refuses to fall, defying gravity. He must feel it, the man amazes me. Coral rows over to the dock and says, "Daddy, wipe your nose, it's all snotty."

It took us over a week to fix the crab pots. The damn things were taller than I am and miserable to work with; chicken wire on a metal frame. It would be awkward and much ado to describe how they work. Suffice it to say that king crab are awfully stupid. Each pot was attached to X fathoms of rope ending with a bright-colored buoy. This plastic buoy was in turn attached to another smaller one that was easier to hook out of the ocean.

Lee owned eighteen pots so we spent a couple of hard days loading them onto the "Dewdrop" and dropping them out on the inlet. We were in mildly high seas when we went to drop the first one over, so Lee hollered from the bridge, "Wait till you're with the roll! *Then* push!" We did and there went Mike head first pushing the pot right into the water. Lee yelled "Mike!" rather ineffectually, but it was all right; Mike broke water a few seconds later puffing and blowing and we hauled him in and he retired to the cabin to change clothes and colors. The water had turned him blue. Lee was always talking about how that water was just too damn cold to stay alive in.

This is the way we pulled the pots every day. Lee gets to the wheel up on the bridge so he can see and takes the boat as close as possible to the floating buoys. I reach down off the starboard side to snag the line, which isn't always that easy, without maybe breaking an arm. Charlie and I together slip it onto a small winch being careful not to crush our fingers off, and when the pot comes up, we hooker to the boom. Then Mike starts up the big winch cause there's maybe a ton of assorted crustaceans in there. In a few seconds, this huge pot is hanging in midair and Charlie and I swing over the right spot with unfaltering machinelike precision jaws set in a Communist mural and yell "NOW!" and Mike lets it drop. Nobody ever got killed for some reason. Then we toss back all the females and squirts, as per F&G directive, while Mike rebaits the pot with chopped herring, already down-packed by Charlie. Shove it back over and on to the next one. All this time Lee's sitting on the bridge smoking his pipe and looking picturesque.

Charlie was our bait man. On the way to the pots every morning, he huffed and chopped our daily new block of frozen herring with a sharp-bladed iron canoe paddle and stuck it in the bait boxes. Whenever something exotic came up with the crab like halibut or a bullhead, it was Charlie's job to carve up the unfortunates for extra bait. And in all honesty, I'm afraid I must say that Charlie loved it; the more so if the fishes were still alive. I think that's how he kept his aggressions in check, which I'll get to next.

By the way, I don't know how you feel about halibut as a table item, but they're damn big fish and it was easy for us to cut a five-pound hunk loose to cook right on the spot. That is, after he calmed down. Halibut flop around as fast as a goldfish, and when the fucker weighs five hundred pounds, it's a good idea to stay clear. If you've been having trouble with your halibut lately, which isn't likely, try it like this: Sauté onions and squash. Add a can of tomatoes and cover the fish with the stuff, and bake it. Take it out about five minutes before you think you should. Drink the extra juice in a cup so you can feel you're doing your ecological bit. It's really damn good.

I remember one morning when Charlie went out on deck, knife in hand, to do in a two-foot bullhead that'd come up the day before. It'd been in the sun all the previous afternoon, and the engine was beating out the rhythm to "Devil with a Blue Dress On" as Charlie brought down his shiv right behind the gills. And that thing let loose a stink that I could smell all the way in the cabin. Charlie said it damn near killed him, but actually he only vomited.

Now this is a strange part of what happened to us out there on Cook Inlet. Hatred. When we were crabbing, we docked at Homer. Not even a walk to the bunkhouse, so we slept, ate, and worked together twenty-four hours a day and the sensitivity we developed to each other's bad points was phenomenal. We've all heard stories of murderous irrationality in Arctic outposts, but man, let me tell you they're *true*. It's a wonder anybody gets out of those places alive.

The first area of friction that comes to mind was meals, and especially when I was frying chicken. So here's the scene: We've been busting our asses all day and everybody's hungry. And as we all know, an average chicken has only two breasts. But there's four of us. See the point? We're *hungry,* and *size* is important. So I put the plate on the table and there's a universal moment of hesitation. Eight eyes pin the best parts. Then, with an infuriating ho-hum affectation of zero interest, four hands reach for two breasts. Poor Lee maintained his cool better than anybody else for some time and always came out on the short end. As in the Olympic Games, a difference of hundredths of a second could draw the line between the joy of victory and the agony of defeat. Until one day, he reacted like he was hooked up to a computer weapons system and grabbed the best in a blur. After that, he took to eating his meals up on the bridge.

Here. I'll try to give you a rundown on a typical hate morning through my own thoughts. I'm getting ready to cook breakfast and I come up into the galley. Charlie was himself wrapped around the insulated exhaust pipe that runs through the floor and ceiling at the end of one of the benches. "Goddamn. Again. Every fucking morning, the warmest place in the cabin and no shame about it. Some people are just decadent. If I wasn't so busy I'd do something about it and there's Mike glaring at him; no balls, why don't *he* do something?"

Okay, so I'm cooking and when I give Charlie his breakfast he says, "Thank you." One: "Is that nessasary? Whatsa matter with him? Does he feel guilty, I'm cooking?" Two: He hardly pronounces his "th" and it comes out "Hang yew." "Is he doing that on purpose? No, he's too dumb. Or is he, the bastard? I oughta dump his food on his head if he wasn't gobbling already."

And then Mike wants his friggin' eggs on a separate plate; can't stand any syrup to come in contact. And Lord, don't bust the yolk, that's worse than cholera. "Awright, wise guy (loony eye zeros in on yolk). Stabo! Die, Commie!" "Here's yer eggs, Mike." (Man, look at his nasty lip curl.)

And that's only breakfast and only through my eyes. I'm an easygoing guy and if I was that wiggy, imagine how Charlie felt about us hating his exhaust pipe. And Mike with his shattered yolk?

Alaskan king crab are spiny; they have half-inch points all over their shells and when we're dumping rejects, sometimes it's impossible to avoid hitting one's dumping partner and of course the victim is convinced that the whole sequence of events was plotted from break of day.

One thing I'll say for Mike though; he was always instantly amenable to reason. On our way home after we'd pulled all the pots, sometimes we had some herring left over for the sea gulls that followed the boat. We'd toss it to them and sometimes they'd catch it in the air, so one day I threw some over my shoulder and hit Mike smack in the eye. He took that as a premeditated, direct frontal attack, and when he went into his Olive Oyl routine he was so funny that I had to laugh. Well, *that* made him so mad that I thought he might hurt himself crashing against something, so I said, "Listen man, I'm sorry. It's just that we're in such close quarters we're getting on each other's nerves." I never saw anybody calm down so fast. "Yeah. You're right," he says as his shoulders relax and the purple leaves his face as the veins in his forehead shrink. Just like that.

The burning boat went down but nobody was hurt. Oh the poor "Dewdrop." She was a fishing lady with a fine big womb for a hold. Honest sea mother type was all and she wasn't built for speed. So one day we'd just tied up at Homer and Lee had gone up on the dock twenty feet above to do some business while we loaded our crab into big haul-up buckets with drain holes in them. Gurry in the eye and on the lip dripping in long yeller streamers when Lee came down off the dock like Spider Man. "Toss off! There's a boat afire!" Fishermen are going nuts all over the place, it's a real pioneer scene like helping each other out and the "Dewdrop" is first out of the harbor. The Crew is up on the bow with instruments of rescue, ropes and hooks, bloody-eyed and looking more like a small lynch mob than anything else. Charlie had a gaff, it was all he could find. "What the Hell, bring 'em up by the gills." And sure enough, away over there on the cold water, there's a plume of smoke. "Maybe there's a girl." I thought, but then BROOOM! every boat passed us up and left us with our banner gone, good-hearted heroic and alone and we turned back to Homer.

Oh it's dark and dank down here in the hold and I gotta tighten some crazy bolt that's bugging Lee. From the look in his eyes, you'd think the whole boat would dismember presently unless I fulfill my mission. The problem is we got a hold full of big old crabs. They're all moving in drunken slow motion, shitting and foaming at the mouth (that's gurry) with the bends from being ripped off the bottom where they live in strange communion and I feel like an emissary from a foreign place. They're all so alien there heaped up waving eye stalks and clasping each other in despair and humping themselves across the floor toward me, all walleyed wrestling with this bolt and feeling sorry for them in the most detached way imaginable. There's others up on deck caught in the chicken wires of pots we're moving to new drop points with their eye stalks turning black in the blaze and the foam crisping on their horny lips and it doesn't ease them any when the sensitive Crew tosses water on them, but they're good to eat and that means money, so all you crab lovers, just forget it. Sometimes we climb around on the pots to untangle them and drop them back in their cold water and you can just feel how nice it is for the poor fuckers to fade into the water and disappear.

Now the plot begins to thicken and I must tell you that I'd never worked before in my life, if you don't consider speed's death grind working and the question *is* open to debate. Is self-destruction hard work or simplicity itself? The difference between the two attitudes is that you can work at drugging through a lifetime and still find yourself empty-handed on that same street corner and the wind is rising in the palmettos and your old lady just left you and your last point's lost (pun intentional) and it's too late to get another and the ground is moving under your feet anyway. Somebody spilled the beans and the carpet's being pulled, they've found us out.

But I worked the other way in Alaska and I remember when we dropped into Seldovia to refuel, a get-here-by-plane-or-boat place and we did our laundry below a whorehouse we didn't have the time or money for. Afterward, we went into a drugstore for candy and there on the shelf by the checkout counter was all kinds of terpin hydrate and paregoric and whatnot, but after a shock of recognition I let it go, thinking, "Yeah, but I couldn't work right." Hell, what with all those winches and shit I coulda lost a hand if my reflexes weren't in order.

And right here, I must say this. You have to agree that we all want to be exciting, to have people want to come *see* us. Like spectacles in our own ways. That's what style is all about. Our choice of personal spectacle. And drugs, now, what they provide is *massive* spectacle. For a select circle, of course, but all the world's a stage and that jazz and drugs provide script for tragedy, lust, ecstasy, control. . . . "Whole boatloads of sensitive bullshit." And where is hard work at? "I haven't *even* got time man, I got work to do." See? No spectacle. So to cool drugs, and dig this, every good thing that they can do has to be recognized and dropped like a politician. Nothing can ever be given up if the renouncee cons himself with scary stories about its bad points. Those are easy to forego, it's the part you like that you gotta cut loose.

So who needs it? Answer: me. No amount of lucidity is a substitute for action, and then tell me this friend. If you got up tomorrow and did exactly the right thing all day, would you like what happened? No you wouldn't and that's why you don't do it you selfish bastard and welcome to the club.

Now where was I? Oh yes. Work. You know what work does? It provides a constant. It structures time. If you're looking for things that "need to get done" you'll never run out. Boredom and laziness and destruction may seem to last forever, but eventually something "has to get done." Inertia by definition always runs out because, let me tell you, there ain't nothing *but* outside forces acting on us every friggin' minute. Is that vague enough, or shall I make it even vaguer? I realize that a fix has to get done also and no two ways about it, but a fix (how many kinds of fix can we name, gang?) goes *in*. To FIX. To adjust, to focus. But what I'm talking about goes *out* and in a choosy way rearranges reality in a way that has the effect of bringing other people to the agreement that when we look at a coffee table, we are actually looking at the same image. You see? I'm flexible, I have nothing against sanity, it's just that sanity requires agreement between people and Hell man, there just isn't enough to go around. Tell you why. Because a human can hurt itself very badly stepping down from what it thinks it is. Then, too, you might have a lot of people fooled into *your* lame self-image, and where can *they* be at? Like you seen what Hitler did. I laugh a lot and I'll tell you what slays me is the blood bath that always comes from this kind of thing. You'd think people would learn after a point. You would. But we seem to be a pretty slow thinking experiment around here and always wind up on that same street corner.

It's only a few minutes later and I just got back from a little place down the street called "Mary's." Couple of pool tables with the ever-present hostile types playing the I'd-just-as-soon-kill-you-as-look-at-you game, but no problem because only one in a thousand is really serious and then you've had it anyway. Came back up the street with a half-full beer can whistling in my hand. It's a windy night and the naked flagpole by the post office is clanking in the wind and the whole sullen night is looming over a great dip into tomorrow. I'm wondering tonight what's going to happen. Will somebody do the right thing at dawn so I can go to his twilight funeral? Will Nixon trip on his ass in China and the whole planet go up in glowing fragments?

Fuck this sound, I should go into something sensible like coaxing giant Jamaican tree frogs to screw in captivity. They won't make it in cages, did you know that? I don't see why not, I do it all the time.

You see, so many of my friends think that knowing what you're doing is a great thing when actually, it's knowing what you're doing and *being able to do something about it* that turns the trick. Did you ever walk out your door and have *no effect* on your day from that point on, try as you might? Man, it makes me scream because we all know exactly what we're doing right down to the *atom*. We *live* in what we're doing, agreed? If you don't agree on that one, you'd best hang up the phone cause you won't make it. But stopping? Or changing? No way.

Big Decision Dept.: I'll put it this way. I got some things on my chest, you understand. I just spent a month not talking to anybody, being damned unfriendly, and living on Clamato (that's clam and tomato juice—great stuff, you oughta try it) and what happened was the other night I just threw up my hands along with some Clamato and said, "Fuck this story line, we could all go up tomorrow." Which takes a load off my mind because I can say more or less what I please, but it does create a problem. You see, the deadline for this book is about four days away. Big deal you say, but it's a hassle for me because I got responsibilities to the big guys. They pay me my advance and I better come across with my pound of concepts, right? So there's a number of things involved, not the least of which was I started this number with a clear objective. (*Reader's Digest*: "Let's start treating junkies as if they might even be people.") But I'm damned if I can be a good boy and stick to the story line. I mean don't worry about it, I'll keep jumping back when it seems like a good time for *me*, because if *I* don't have my heart in what I'm talking about, *you* sure as shit won't like my presentation.

Tirade one: (and this is really pretty important. I'd appreciate it if you'd take me seriously for just a minute. I don't ask that very often.)

If insanity means an outlook so different from the average clown's on the street, then I've been a lunatic for as long as I can remember. I refuse to go into reasons for such an opinion. Far as I can see, there *are* no reasons. That old bugaboo about cause and effect doesn't exist because once anything obtains, the "reasons" for it have ceased to exist. And any scientists in the audience can chuckle uneasily and go ahead and bust their asses for the rest of their lives. But hopefully, someday some great joyous day of dancing and nakedness, "cause and effect" will go down the same drain with the angels and the pins and we'll start dealing with what's *happening*.

Isn't that enough, or do I have to say that the

whole question of "why?" is a crock of shit. An ambiguity and a pissyassed attempt to justify avoiding action. Who *cares?* If I know "why?" will it make a difference? Maybe. But then I can always fall back on, "Why did it make a difference?" Like is that word the original sin? I ask you, are we in a strong enough position to ask such a question?

Sure, sure I admit to making a plea for the integrity of insanity, though I, like you, can see neither rhyme nor reason to some of our backward people. I must mention, though, the power of the insane. Like if I say "tree" you will imagine a different tree from what I do. For all you know, mine might have silk stockings knotted in the branches. I say this because I knew a girl who did just that: decorated "her tree" with stockings off in the forest and she had a pull rope to bring up her food. But she pissed in the bucket. Now, to *me, that's* crazy, but maybe she just had a thing for body salts, I dunno. But where the power comes in though, and all I can do is ask you to believe me, is that everything within twenty yards of her tree died. She carried around with her a veritable halo of desolation. Damnedest thing I ever saw.

Okay, let's assume that you're out of your nut. What I want you to understand is that no matter what you said to me I'd never call the cops on you. Is that clear enough?

Now you know and I know that we're spending a lot of money on this planet. But what I'd like to see is a great deal more spent on the "insane." Rather than a liability, loonies are our *greatest* planetary resource, and that's no shit brother. If we spent the money we're blowing on advertising, for example, on training people that would be able to go into a given madness and were able to report *back*, why, that'd be a spent buck with value. That'd make Soviet psychic research look like peanuts. It's theoretically possible to go out as far as other galaxies, but unless our race learns how to go *in* (and take my word for it I'm a nice guy and have no reason to lie to you, them galaxies are just across the table compared to the distance we can travel *in*), this whole scene is just gonna wind up some kind of aborted experiment. . . . By the way, there's two kind of cops. Cops that believe in what they're doing and the other kind. Sometimes it's hard to tell the difference. As far as I'm concerned, they can all drop dead, but the distinction has to be made and I just did it— good for me and don't shoot I'm harmless.

Tirade two: I once saw an intellectual trying to look up "mojo" in the dictionary.

Oh right. I told you I'd tell you about Lee's frugality. Waste not, want not, he *lived* there. Okay, I can understand a man wanting to save a buck, but Lee was like strong on the point. Lemme tell you what happened. We had a little box up on the bridge where we kept our groceries and it usually got cold enough at night to preserve everything. So one day I went in there and way in the back, I found some black hamburger that must have been there since the Mesozoic, and I took it to Lee as a joke. "Look at what's become of this cow," I said, and Lee, may I succumb on the spot if this isn't true, said, "Well, we better eat it tonight." I speak the truth, white boy, and I had to air out the cabin when I unwrapped that carrion and had to rinse it three times. But we ate it and didn't get sick at all.

Now I have a few words to say to salesmen in general and ad-men in particular. As calmly and as closely as I can tell you, you're just a mob of wretched traitors. Like scum, you know what I mean? Creators of diseases. You see, psoriasis is frightening to some naïve persons and you sneering sophisticates can shove it, too. You're walking all over people who don't have the strength to resist and you're doing it in the most contemptible way possible. By further manipulation of fears that you yourselves have created or maintained. You go around telling them you can make them better than what they are and so help me God, if I could catch you out and know you when I saw you, you'd be in a terrible fucking position. When I think of some poor skinny miserable girl sitting at a mirror and rubbing her face endlessly, hopefully, tearfully with your shit product for your goddamn buck . . . Bad medicine for you to be selling ersatz magic, because, take it from one who knows, I don't care and it makes no difference if you believe me, but Roscoe, real magic exists and you're gonna get yours. You can bet on that one.

I'm writing this in Savannah Beach, Georgia. Nobody ever wrote a song about Savannah Beach, Georgia. We've just waited out the cold, gray, fucked-up winter in this bar town with just a few drunks lurching around and driving into canals and now it's starting to get warmer. Pretty soon the sun'll come out and all the little look but don't touch chickies will be parading around and drunken teenagers will be falling down in the hot sand. But stick to your own age group, that's my motto, and I can sit on the high stairs outside and get a hot back.

We live over a dime arcade, inflation you dig, and from 10 A.M. to 10 P.M. it's "Boing! Zonkotwang! Kachow!" A friend of mine used to live here and at the bottom of the stairs there's kind of an alley where young kids would duck in to smoke their reefer. Nobody ever notices you if you're off the horizontal, like in a hole or up some stairs, and Dave used to take fiendish delight in creeping down the steps while they groped for their matches. Come up behind them and click! goes the lighter in his red-haired beefy hand. Scare the kids half to death and cops hate him, too.

Wham! Bam! "Du-h-harrgh!" And them crazy broads in the audience. "Kill him Chief! Mash dat fat guy!" And these cats are floppin' on the mat like great walri and you can just imagine the locker-room smell in the joint. My God but the way they carry on! Quivering pockmarked skin, crotch shots you couldn't get away with anywhere else and wouldn't want to, referee's slapping themselves in the face and giving out with obscure referee shit and everybody's wigging out and nobody hardly ever gets hurt.

Been away again. I just got back from going down the back steps and crossing a junk-filled vacant lot, being careful not to step in some peas I threw out yesterday. Our house faces the back of Nickie's Lounge and the Dragon Palace, a Chinese restaurant, and I'm always getting spooked by one of the old Chinaman's rabbits that lies in invisible wait and then bolts across my feet I swear I'm gonna fricassee that son of a bitch.

So I pulled myself through the door to get a beer. That's at Nickie's and the back door is five feet off the ground due to a fuck-up on the administrative level. It's cool and dark and boring inside. Twenty boozed-up eyes watch me scrabble in. "Are you the one? New blood? Will you make my day a new beginning?" Uh, uh, no way. Just a beer and a few friendly words with Nick who's from Sicily. He lets everybody think he's a big Nostra cat hiding out in Savannah Beach. He's got a scar on his face, which helps, and an incredible predilection for sixteen-year-old girls. He's never without them either and I stepped in the damn peas on my way back.

Karen, that's my wife, she works in a club down the street to keep a roof over our heads and here I am not even turning out a turnip. You've got to be a damn good writer to be more valuable than a turnip, what with the current food shortage.

Some drunk kidnapped her the other night. This is true, he'd been hanging around the club for about a week acting the nice guy and it was cold out and he said he'd give her a ride home and when she went to get out of the car, the son of a bitch speeded up. "I just want something I can't have," he says after offering "a *lot* of money." Evil beady cracker eyes gleaming in the passing lights and white knuckles on the wheel. Karen talked him out of it though, and even got him to bring her home after going eighteen miles and he never actually jumped her, but that's a dangerous situation I don't have to tell you. She gave him the old contradictory stimuli bit with strobe statements alternating between, "You know, I just wouldn't have *believed* this of you; you seemed like such a nice *attractive* guy," and "Listen you bastard, the cops on this beach are practically family to me and I know you and I know your car and people saw us leave, so you turn around this goddamn minute!" "Suddenly you're making a lot of sense to me," he says, but damn man, I was horrified at what might have happened. Ten years from now in *True Detective* I pick up a copy and see my wife's remains "stabbed repeatedly in the abdomen until the blade broke off in her body." I used to think I was a married man, but not no more.

B.J. on the other hand, wasn't like Karen and didn't have whatever it was it took and she flipped her bird up there in the Cove. Just went round the bend and started hating us all in an enduring way, so she took a plane out early. A few days back I thought to myself, "Well, that scene should be good for a few hundred psychological words, at least." But I'll spare you the bullshit. What really happened was she didn't like it there, got mad, and went home. So let's leave it at that.

About the time that B.J. left, crab season was near kaput. So Lee started mouthing the magic words: "Moose Valley." All season, he'd promised us that when the work was done we'd shoot us a moose, carve open his guts, and pack out the steaming flesh for a feast. Maybe even dry ice some of it to take back to the school. I personally wanted to make moose stew for the folks back home.

So we were all very happy if not downright excited as we loaded up the skiff for the hour trip around the Cove to a little spot where a tiny thin trail led up steeply into the spruce. It was a ten-hour hike from there to Moose Valley, very tiring, but exhilarating because Lee told us to keep our guns ready all the time in case we came across game. Lee and Charlie were the only ones with weapons but Mike and I cared not a whit, thinking the guns were useless without our eagle eyes.

All the way through the forest, Lee pointed out mysterious signs of game past and I was waiting for him to say, "That's where the gnomes dance," or "Whatever you do, don't look to your left." No such luck and we found the little cabin that Lee and his friends had built some years before. It had half an oil drum for a stove, very effective, and three bunks. And it was in virgin wilderness. Well, not precisely virgin, I picked up a Juicy Fruit wrapper on the ground nearby—not offensive at all like heavy litter; rather friendly actually.

We stayed four days and got very hungry and we didn't even see a moose, much less draw blood. As hunters, we were the most grotesque piece of miscasting you could imagine, clattering over rocks and thrashing through the underbrush. Buncha Keystone Cops and every moose within five miles must have chuckled lightly to himself as he moved dappled and spectrally away.

The third morning I got up before dawn and went with Charlie's beautiful rifle to a spot Lee favored. I sat there staring into the clearing mist like a wigged-out revolutionary studying maps of sewer systems, and I must have seen the entire moose population of Alaska, all of which changed into vegetation by way of self-defense as I took my deadly aim. We'd brought very little in the way of food with us, just some rice, so about noon I said fuck it and went back and got Coral's .22, which she used to aim at the Crew. I shot us a spruce chicken that we cooked very badly and the next day, Lee missed a black bear, which would have made many good meals. You can eat a black bear but no other. Oh, and speaking of hunting for food, I have it from a trust-worthy medical source that the human body is no longer fit for consumption. Our flesh is lousy with vile transients and if that doesn't say something about us, I don't know what. Yer wife may be deli-cious, but lop off a hunk for the frying pan, you'll get sick as a dog. Tsk, tsk, so we all went back to the cabin with watered mouths to gnaw the chicken bones.

We left the next day, that makes five days doesn't it and here's a strange thing that happened to me on the way back that might give you a glimmer of what your beastly rational intellect can do for you. We started before light and stopped about dawn to rest by a crescent-shaped lake. Mountains were all around us and in the distance and trees encroaching on our meager path with ferns were alive with tiny crawling things as we sat down to ease our packs. We heard a loon calling from over there somewhere —a very earthly primal sound that hit me in the heart first and then crawled through my guts like a friendly warm spider. And here's the rub. I thought to myself that that scene was so eternally beautiful that I should remember it forever. And I *do*. I remember myself sitting there thinking I should remember it forever. See the problem there? How many times have your own memories got jammed up by the *duty* of happy recollection? That's what they'd call "jive-ass" on the corner of East Fourth and Avenue B. Them junkies are really all right sometimes.

A few days after we went mooseless back to the Cove, Mike and Charlie left on a seaplane. It was another odd moment for me because I am a very suggestible man, to say the least. That is paradoxically to say that Newton's body at rest tends to stay at rest unless acted upon by some outside force, doesn't obtain with me. No, I tend to stay at rest for a long time after the action begins before deciding the force is a valid basis for action. Now for sixty-four bucks and a cure for cancer, what am I? You guessed it! Lazy!

No, seriously. Not acting until the right time, I was still back near Moose Valley riding that loony wail like a broomstick into my far past—I'm not lying—and when their plane took off I was suddenly brought back to the Cove on the end of a psychic leash. It hurt. There was this glistening hunk of steel agonizing into the air with what I felt and still do are two of the best folks in the world in its dream-cold guts. Did you ever have a nonimage texture dream? Completely tactile and usually horrific? That's what that plane was like—all metal and

353

hard, and with the mere suggestion of metal came a flood of images there on Lee's wooden porch:

Thin steel in the vein.

Steel skeletons left when the brick and concrete falls and it's bound to.

Steel-jacketed bullets ordered by the Geneva Convention because they go right *thru* you instead of expanding and blowing your filthy old guts all over the ecology and if that wasn't a demon grange I don't know what is as soldiers file down their bullets in every Godforsaken war hole in the world.

In other words, it was cold, technical and American that plane. Reality. And I felt like a chimp.

So they were gone and the next thing I can remember after a lot of packing and sneaking out from under early blizzards on the Alcan is being back in St. Louis.

"My Street Days Are Over."

You see, we'd just got into town and I'd just taken a deep breath of the pollution and I said to myself I gotta get out on the street tonight to see what's up. So when we got to Lee's mother's house, I bid adieu and said I'd be back sometime reasonable.

No booze, no woman, no music for months. So I do the logical thing and bop into a bar for a martini and sit down happily figuring how to increase my fun. Only, I don't stop there and go through three or four and repeat the scene in a couple other places.

"Standard removal of front brain Burroughs' excess" and by this time, I'm pretty high. What's next? Why, the bathroom, of course. So I go up to the room, which has one stall and a sink. A marine's pissing in the toilet. Now, I did one of two things: I either (1) washed my hands while delivering a lecture on how "You're all a bunch of murderers anyway," or (2) pissed in the sink. Maybe both, all I remember is being kicked down the stairs wondering how badly I was being hurt, lights flashing, getting a hard boot in the face, and losing my hat. Then I was back on the street wondering where to go.

Now any sane man would have said, "Well, Hell," and gone home to bed. But not me. I don't recall *ever* having any sense, so what I do is call a cab and I'm so drunk I don't even bother to ask the driver, "Where can I locate a woman?" No. I say, "Y'know where there's a whorehouse?" The driver takes one look at me and grins. "MMMM-HMMMM!" he says and the next thing I know, I'm beat for a hundred bucks' worth of traveler's checks (which I myself must have signed) and for getting laid. The police picked me up a few hours later wandering down the street with my boots unlaced and raving about where the hell did them chicks go?

So you see, my street days are over. I could probably revert damn quick in a crisis, however, because any given race or culture *has* to be descended from the criminals of the one before.

355

It looks as if Alaska was one of the best things that ever happened to me. I sure needed something after all that dope. And now all I have to do for the moment is wrap up this book here. We've been through a lot of shit together what with Lexington and everything else, so what I think I'll do is a little review and clarification.

Now, I don't think it was even too long ago that a group of old men sat down and made the use of narcotics illegal. It was the Harrison Act, I believe, but I don't really know much about these things, so if I hit on the wrong act of Congress, I beg your pardon. But the effect was simply marvelous. In the short time it took to vote away the right of an individual to administer medicine to himself, an entire new class of criminals was created. Just add legislation. And of course to deal with these bad guys one must also have new good guys. The Federal Narcotics Bureau, run by a bunch of guys whom I wouldn't even have at my table, is one of the most notorious stumbling blocks in the way of progress that Western man has yet produced, so leave us give credit where credit is due.

Junkie kids in junk neighborhoods are usually resented and hunted because they have to steal to support their habits. I'm talking about heroin now, but five'll get you ten that no matter where you live in the United States today, that your little Johnny or Suzy are, at most, over seventeen, they've dipped into the pharmacopoeia by now. There is no sanctuary even in elementary school. I have seen dealings in hard narcotics by the Junglegym. I know this is difficult to accept, but I hope I've frightened you a little. The time has come for all good people to come to the aid of their children. And not with threats or belts.

Two things are working against today's youth (and I'm talking about youth at the moment because I can't please everyone at once). One is availability. It seems to me that in all ages and levels of so ciety, if you put something pleasant in front of someone, they're going to take it. And the other is Lack of Strong Motivation in Any Other Direction. And I don't mean, be a pal, urge the Boy Scouts or Little League. I mean something *real*. Do you have anything real to offer? Now *do* you?

Want to lick the drug problem? Make it legal. That would solve the biggest part of it right away and besides, what kid is gonna go to a guy on the corner who cuts the stuff with milk sugar or worse when he can go to a pharmacy and get it safe, uncut, and legal? This approach would put the dealer out of business and stop the stealing and who can shriek criminal! when they're not a victim? Besides, street dope gets expensive after a while, and speaking of expenses, anyone who claims that junkies are stupid should take into account that a thirty-dollar-a-day habit 365 days a year comes out to over ten thousand dollars. Hmmmm? (Side thought: It should be obvious that this enormous amount of manpower, especially among the young and restless, is being consciously invalidated by and because of certain sensitive political areas. Remember what we did to the Indians with whiskey when we first started it.)

The scene as it stands today? Well, twenty, even ten years ago, drug addiction was a private thing, hidden as much as possible from family and friends. King Heron stood in shadows. Well now He's strutting in the sun. Whole gangs of kids are banging H with the same rusty needle in that old clubhouse on the vacant lot. One kid will turn on as many as ten others and tell them where to score for themselves. (And most parents worry about masturbation.) So you can see the mathematics.

But a few more words of defense here. I will freely admit that there is a very visible minority of junkies whose values and morals are enough to gag a maggot. But here's the rub. Owing to the Federal Narcotics Bureau, which is possessed of more zeal than literacy, the public has been presented with this image alone. *Dope Fiend!* There have been many times when I myself have been looked at with a sort of odd curiosity as in a glass cage, a specimen of "Junkus Horribulus." But that's the image, that's how we're seen. Slavering pincushions just waiting to get at your daughter. And for Christ's sake, let me get this even straighter and once and for all. A stoned junkie is the most inoffensive, asexual creature on the face of the earth. He has the sex drive of a Galápagos Island turtle, which animal has been known to go for years without sex and then fall asleep in the middle of it. This very popular term "dope fiend" implies that the poor sick clown is a goddamned visitation from nether regions. Wow. So how do we go about helping junkies when we can't even *see* them?

Show you what I mean. Let's take a look at it from this angle: I don't mean to be overly accusing and I obviously exclude present company because if you've read this far . . . well. But it seems to me that a vast majority of people seem to think this way: You are returning home to Lexington from New York City. The train rocks and chatters gently through a winter night as you strike up a conversation with a pleasant-looking young fellow because he looks a bit anxious and in need of company. He looks as if he has a cold but that doesn't bother you —you're a nice liberal type and so what if the kid's a little unkempt? What's youth for anyway? Besides he looks intelligent even if his teeth need attention and you've just had a couple or three bourbons in the bar car so you're feeling sociable. The kid doesn't seem too happy to have you around and he's getting more nervous by the minute. But you figure he'll warm up and wonder for some reason if, maybe, his mother's dying in Lexington and he's on his way to see her. Suddenly he excuses himself and rushes to the bathroom, returning white as a sheet and trembling visibly. You are concerned now, and come right out and ask if there's anything you can do. A desperately ill human being comes briefly to the surface of his eyes to silently tell you "no" as he tells you that he's a junkie on his way down to Lexington Farm. "I'd do most anything for a shot about now," he adds, thinking he's found someone he can at least say it to.

Now you're a little nervous and his conversation has become invalid because you gotta be stupid to take dope (remember that ten thousand dollars) and besides your bourbons are wearing off, leaving you with a slight headache and maybe that scraggy hag that was giving you the eye in the bar car wasn't so bad after all and you *do* have a roomette, so you take your leave, heading for the bar and thinking something to the effect of "Goddamn! There's enough misery in the world without having to watch it, let alone sit next to it."

It's snowing when you steam into Lexington station and you see the kid stumble off a couple of cars down in his green silk long-sleeved shirt and black slacks. Expensive shoes but no coat. It's late now and the wind is rising as you take the only cab, thinking, "Poor kid. Couldn't be over twenty-one. It must be awful . . . Well, he got himself into it . . . I wonder what's in the icebox?"

> "And the longest train that ever run,
> run from Bellevue to Lexington."

> Just keep your thumb on the plug, baby,
> that's all.

AFTERWORD

"The Trees Showed the Shape of the Wind"

KENTUCKY HAM is illuminated by a mysterious vitality and a clear light; mysterious, because the source is hidden from the reader and from the writer himself.

I intersect some of the events described in this book... I had received a distress call from Mother: Billy, who was supposed to join me in London, had been arrested for forging a prescription. I was myself strung out on tincture of opium at the time. I thought the habit was small, and brought nothing with me to Florida, where Billy was living. A search at Customs seemed quite likely. The habit turned out to be not so small and a period of excruciating withdrawal lasted for a month.

I see this period through the painfully sensitive medium of junk sickness... I am talking to the lawyer and I hear him say quite distinctly in my head: "Lousy father." And seeing myself through his eyes: the seedy, shifty, addict father.

The house at 202 Sanford Avenue in Palm Beach was a one-story bungalow with three bedrooms and three bathrooms. I slept in a small back room with sliding windows that didn't slide, because the aluminum fixtures were corroded by the salt air. It was here that an extremely vivid technicolor dream occurred.

The dream set is a deserted futurama of Palm Beach: sidewalks and street blocked with palm branches, robins all over the empty houses. I find a .38 snub-nosed revolver and some ammunition in the drawer of a deserted house. Billy is missing, and I know that he is in some terrible danger. He has fallen into the hands of Helen and Van, seedy medical practitioners specializing in illegal operations in future time. From present time we cannot know the nature of these operations, but on some deep level I *do* know, and I do know exactly who Helen and Van are. I am running across a ruined, weed-grown golf course, the .38 in my hand... suddenly I stop: "We're too late!" In the next scene, Billy comes into the house on crutches, horribly crippled, and won't speak to me.

Billy was afraid to fly, and he took three Miltowns before getting on the plane to Atlanta, on his way to the Federal Narcotics Hospital at Lexington, Kentucky. When we got to Atlanta, he refused to go any further by plane. So I took a propellor flight and he planned to rent a car and drive up. Thre was heavy snow, and bad driving conditions, and he was late. I was waiting in bed, having left instructions that he should be shown up to the room whenever he arrived. I remember being overcome by grief, and I was convinced he had suffered a fatal accident. But he hadn't; he was just delayed, and did not show up until the following morning.

I think people have many fatal accidents that are not seen as such at the time. Like the old joke about the razor: "Just try and shake your head ten years from now." People die in installments, a bit here and a bit there.

Our time together in Tangiers was strained and hollow, like the time he called me long distance from a hospital in Florida after a car accident. I could hear him, but he couldn't hear me. I kept saying, *"Where are you, Billy? Where are you?"*—Strained and off-key, the right thing said at the wrong time, the wrong thing said at the

362

right time, and all too often, the wrongest thing said and done at the wrongest possible time. We never really came close in Tangiers. I remember listening to him playing his guitar after I had gone to bed in the next room, and again, a feeling of deep sadness.

In his two short books, Billy conveyed a great deal about life and youth in the Sixties: the glue sniffing, belladonna trips, freak-outs, casualties, the drop-outs and losers, in and out of sanitariums, the arrests and harassment under the weight of Anslinger's reign of terror. And his remote, ghostly picture of my mother, Laura Lee Burroughs, is one of the most touching Mother figures in fiction. The Victorian antiques and bric-a-brac... porcelain dogs and music boxes and paper-weights with snow scenes, the sad unhappy face, a plaintive phantom presence in the smell of jasmine...

For all her gentleness, Laura had authority. She was a real lady. Once she walked in when two narcs were sitting in her living room, waiting to talk with Billy, and she said: "Get out of my house and don't come back." They got and they didn't.

"The wind moaned from the face of the moon and the trees showed the shape of the wind." SPEED and KENTUCKY HAM show "the shape of the wind" that swept through the world in the Sixties, one of the great cultural revolutions of history, "perhaps the last and greatest of human dreams."

WILLIAM S. BURROUGHS
June, 1984